THE EPIC
WOMEN OF HOMER

THE EPIC WOMEN OF HOMER
EXPLORING WOMEN'S ROLES IN THE ILIAD AND ODYSSEY

EIRENE S. ALLEN

AN IMPRINT OF PEN & SWORD BOOKS LTD.
YORKSHIRE - PHILADELPHIA

First published in Great Britain in 2025 by
PEN AND SWORD HISTORY
An imprint of
Pen & Sword Books Ltd
Yorkshire – Philadelphia

Copyright © Eirene S. Allen, 2025

ISBN 978 1 39905 863 6

The right of Eirene S. Allen to be identified as Author of this work has been asserted by her in accordance with the Copyright, Designs and Patents Act 1988.

A CIP catalogue record for this book is available from the British Library.

All rights reserved. No part of this book may be reproduced, transmitted, downloaded, decompiled or reverse engineered in any form or by any means, electronic or mechanical including photocopying, recording or by any information storage and retrieval system, without permission from the Publisher in writing. No part of this book may be used or reproduced in any manner for the purpose of training artificial intelligence technologies or systems.

Typeset in Times New Roman 11/13.5 by
SJmagic DESIGN SERVICES, India.
Printed and bound in the United States of America by
Integrated Books International

The Publisher's authorised representative in the EU for product safety is Authorised Rep Compliance Ltd., Ground Floor, 71 Lower Baggot Street, Dublin D02 P593, Ireland.
www.arccompliance.com

For a complete list of Pen & Sword titles please contact
PEN & SWORD BOOKS LIMITED
George House, Units 12 & 13, Beevor Street, Off Pontefract Road, Barnsley, South Yorkshire, S71 1HN, England
E-mail: enquiries@pen-and-sword.co.uk
Website: www.pen-and-sword.co.uk

or

PEN AND SWORD BOOKS
1950 Lawrence Rd, Havertown, PA 19083, USA
E-mail: uspen-and-sword@casematepublishers.com
Website: www.penandswordbooks.com

CONTENTS

Epigraph vi

Preface vii

Introduction xiv

PART 1   QUEENS 1

PART 2   CAPTIVES 23

PART 3   GODDESSES 53

PART 4   HEROES 89

Afterword   The World in Homer 142

Appendix 1   Word Guide 157

Appendix 2   Gods and Heroes of the *Iliad* and *Odyssey* 167

Appendix 3   The Narratives of the *Iliad* and *Odyssey* 175

Notes 188

Bibliography 193

Index 203

See, look at that
The hydra of Lernea that he slew,
The son of Zeus, with his golden sickle.
Look with your two eyes, dear ones.
I see beside him another
Lifting a torch blazing with fire.
Is he from the authoritative story told to me as I thread my spool,
The warrior Iolaos, who
Took up in common the labours of the son of Zeus?
(Euripides, Ion, lines 190–200)

Hector, you are impossible to persuade by words.
Because a god has given you warlike ways among men,
You therefore also wish to be skilled in counsel among others,
But you yourself are not able to hold every ability at once.
For a god gives to one man warlike ways,
To another the dance, to a second the lyre and song,
In another far-seeing Zeus places understanding
Of what is noble, and many men reap the benefit of it,
And he saves many people, and he himself knows this best.
(Iliad, 13.726–734)

PREFACE

ANYONE WHO WRITES about Homer is inevitably confronted with the vast unknowability of her subject. By this, I don't mean only Homer himself, or the epics attributed to him. I mean the impossibility of consuming everything that has been written about Homer across the two-and-a-half millennia during which he has been received, without interruption. Only to contemplate that a set of texts, composed in a language unique unto themselves, has been experienced continuously, across unfathomable social, religious and political transformations, is profoundly humbling. So much more so, then, to consider the endless works of art, scholarship and history that have been created in conversation with Homer.

I say this to underscore the impossibility of making grand claims to knowledge about Homer. Here, it feels appropriate to invoke the wisdom of the bard in book three of the *Iliad*: 'Not even if I had ten tongues and ten mouths, / An unbreakable voice and a heart of bronze, would it be possible' for one book – or ten or a hundred – to capture all there is to say and know about the subject. It is not possible to exhaust the meaning of these epics. I say this now, before we begin, so that we can set off together with the proper measure. As Homer's virtuous Phaeacian leader Alcinous tells Odysseus, it is 'best in all things'. Each of us who writes about Homer shares the Homer we receive, cumulatively, through each reread or re-listen of the epics and in conversation with everything we have read or heard about the epics.

My Homer is not a man or a woman telling me a story (or two men or women telling me two stories). The scholar Barbara Graziosi has insightfully noted that modern readers responding to the 'intelligence' in the epics assume that this intelligence must belong to an individual. We struggle to imagine how such inspired and cohesive texts could be the products of anything other than a single genius, or two geniuses, if one prefers. The debate over this – as with so many other aspects of Homer and his epics – is vigorous. Following the scholar Gregory Nagy, my Homer is neither an individual nor a committee but a community of voices speaking the same special language about the same sacred subjects. Over long stretches of time, these voices evolved, by some alchemical process that will likely never be fully divined, into the two epics that we now know by the names *Iliad* and *Odyssey*. My Homer is both two epics that are complete in themselves and a multiplicity of voices engaged in an extended dialogue concerned with the impact of immortal forces on mortal bodies.

The Homer I strove to share in these pages is a cultural consciousness that is reflecting on human experiences, both transcendent and acutely particular, and inviting its receivers to think with and through them. This Homer is meditating self-consciously on the systems that have been constructed to ascribe meaning to suffering and to promote social cohesion and connection, even knowing already that these systems will, at some point, inevitably fail. Seeing Homer as a communal consciousness in dialogue with itself, continuously shaped and reshaped over time, provides one possible explanation for why in Homer we can find anything, everything, of consequence in human experience. Extreme rage, enduring love, bitter resentment, gentle care, corrupt leadership, forgiveness of the unforgivable – all are woven into the epics so that even in their most alienating moments (and there are many such moments), these epics can still speak directly to us, whenever and wherever we are in time and space. To see and hear the multiplicity of voices – perhaps especially the women's voices – and the dialogues among them, however, requires holding this duality: that however familiar Homer's epics may feel, they are also distant. They belong to and exist in their own world, their own language, their own storytelling ecosystem. This ecosystem is a vast, elaborately constructed tapestry, each thread representing an individual life force woven into the cosmic whole.

As modern readers, we are trained to enter texts seeking cohesive narrative wholes. If these texts are called 'poetry', we are trained to find a meticulously constructed metre. When confronted with apparent narrative inconsistencies or metric anomalies, as we are in the Homeric epics, we may assume such inconsistencies are errors on the part of an 'author' or 'editor' and dismiss them as unsophisticated or inferior 'literature'. We may overlook that the Homeric epics were not texts produced in a literate age but songs that were carried forward across time and place breath to breath for hundreds, perhaps even thousands, of years before they were written down. The inconsistencies that trouble modern readers may not have registered as significant for the earliest receivers who recorded them. Perhaps they exist to make the point that narratives are not stable things but always in motion, shaped by the teller of the moment and carried relentlessly forward in a steady beat. This beat may falter but never falls as it strives, through a chorus of voices, to achieve unity of the totality, which remains stubbornly out of human reach.

In the archaic and classical Greek worlds from which our texts, the *Iliad* and *Odyssey*, emerged, Homer was neither fiction nor history, as we might define these categories today. Homer was a timeless tradition of invoking the power of gods and heroes by retelling sacred stories about them. The Greek word *mythos*, our 'myth', meant (among other things) 'an authoritative story', as discussed by Gregory Nagy. Continually retelling these authoritative stories was a way to channel the eternal. With each retelling, past and future collapsed into 'now'.[1] Our *Iliad* and *Odyssey*, then, are not discrete works of literature but slices from a larger narrative about the nature of the cosmos. When we know how to read the signs, we can perceive the whole through the part.

The essential place of women in this Homeric world has tended to melt into the background in translations that strive to fashion a straightforward narrative from each epic by conforming to our expectations as literate readers of fiction. Likewise, metered English translations, though often very beautiful, have for me felt distant, inevitably and to varying degrees, from the Homer I experience in the ancient Greek texts, which moves like a powerful, timeless tide, cyclically crashing into the shoreline dramatically then receding gently away. When I began translating speeches and scenes which focalise women, I did not set out to render them in English verse but to convey as closely as possible what I experience when I read the Greek. I held myself to translating line by line, even when it seemed virtually impossible. I did not do this because I believe it to be the 'correct' or 'only' way that Homer 'should' be translated. Rather, I hoped to attune my mind to oral poetry's layering, digression-and-return style, the dynamic simultaneity of repetition and variation and the endless mysteries and ambiguities that anyone who attempts to render Homer into a modern language inevitably confronts. In the Greek, every word is an atom to be split open, with endless meanings spilling out.

I hope for anyone who encounters these translations to feel in Homer the presence of something ancient and powerful and strange but also eerily compelling in its familiarity. As such, I did not strive to make reading Homer in English either easy or difficult; I strove to excite the sense of wonder I feel reading Homer in Greek, which is like unwrapping a giant present and then realising there are endless smaller presents inside. It takes time to unwrap them, but each is a thrilling new discovery and avenue for inquiry. I did not strive to offer the story in the *Iliad* and *Odyssey* but a way of thinking with the *Iliad* and *Odyssey*.

As an example, take the words Hector speaks in his *Iliad* book six conversation with Andromache, in which he describes what he would be if he hung back from battle and what he is when he throws himself into battle:

> I would shame myself to the Trojan men and the Trojan women
>   of the trailing robes
> If aloof, I shrank from battle, as a *kakos* would,
> Nor does my consciousness command me thus since I learned
>   to be an *esthlos*.
>
> (Lines 442–444)

These words – *kakos* and *esthlos* – are like bottomless duffle bags into which any number of meanings can be stuffed. They are singular adjectives with masculine, feminine and neuter forms that, in their essence, can be understood as *bad* (or *harmful*) and *good* (or *beneficial*) respectively. The noun these two adjectives modify in Greek is implied in their form, which here is masculine singular, thus *man*.

In English translations of this passage, these words are often translated as *coward* (meaning *a cowardly man*) and *brave* (meaning *a brave man*) respectively because these are the English words that seem most suited to the context, whether one is criticising or praising Hector. Thinking about him in this moment, his city under siege, with a dire prophecy that it will eventually fall hanging over it, I wondered if Hector would think of what was asked of him as being rather straightforward: A bad or harmful man runs away from necessity; a good one meets it. Yet Hector's choice to be 'a good man' ultimately causes harm. The two meanings that seem clearly to be opposites fuse together. In hopes of offering readers an opportunity to think about what it has meant to be a 'good' or 'bad' man across time and under different circumstances, I am concerned not to overdetermine the meaning but instead to leave it open to exploration that invites dialogue, within our own time and with the past:

> I would shame myself to the Trojan men and the Trojan women
>   of the trailing robes
> If aloof, I shrank from battle, as a bad man would,
> Nor does my consciousness command me thus, since I learned
>   to be a good man.

Translation demands countless choices like these, mulling over how to adapt the grammar and meanings of one language into the grammar and meanings of another. While I strove to stay as close to the Greek as possible by translating line by line, to be literal is impossible. Greek does not function and mean as English does. Interpretive choices cannot be evaded. This inevitability is not an invitation to a free-for-all but a sobering responsibility for the translator to juggle what can seem like competing priorities. Do we prioritise narrative and semantic clarity? Do we prioritise metre? Do we prioritise meaning? What do we do when we can't find one or even three words that convey what the one Greek word does? Which meaning do we choose when the Greek word holds multiple meanings simultaneously? What do we do with the different dialects and usages that appear in the Greek text? How do we negotiate ritual function and performance context? To what extent can we incorporate them? No one translation can convey all that Homer is and does.

My priority was to illuminate Homer's women, who I believe can be best seen, heard and appreciated in the context of their own creation, which is the oral tradition of retelling stories in the context of a ritual. Consequently, I prioritised retaining features of the Greek that suggest its origins in oral composition and its concern with the sacred, and I opted for words and phrases that would at times defamiliarise concepts which have become loaded with modern meanings. Operating on the principle that each line in orally transmitted verse would function as a complete thought (though not necessarily a complete sentence), I held myself to line-by-line translation and retained repetition as consistently as possible. In concessions to clarity, I have occasionally added words that are implied in the Greek texts, e.g. occasionally substituting proper names for pronouns and adding implied nouns and various forms of the verb 'to be', among others.

To capture what I experience as the powerful tide of Homeric lines, I use punctuation loosely, incorporating full stops sparingly and favouring commas to divide phrases that might otherwise run together incoherently. As an example of what I mean by 'powerful tide', consider the following four lines (91–95) from book two, when Antinous is describing Penelope's ruse:

> She makes all have hope and makes promises to each man,
> Sending forth messages, but her way of understanding has other intentions.
> She pondered another trap with her perceptions,
> Setting it up on a great loom, to weave in the large room,
> A subtle and well-fitted thing, she spoke among us straightaway.

In the Greek text, the adjectives in the phrase 'a subtle and well-fitted thing' in line 95 are in the accusative case, which correspond grammatically with the word 'trap' in line 92, which is also in the accusative case. But the presence of that phrase in line 95 with Penelope speaking tricksy words to the suitors makes it impossible for me not think of it also as a description of her, not grammatically but in her characterisation: she *is* subtle across the *Odyssey* and well-fitted to the task of tricking the suitors. If I were rendering this phrase in English for maximum narrative and/or grammatical clarity, I would not be translating line by line, and I might thus opt to pair 'subtle and well-fitted thing' with the noun 'trap' and eliminate the unnecessary 'thing' – which I have added as the implied noun – along the lines of 'a subtle and well-fitted trap'. But then I would lose the flow of allusion that so elegantly captures Penelope's character. As often as possible, I incorporate exploration of translation choices into my discussion to make the relationship between translation and interpretation as transparent as possible. All line references are for the Greek text. A Word Guide in Appendix 1 delves deeper into my thought process around specific words and the challenges they pose for translation. Appendixes 2 and 3 are references to aid the reader first with the Homeric figures referenced throughout my discussion and second with the larger narrative into which the women's stories are woven.

While all mistakes and misunderstandings are my own, my approach and translations are inspired by many dedicated scholars who have devoted, in some cases, a lifetime to the study of Homer. The works of Gregory Nagy (whose awe-inspiring work has been a constant companion), Laura Slatkin, Casey Due, John Miles Foley, Susan Edmonds, Egbert Bakker and Barbara Graziosi have been especially illuminating to my understanding of Homer as a cultural construct, oral storytelling traditions and the roles of women within them. I am also grateful for all the translators of Homer – in English and modern Greek – whose work made these texts accessible to me before I studied ancient Greek and who inspired me to do so in order that I might read them for myself.

Homer, sum total, shows us that we survive and thrive together in ways that we could never do alone. I wish to thank my dear family and friends for their support and encouragement. I am thankful also for the support of the lovely team who worked with me at Pen and Sword – Sarah Hodder and Sarah-Beth Watkins – and for Cecily Blench and her work on my manuscript. I also wish to thank Hillary Yip for her beautiful artwork. My understanding benefitted tremendously from conversations with my professors, classmates, students and friends, especially Lauren, Mariana,

Preface

Maria, Theo, Alison, Martin, Robin, Anthony, Susan, Abby and everyone who passed through our Tuesday translation group. No words can fully express my gratitude for Helen McVeigh, to whom this book is dedicated. Her HM Classics Academy has created a beautiful community of learners from around the world. Her tireless dedication, generosity and love of Homer inspire me every day. I am eternally thankful for her constant support, friendship and encouragement and for many happy hours poring over Homer's Greek together. This book would not exist without her.

INTRODUCTION

Andra

The Greek text we know in English as the *Odyssey* famously begins with the word *andra*. Whether in English verse or prose, from George Chapman's 1615 translation to those most recently published by Peter Green and Emily Wilson, this word has commonly been translated as *man*, as in the notable examples below:

George Chapman, 1615:

> The man, O Muse, inform, that many a way
> Wound with his wisdom to his wished stay;

Thomas Hobbes, 1675:

> Tell me, O Muse, th' adventures of the man
> That having sack'd the sacred town of Troy,

Alexander Pope, 1725:

> The man for wisdom's various arts renown'd,
> Long exercised in woes, O Muse! resound;

These translations announce that the *Odyssey* is the story of a man and encourage us to anticipate a biographical narrative about *his* journey.

When the bard invites the goddess to begin the story of this *andra*, Odysseus, wherever she wills, she chooses to start at a council of the gods. There, Zeus and Athena deliberate how to achieve the successful return home of Odysseus, who Calypso is holding captive. Athena advises her father to order the release of Odysseus while she herself departs for Ithaca to inspire courage in his young son, Telemachus, whose home is being

Introduction

besieged by suitors hoping to marry his mother, Penelope. The narrative then shifts to Ithaca – where Athena counsels Telemachus – and remains there for the first four of the epic's twenty-four books. Odysseus remains out of reach, hidden by Calypso, whose name shares a root with the Greek verb 'to conceal'. The narrative likewise conceals him from us, concerning itself with events at Ithaca and the trials facing Telemachus and Penelope.

If this is the story of a man and his personal journey, why does the narrative spend so much time in Ithaca with Odysseus' wife and son?

An answer can be found by returning to the first word of the epic, *andra*, which in both ancient and modern Greek can mean either *man* or *husband*. The word's dual meaning captures the interwoven natures of Odysseus' individual and social identities. Without Penelope, Odysseus would not have his identity as an *andra*. Thus, his identity as a man is defined by his relationship with a woman: without Penelope, Odysseus would not have his identity as a *husband*. This duality persists in Roman poet Horace's Latin translation: he uses the word *virum*, which carries the dual meaning *man* or *husband*, not the word *homo*, which does not. In the absence of a single word that holds the meaning of both man and husband, translations of the modern period have favoured rendering *andra* as *man*.

When we restore the dual meaning of *andra*, we restore the essentially, and perhaps for us paradoxically, social nature of Odysseus' subjectivity: he is not an *I* but a *we*. At Troy, the *we* was the men Odysseus fought alongside, both those he brought with him from Ithaca and the larger Achaean expedition that his contingent joined. Now that the war is over, the *we* Odysseus belongs to lies far away in Ithaca. Recognising him as a husband confers a purpose to his wanderings, referenced in the opening lines: to deliver him from the war to his wife and home, the locus of his identity as an *andra*, a man and a husband.

> A husband, a versatile man with many plots and schemes,
> relate to me, Muse, of him who very much
> Was made to wander, after sacking the sacred citadel of Troy.
> He saw many people and cities and came to know their way of understanding.
> He experienced at sea many sorrows upon his consciousness,
> Striving to recover his mortal identity and the return home of his companions,
> But not even he could rescue his companions, having very much desired to
> For they destroyed themselves by their own recklessness,

> Being disconnected, the sacred cattle of Hyperion, the Sun,
> They devoured them, and the god took away their day of returning.
> From any point whatever, goddess, daughter of Zeus, tell us too.
> *(Odyssey*, lines 1–10)

The reference to Troy reminds us that Odysseus is one of many husbands who undertook a return journey like his, some who survived and some who did not. His story, the *Odyssey*, is one in a pattern of homecoming hero stories, several of which are woven into the epic. Odysseus is preeminent among them because he not only survives the war and the peril-filled journey home but also recovers his mortal identity as the husband of Penelope, the father of Telemachus, the son of Laertes, the leader of Ithaca. He achieves his return because his wife is his perfect counterpart, equally capable of enduring and equally capable of deploying her strategy in the battles she faces at home during her husband's absence.

The story of Odysseus is not, then, the story of a man but the story of a marriage, a family, a community. The challenge of interpreting Homer is entangled with the challenge of translating Homer, and it is here that Homer's women have tended to get lost.

Histos

In the *Odyssey*, our first glimpse of Penelope comes three-quarters of the way into the epic's first book, immediately following the discussion between Telemachus and Athena. From the women's quarters, Penelope hears a bard, Phemius, singing to the men assembled in the hall below about the failed homecomings of the Achaeans. Troubled by the song's content, she descends to confront Phemius and, in a much-discussed passage, is told by Telemachus to return to her own rooms and her own work:

> But going into the house, take care of your own works,
> The loom and the distaff, and urge your handmaidens
> To go to their work, for public speech is the concern of men
> Alone, and mine most of all, for might in the house is mine.

Read in modern English, Telemachus' imperative can sound uncomfortably like a scolding. Much has been made of this young man, still unsure of himself but infused with fresh courage after his encounter with Athena, patron of heroes, ordering his mother to return to her handicrafts.

Introduction

This same imperative in ancient Greek, however, is heavy with allusions. The terminology of weaving and the terminology of ship building flow from a related lexical web in which the Greek words for loom and distaff both figure.

The Greek word *histos*, which most literally means *standing beam*, is the word used for both *loom* and *mast*, and it shares a root with the word for the noun sail (*histion*). Reyes Bertolin argues that the loom and mast in Homer are both 'gendered' objects related to the authorities of women and men respectively. That our *loom* and *mast* collapse into the single word *histos* suggests gender symmetry encoded in the Greek language that cannot be rendered in translation.[1] On a related note, Stella Spantidaki observes that a single Greek word can provoke 'semantic harmonies' for the listener, which invite a series of 'mental associations'.[2] This in turn invites us to reflect that the earliest receivers of Telemachus' words would not hear *histos* as we hear *loom* and *mast* in translation, as two separate and unrelated activities that exist in some sort of hierarchical relationship.

In book five, when we finally meet Odysseus on Calypso's Island, he will craft a raft with which to escape, and this raft will be fitted with an *histos* (mast) and an *histion* (sail). In book eight, Odysseus will be tied to the mast's feet, called *histopedes*, also the word for the feet of a loom. Both of these nouns are related to the verb *histemi*, meaning *to make something stand upright, to set up* or *to stand*. This is the verb used to describe Penelope when she arrives in the hall to complain to Phemius and stations herself beside one of the posts that hold up the roof. It is also the verb used to describe Athena when she arrives in Ithaca in book one.

These interwoven meanings are invisible in translation, but Telemachus' language in the Greek text evokes deep-rooted associations among essential activities in the ancient Greek world: weaving, sailing, fighting. Seen through this lens, his language seems to allude both to the shared authority of men and women and to the shared circumstances of Odysseus and Penelope. Both are trapped, Odysseus by Calypso and Penelope by the suitors. To slip free of these traps, each must deploy their shared skills of craft and strategy. To achieve their reunion, they must be of one mind, understanding and purpose, trusting that the other is doing the same.

In the absence of mass production, weavers provided an essential function both in everyday life, producing garments for the members of their households, and in sacred rituals. At the Panathenaea, widely believed to be classical Athens' most important religious festival, a procession would deliver a *peplos*, or dress, woven by prominent Athenian women to a cult statue of Athena that resided on the Acropolis. The priestess of Athena oversaw the preparation of the wool and the weaving of the garment, a nine-month-long process that culminated in a dedication at the Erechtheum. By the fourth century BC, the tradition is believed to have evolved into a ship procession, and the *peplos* to have grown to the size of a sail. It has been argued that the ship with a *peplos* embodied the shared knowledge and techniques of weaving and sailing.[3]

The connections extend to other objects and movements associated with weaving and sailing. Both looms and sailing ships made use of wood and cloth. Both had forked devices on which beams and oars, respectively, rested. Both used weights, which looked and functioned similarly: loom weights and ships' anchors were both shaped like pyramids and served as stabilising devices. The Greek word *spathe* could refer to both weaving implements and swords, and the motion of weaving, which included beating the weft threads, resembled the motion of rowing, which involved beating the water with oars. These, in turn, evoked the fighting motions of warriors, hence the applicability of the word *sword*.[4]

These complex associations are woven tightly together in the Greek language in ways that cannot be reproduced in translation. Awareness of them invites us to consider the ways in which the loom and the ship may have coexisted in the Greek cultural consciousness as complementary spheres of authority, both essential to the productive functioning of an island-dwelling family and community. In the passage above, Penelope has descended from her rooms to ask the bard for a different song. Telemachus' instructions to his mother to 'take care of your own works, / The loom and the distaff' urge her to shape the song of the hero's homecoming herself by returning to the mediums of her authority and strategy, her loom and her distaff, which in the ancient Greek language are also the mediums of Odysseus' return home.

Diplaka Porphyrein

In book nineteen, Penelope describes to a disguised Odysseus the ruse she used to hold off the suitors:

> While they urge for a wedding feast, I myself spin traps.
> My first, which a *daimon* breathed into my consciousness, was
>   a large cloth.
> Setting it up on a great loom, to weave in the large room,
> A subtle and well-fitted thing, I spoke among the suitors
>   straightaway.
>
> (Lines 137–140)

Introduction

The 'scheme' Penelope spun is both metaphoric and literal. Her ruse was the funeral shroud that she claimed she needed to weave for Laertes, her father-in-law, before choosing a new husband from among the suitors besieging her. As long as the shroud was in progress, she could hold the suitors at bay. In this way, she kept events at Ithaca in a state of suspended animation, holding Odysseus' place and buying him time to return.

Women are also described weaving in the *Iliad*, twice and at equidistant points. The first arrives three books into the epic, the second three books from the end. Both occur at pivotal moments in the narrative when events are about to take or have taken a cosmic turn. Identical phrases, which appear only in these two places, describe the object of each woman's labour: *diplaka porphyrein*, rendered above as *a dark, gleaming, double-folded mantle.*

The first weaver described is Helen, the daughter of Zeus whose removal from Sparta has brought the Achaeans to the gates of Troy. At the moment the bard turns his attention to Helen, the war over possession of her has halted. Instead, a duel will be held between her first husband, Menelaos of Sparta, and her current one, Trojan prince Paris. Both sides have agreed to abide by the results of the duel, whose winner will claim Helen and her treasure.

Messenger goddess Iris has been sent to fetch Helen and bring her to the Trojan walls to watch the contest between her past and current (and hence future) husbands.

> Iris found Helen in a large room weaving on a great loom,
> A dark, gleaming, double-folded mantle, she was sprinkling
>   into it the many contests
> Of the Trojans, tamers of horses, and the Achaeans, clad in
>   bronze,
> Who on account of her were suffering at the hands of Ares.
>   (Lines 125–128)

This portrait of Helen presents her narrating the story of the Trojan war. As a bard does with song and a potter with clay, Helen instantiates the story. Her medium is thread and cloth, what Elizabeth Wayland Barber in *Women's Work* refers to as 'women's paper' in the ancient world. With thread and cloth, women could record events, convey messages to each other, and express entreaties to superhuman forces. In one sense, Helen is the passive object of the contest; simultaneously, her weaving the war story suggests that she participates in the creation of that story, as Penelope uses her weaving to shape the story at Ithaca.

The wife of Trojan prince Hector, Andromache is the second weaver described in the *Iliad*, in book twenty-two. Her husband, Hector, has been killed, but no messenger has yet arrived to bring Andromache the news. She continues at her work, unaware that the best defender of Troy has fallen, portending the fall of Troy:

> But in an inner room of the high house, she was weaving at her loom
> A dark, gleaming, double-folded mantle, she was sprinkling into it patterns of dappled flowers.
> (Lines 440–441)

Unlike Helen, Andromache is not weaving a story but creating flower patterns, which may have been connected to inscribing prayers for protection.[5]

Modern translations vary in their renderings of the phrase *diplaka porphyrein*. Some translators opt to retain the repetition, using identical language in both books three and twenty-two. Others choose to vary the phrase according to their own metrical needs and contexts. What concerns us here is not so much what each translator chooses to do or not do and why but noticing what the repetition (of phrases) within the variation (of context) invites us to perceive at these two critical turning points about two women striving to survive in a city under siege.

Both women have husbands on the field of battle. Both are weaving *a large, gleaming double-folded mantle*. Both, in the course of their weaving, communicate with superhuman forces, Helen with Iris and Andromache (potentially) through prayers. While Helen weaves in a large room, Andromache weaves in an inner room. While Helen tells the story of the war, in which she herself lies at the centre, Andromache hovers at the fringes, praying for deliverance. While Helen is the cause of the war and will survive the fall of Troy, returning to her former husband and home, Menelaos and Sparta, Andromache will experience a reversal of fortune, from having been the wife of the most revered Trojan prince to being enslaved by the Achaeans. In the moment she is depicted weaving, this reversal has unbeknownst to her already occurred. The death of Hector has sealed her future fate and rendered her woven prayers futile.

Both women echo in Penelope. Though the field of battle lies far from Ithaca, its effects ripple outward, reaching Penelope and her household. Her husband's extended absence has left her home vulnerable, and it has come under siege by an unwieldy horde of suitors who court Penelope against her will. Like Andromache, she prays for the protection and safe return home of her husband, whose fate at times remains hidden from her. Like Helen, Penelope is both an agent who weaves a story with a great loom in a large room and an object who the suitors fight to possess. Each of these women is an iteration and variation of the other, their fates discrete but interconnected, emerging in communion with the eternal forces with which they interact.

Daimoni

Immortal intervention brings the *Iliad* book three duel between Menelaos and Paris to an abrupt end just as Menelaos appears on the brink of prevailing. Seeing one of her favourites in danger, the goddess Aphrodite obscures Paris in a mist, snatches him away and spirits him to the safety of his incense-scented bedroom. Disguised as a woman dear to Helen, Aphrodite then summons her to Paris' bed. Recognising that she is in the presence of the immortal, Helen confronts her:

> *Daimoni*, why do you long to deceive me with these things?
> (Line 399)

Helen's resistance to Aphrodite's demand provokes the goddess's wrath, and the chilling threat she issues coerces a terrified Helen into compliance:

> Covering her face with her bright, radiant robe, she walked
> In silence and escaped the notice of all the Trojan women; a
> *daimoni* led her.
> (Lines 419–420)

Broadly, the Greek word *daimon*,[6] which appears in both masculine and feminine form in Homer, means immortal power. More specifically, as Nagy observes,[7] it is used to refer to immortal power interceding in mortal affairs. Though localised in Troy, the above scene replicates the event that launched the war: Aphrodite leading Helen away from Sparta. While that event lies outside the boundaries of our *Iliad*, the dynamic within it replicates in this scene: Helen's will submits to Aphrodite's. Within the larger narrative that stretches beyond the scene and our *Iliad*, her will submits to the plans of Zeus, the architect of the Trojan war. Helen addressing Aphrodite as *daimoni* in the scene above draws attention to Helen's captivity, not only within the physical space of Troy but also to the plans and intentions of the gods who determine mortal outcomes.

The book nineteen scene from the *Odyssey* discussed above in which Penelope explains her ruse with the shroud to a disguised Odysseus portrays a similar dynamic of immortal interference in mortal concerns, though to very different effect:

> While they urge for a wedding feast, I myself spin traps.
> My first, which a *daimon* breathed into my consciousness, was a large cloth,
> Setting it up on a great loom, to weave in the large room,
> A subtle and well-fitted thing, I spoke among the suitors straightaway.
>
> (Lines 137–140)

Without naming the goddess, who is presumably Athena, Penelope acknowledges that the ruse, which enabled her to hold off the suitors, was god-breathed. Like Helen's, Penelope's actions emanate from a goddess who engineers human events. But while the wills of Helen and Aphrodite conflict, those of Penelope and Athena converge in a common purpose: to ensure the successful return home of Odysseus.

As with *andra* and *histos*, *daimon* holds a duality that is difficult to convey in a single English word: the convergence of eternal and ephemeral, immortal and mortal, within the figure of the hero. As expressed in Penelope's explanation of her ruse, immortal power flows through heroes. In the epic, this manifests both in the ways gods work through heroes, as depicted in the scenes above, and in the acknowledgement of heroes' ancestry: their genealogy traces back to the gods. The immortal within the hero cannot, by definition, die, which signals that, though their life forces are contained in mortal bodies, heroes are destined for immortalisation. The presence of the word *daimoni* in the scenes above calls attention to this duality as it applies to Helen, whose actions are set in motion by a goddess, and Penelope, whose ideas are set in motion by a goddess.[8]

In the historical world of archaic and classical Greece, from which our *Iliad* and *Odyssey* emerged, the heroes of mythical narratives were recognised as superhuman forces and worshipped with rituals and sacrifices. Though the epics do not explicitly reference the historical practice of hero worship, ancient receivers of the epics would presumably have understood the religious significance of heroes. For modern readers, however, the concept of the hero has tended, over time and for a variety of reasons, to become conflated with male warriors. Hector and Odysseus are widely recognised as heroes from myth, Andromache and Penelope less so, though in historical times all could have been figures of cult who were worshipped in sacred rituals.

Two pivotal scenes, one in the *Iliad* and one in the *Odyssey*, suggest the heroic status of Andromache and Penelope, signalled through the word *daimoni*. In *Iliad* book six, Andromache, aware that Hector will not willingly retreat from battle and fearing where it will lead, tells him,

> *Daimoni*, your might will despoil you.
>
> (Line 407)

After lamenting what will happen to her after he is gone, she urges him to remain safely inside the city walls and from there to protect their most vulnerable entry points. Though he recognises the truth contained in Andromache's lament, Hector has learned always to be the first in battle to win 'great fame' for himself and his father. He instructs Andromache,

> *Daimoni*, do not grieve excessively for me in your consciousness
> For no man will hurl me into Hades beyond my allotted portion.
>
> (Lines 486–487)

As with Aphrodite and Helen in the scene above, the wills of Hector and Andromache are here in conflict. She wishes him to remain home and safe, but Hector recognises that the way to fame lies, for him, through battle and death. Hector's will ultimately prevails, and Troy falls, leading to the enslavement of Andromache and the other women of Troy.

The dynamic between Odysseus and Penelope in their book twenty-three scene is likewise a contest of wills. Unlike Hector and Andromache, however, Odysseus and Penelope are united in a common purpose: their reunion. At this point in the narrative, the suitors have been killed, Odysseus has been bathed and Athena has beautified him, but Penelope continues to keep her distance, prompting him to exclaim,

> *Daimoni*, in you among all women
> Has been given a hard heart by those who dwell on Olympus.
>
> (Lines 166–167)

Penelope responds, clarifying that her behaviour towards him is not intended to set herself apart from him:

> *Daimoni*, I am neither exalting myself nor disregarding you.
> (Line 174)

Following this exchange, Penelope orders a bed to be brought to Odysseus, the same bed which he himself crafted. It is her final test to confirm his identity, since she and he alone know that the bed could not be moved: it is built into a tree that lives in their bedchamber. Her suggestion that the bed could be moved prompts an aggrieved outburst from Odysseus and a long explanation of how he built it, which confirms his identity. In their contest, the wills of Penelope and Odysseus merge: Odysseus' knowledge of the bed proves that he is her true husband, leading to the couple's reunion. The outcome of the contest is their coming together, their reunion.

In these two scenes, the heroes referring to each other as *daimoni* suggests that each recognises the presence of immortal power in the other. For readers of modern translations to perceive this, however, hinges on how this word is rendered, and the immortal dimension of *daimoni* is often left behind in modern translations. This is especially the case when the term is applied to Andromache. Translators often render Andromache addressing Hector by either an endearment or an allusion to his power, e.g. 'strange power', 'possessed', 'reckless one'. Hector, however, has been rendered addressing Andromache either by her proper name or an endearment, e.g. 'dear one', 'dear heart', 'my dearest'. In the scene between Odysseus and Penelope, the repetition in their exchange of addresses is retained but the immortal component is typically not. Translators often render them calling each other some version of 'strange one'.

As noted above, however, the application of the Greek term *daimoni* seems to mark Andromache and Penelope as heroes, like their husbands: superhuman forces contained in mortal bodies who are destined for immortalisation and cult honours. Given that the epics do not overtly reference ritual hero worship, it remains for us to consider what kind of immortalisation the epics themselves promise for heroes like Andromache (and Hector) and Penelope (and Odysseus) and how this form of immortality interacts with the ritual worship of heroes.

Kleos

In the scene between Hector and Andromache discussed in the previous section, the Greek phrase for 'great fame', which Hector has earned for his father and himself by being first in battle, is *mega kleos*. Typically translated as *fame* or *glory*, *kleos* refers to a specific kind of fame or glory: that which is conveyed through epic song, thus fame or glory that is heard.[9] To achieve *kleos* is to have one's name breathed into, received by and carried forward in the social world, from one generation to the next. Two notable scenes in the *Iliad* and the *Odyssey* illuminate this cyclical dynamic and the function of the Muses, the immortal daughters of Zeus and Mnemosyne (Memory), within it.

In book two, the bard of our *Iliad* appeals to the Muses to provide the names of the Achaean leaders and their ships because no mortal alone could know them all:

> Tell me now Muses who have homes on Olympus,
> For you are goddesses, you are present, and you know all things.
> We hear only the song that brings fame but know nothing.
> Who were the leaders and rulers of the Danaans?
> I could neither speak of nor name the masses of men,
> Not even if I had ten tongues and ten mouths,
> An unbreakable voice and a heart of bronze, would it be possible,
> If not for the Olympian Muses of aegis-bearing Zeus
> His daughters, who can recall to memory how many came upon Ilium.
> (Lines 484–492)

His appeal suggests that bards are the instrument of the Muses. They do not need to know or have seen the events they sing about.[10] They need only hear, and channel, the voice of the Muses. While exploits of heroes may have been known or heard within their personal communities, only immortal memory could hold the sum of all knowledge – in this moment, represented by knowledge of the full Achaean contingent. Wardens of eternal memory, the Muses collect knowledge of all 'the songs that bring fame' and filter it back into the mortal world through the breath of bards. This cycle is suggested in a book eight scene in the *Odyssey*, when the Muse provides a song for Phaeacian bard Demodocus:

> The Muse prompted the bard to sing the famous deeds of men,
> A song whose fame had reached the wide sky,
> About a quarrel between Odysseus and Achilles, son of Peleus.
> (Lines 73–75)

This quarrel between Achilles and Odysseus became so renowned that it reached the 'wide sky', signifying not only the mortal world but also the realm of the immortals. By reaching the 'wide sky', the song became incorporated into the eternal memory of the Muses who could then provide the song to Demodocus, however far removed he was in time and place from the event itself.

If songs of fame originated in local communities, how did they travel beyond them? In Homer, women are portrayed as integral to this process. They are not only heroes whose famous deeds become the subject of song, as suggested by Andromache and Penelope being marked as *daimoni*, but also shapers and conveyers of famous deeds. We have seen the latter in the figures of Penelope controlling the timeline of events through her weaving and Helen weaving the story of the Trojan war. Andromache too has an essential role to play.

In the *Iliad* book six scene between Andromache and Hector discussed above, Andromache laments the suffering that will fall on her and Hector's son after his death. In his response, Hector shares her concerns but insists that he cannot refrain from fighting. He further notes that, after his death, when she has been enslaved by the Achaeans, Andromache will become a medium through which he is remembered:

> And seeing you pouring tears, some man will say,
> 'This is the wife of Hector, who was first in battle
> Among the horse-breaking Trojans whenever they fought around Troy.'
>
> (Lines 459–461)

Andromache's public expressions of grief will ensure that Hector's name continues to be spoken and his 'famous deeds' remembered.[11] Andromache's laments will become Hector's song of fame, which she will carry beyond Troy after it falls. Her survival will ensure that his name continues to be breathed.

Odysseus' 'song of fame', our *Odyssey*, reaches its climax not in his death but in his successful return home. Yet his pain and his fame are interconnected, as Penelope is aware. After Odysseus warns her that further trials await him, she asks him to reveal what has been prophesied:

> Tell me about this trial, since I suppose hereafter,
> I will hear it told. It would not be inferior to learn it straightaway.
>
> (Lines 261–262)

Introduction

Penelope's response reflects her recognition that Odysseus' future suffering will become the subject of song, as her own fame has grown from her ruse to hold off the suitors who are besieging her. Her insistence to hear the prophecy seems to surprise Odysseus, who replies,

> *Daimoni*, why do you again urge me exceedingly, encouraging me
> To tell it? But I will speak, and I will conceal nothing.

Perhaps it also surprises the modern reader, who may not understand why Penelope, immediately upon being reunited with her husband, insists on hearing about future trials that will separate them. Trying to make sense of this scene's narrative or psychological logic can obscure the significance it communicates within a culture in which breath, not text, is the conveyer of famous deeds. As Aphrodite leading Helen to Paris replicates within the *Iliad* the plans of Zeus leading Helen to Troy beyond the *Iliad*, this scene between Penelope and Odysseus replicates within the *Odyssey* the origins of epic beyond the *Odyssey*. These origins lie in (among others) men and women exchanging stories about remarkable events,[12] as Penelope and Odysseus do in the rest of the scene. She describes 'all that she endured' in Ithaca, and he responds by sharing the pain he inflicted on others and suffered himself, which is a summary of the story Odysseus himself narrated for the Phaeacians in books nine through twelve.

The form of immortality that Homeric epics promise their heroes is this: to be woven into the web of stories that never die but are continuously breathed into existence and carried forward. This promise to become eternal in memory was actualised through the incorporation of Homeric epic at sacred events. In archaic and classical Greek city-states, epic material attributed to Homer was recited at festivals held to honour the gods and heroes of the city, notably at Athens' Panathenaea mentioned above. The precise relationship between what was performed at these festivals and our *Iliad* and *Odyssey* remains debated, reminding us of the distance between what ancient people considered 'Homeric' and what we in modern times do.

For us, Homer is two texts that we receive as 'books' and read or listen to, typically alone. In the earliest ancient sources, 'Homer' represented a vast web of ever-expanding stories about gods and heroes whose power a community could invoke and appeal to by retelling them in sacred, communal settings. As long as the ancients perpetuated the cycle, their heroes were rendered eternal by being rendered eternally present. Though we will likely never know precisely what versions of our *Iliad* and *Odyssey* were recited across the ancient Greek world, the gods and heroes within these and other Trojan war epics were woven into this vast web of infinitely variable but interconnected stories.

The words *andra* and *histos* discussed above are just two of many instances of interconnections within Greek language and thought of elements that we moderns tend to put in separate boxes.

Together, these two words speak to the centrality of weaving not only literally, as an indispensable craft in the material reality of ancient life, but also for the metaphorical power of weaving. It signifies the mutual dependence and cooperation on which ancient men and women relied to thrive. As the ship required the woven cloth to sail, to build the loom required wood. As strategy could mitigate might, might could implement strategy. Masculine and feminine were oppositional, and they were complementary.

Though men and women in Homer (and in historical ancient Greece) occupy separate spheres of authority, these two authorities are framed as mutually dependent. Neither can survive, let alone thrive, without the other. This notion of mutual dependence is perhaps most acutely expressed in a speech of Polydamas to Hector in *Iliad* book thirteen, when the latter refuses to heed the former's counsel:

> Hector, you are impossible to persuade by words,
> Because a god has given you warlike ways among men,
> You therefore also wish to be skilled in counsel among others,
> But you yourself are not able to hold every ability at once.
> For a god gives to one man warlike ways,
> To another the dance, to a second the lyre and song,
> In another far-seeing Zeus places understanding
> Of what is noble, and many men reap the benefit of it,
> And he saves many people, and he himself knows this best.
>
> (Lines 726–734)

Polydamas is speaking here specifically of men, but when we focalise Homer's women and interpret the men through their relationships with them, Polydamas' point is revealed to resonate beyond the battlefield and beyond the domains of men alone. Hector is the acknowledged leader of the Trojan forces because of his might and valour. His willingness to accept the greatest risk by fighting on the front line makes him valuable and esteemed. It also makes him dangerous, not only for his antagonists but also for those closest to him because, as Polydamas cautions, Hector's pre-eminence in battle does not mean that he is the best at everything. Fighting skill is one among many skills that lead to a beneficial outcome, and each skill must be honoured and heeded. Polydamas' observation is reflected in the organisation of Olympus: Zeus is the acknowledged leader due to, as he repeatedly references, his preeminent might, but he cannot trample over the domains of others without consequences. Each god and goddess has a unique authority and skill that is essential and that must be worked with and respected. So too in the mortal world.

The cosmos itself was conceived as a fabric into which was woven each individual life spun by the Fates. This fabric could not be woven without the individual threads, and the individual threads derived their meaning and purpose by being woven into the fabric, which expanded without end. Each new thread enfolded into it varied from and expanded on familiar themes. The songs of Homer manifest this cosmic fabric; through any one story, one can access and be drawn into the whole of it. To hear the voices of Homer's women requires becoming attuned to the patterns that shape that whole. As such, the translations and discussions that follow strive neither to render the women of Homer familiar and palatable to modern sensibilities, nor to universalise their experiences as representative of women across time, nor to judge the world they inhabit as acceptable or unacceptable. Rather, they strive to illuminate the place of these women within the cosmic web into which their creators wove them. By examining the unique thread that each woman represents, we strive to perceive her essential place within that web.

We will begin with the 'queens', the women who are framed as authority figures within their respective communities, to consider how feminine authority is conceptualised and how it interacts with masculine authority. Following the leaders of women, we will explore the captives, whose narratives draw acute attention to its prevalence as a condition of ancient life. From the captives, we will shift to the goddesses, who are as essential in Homer as they were believed to be in the historical ancient world. The final category we will study are the heroes, the women in Homer who are arguably most significantly coded as heroic and most overlooked as such.

PART 1

QUEENS

THE 'QUEENS' IN this section are leaders of women who are married to leaders of men. Though they could slot into other categories as well, these are women who in Homer offer paradigms of feminine authority, which is portrayed, in immortal and mortal realms alike, as both complement to and competitor with masculine authority. To approach how the ancient Greeks may have conceptualised this seemly paradoxical notion of feminine authority benefits from insight into how the feminine itself is conceptualised within the tradition of retelling sacred stories. For this, it can be illuminating to look not only within Homer but also across ancient sources broadly located within the same time and culture.

Hesiod's *Theogony*, a cosmological epic dating with Homer to the archaic period, offers insight into the feminine concept via its narrative concerning the creation of the first mortal woman. Zeus orders her creation as a response to Prometheus, who provided men with the benefit of fire against Zeus' will. The creation of woman can thus be understood to restore balance in the mortal world against the advantage men acquired through the technology of fire. Her production is portrayed as a joint project of the craft goddess Athena and the craft god Hephaestus, under the direction of their father, Zeus:

> Straightaway, against the usefulness of fire, Zeus prepared a
>   danger for men
> For renowned Ambidexter[1] moulded from the earth
> The likeness of a venerable maiden, by the will of the son of
>   Cronus.
> The goddess owl-eyed Athena dressed and adorned her
> In a glittering garment with a veil over her head
> Held by a diadem crafted by hand, a wonder to behold.
> A crown of flowers of fresh-budding grass,
> Pallas Athena placed it round her lovely head,

> And round her head she set a gold band,
> Renowned Ambidexter crafted it for her himself,
> Working it in his hands to please father Zeus.
> Many cunning designs were worked into it, a wonder to behold,
> Of fearsome animals, the kind that land and sea nourish,
> He put in many of them, charm and grace were breathed into all,
> Wondrous, resembling living things voicing utterances,
> But after he made ready the beautiful danger against the useful,
> He led her out where gods and men assembled
> Made glorious by the adornments of the owl-eyed daughter of a mighty father.
> Wonder held both the deathless gods and mortal men
> As they beheld the sharp trap unmanageable by men,
> For from her is the race of women.
>
> (Lines 570–590)

Perhaps crucial to perceiving masculine and feminine as inextricably interwoven, Hesiod describes the creation of woman as the work of both Athena and Hephaestus, both children born from the parent of the opposite gender. Athena is born from Zeus after he absorbs her mother, Metis (meaning *cunning* or *resource*), and Hephaestus from Hera, seemingly in opposition:

> Without mingling in love, Hera to renowned Hephaestus
> Gave birth. She was quarrelling with her husband and put forth all her might.
>
> (Lines 928–929)

Hera's apparent competitiveness with Zeus inspires her to birth the god Hephaestus, who mirrors the daughter born of Zeus, Athena: both are associated with crafts, Hephaestus with the forge and metalworks, Athena with handcrafts and strategy. Thus, the competitiveness between Hera and Zeus is also generative, producing gods whose domains complement and supplement each other. Simultaneously, while the power of Zeus is affirmed through his ability to absorb Metis and assume control of her domain and daughter, the power of Hera is affirmed through her ability to birth a god by her own will and might.[2] In the immortal realm, masculine and feminine are thus portrayed as mirrors of and responses to each other. In competition, they can be complementary and generative when the strife between them achieves symmetry and balance. In the mortal world, the creation of women provides a challenge for men that balances the benefit of fire they received from Prometheus. In both the immortal and mortal realms, then, woman can be understood as a leveller.

In Homer, masculine and feminine authorities are portrayed as similarly complementary, competitive and interdependent. Masculine authority is generally associated with physical power and public speech and feminine authority with strategy and craft. The epic references the narrative Hesiod develops in *Theogony*: that Zeus gained his position as leader of the immortals through his might, by defeating earlier generations in battle. In the mortal realm, warriors distinguish themselves through their physical feats and as leaders in public assemblies. The wives of warriors – notably Andromache, Helen and Penelope – are all weavers who generate not only garments but also strategies and stories.

Yet these domains of masculine and feminine are mutable, among both gods and mortals in Homer. Hephaestus is a craft god, thus associating him with strategy, and his materials are metals and fire, thus associating him with physical strength. Athena is a war goddess who is depicted defeating Ares on the battlefield, thus associating her with might. She also weaves garments for the goddesses of Olympus, thus associating her with craft, and her schemes enable the reunion of Odysseus and Penelope, thus associating her with strategic planning. This mutability signifies the need for masculine and feminine to be integrated into a functional whole. A productive community, whether mortal or immortal, must achieve and maintain harmonious balance among its parts, a challenge that Homer portrays requiring constant and exhaustive effort.

His epics depict this balance as difficult to sustain in the immortal world and perhaps impossible in the mortal one. On Olympus, the conflicts between Hera and Zeus invite cosmic instability that threatens all involved. In the mortal realm of the *Iliad*, no matter how well or poorly Priam and Hecuba work together (or, in the *Odyssey*, Laertes and Anticleia), their rule remains vulnerable to internal and external threats, not only the disastrous decisions of their son, Paris, and the destructive consequences his behaviour invites but also the dictates of the Fates and the will of the gods. But as the queens of both the mortal and immortal realms demonstrate, when masculine and feminine powers work in harmony, they bring not the mere compliance of those they lead but cooperation. In this way, these leaders of women establish a model for how all parties can work together for the benefit of the community.

Hera

In the *Iliad*, the first speech of Hera, wife of Zeus, takes place at an assembly of the gods that appears at the close of book one. Each pivotal event leading up to this assembly has spiralled out of and echoes the conflict that set the war in motion: Trojan prince Paris taking Helen from Sparta to Troy. The *Iliad* begins with preeminent warrior Achilles and Achaean leader Agamemnon quarrelling over the latter's refusal to return the woman he had claimed as his war prize: Chryseis, the daughter of priest of Apollo Chryses. After Agamemnon was forced to relent and return Chryseis to her father, he confiscated Briseis, Achilles' war prize, for himself. As Achilles' grief over the loss escalated into rage, he appealed to his mother, the sea nymph Thetis, to use her influence with Zeus to restore her son's honour. Though aware that doing so would trigger strife with Hera, Zeus nevertheless agreed, for he owed Thetis a debt. As told by Achilles in his conversation with his mother, when the other Olympians had bound Zeus, seeking to overthrow him, Thetis had released him. She had then summoned Briareus, the hundred-handed giant, to subdue the mutinous gods, restoring Zeus to power. Zeus is thus beholden to Thetis for the stability of his reign, but his promise to honour her son at the expense of Achaean lives will mean angering his wife, Hera, whose support lies with the Achaeans, which could, in turn, threaten the stability of his reign.

By the time the first assembly takes place, a duality (resonant of the creation of the first woman as portrayed by Hesiod) has been established as a pattern: women can be both active agents who provoke conflict and passive objects within these conflicts. Each of these women is vulnerable to masculine might as an individual, but each is also part of a larger community that will, when possible, seek redress on her behalf, potentially leading to further escalation of conflict. This may be as true of Helen, daughter of Zeus, and the immortal Thetis as it is of Chryseis, who has been captured and enslaved. The queen of the gods, the wife of Zeus, Hera provides another variation on the pattern: she is the honoured wife and counterpart of Zeus, who Homer also repeatedly portrays, in her interactions with him, as his antagonist, simultaneously vulnerable to his power and capable of activating an uprising against him.

Her first speech in the epic is to reproach Zeus for plotting without her knowledge, prompting him to assert his dominance. He acknowledges her right, as his wife, to know his decisions before the other immortals but equally affirms his right to keep his own counsel when he deems it necessary. Yet Hera persists in questioning Zeus, revealing that she perceived his exchange with Thetis and now fears for the Achaeans. Provoked by this further challenge to his authority, Zeus calls Hera a *daimoni* – a superhuman force attempting to shape mortal outcomes – whose notice even he cannot elude:

> *Daimoni*, you are always thinking, and not even I can escape your notice.
>
> (Line 561)

The verb Zeus uses in the second part of his speech above is *lanthano*, meaning *to escape unnoticed*, the same verb used in *Iliad* book three to describe the effect of Aphrodite leading Helen to Paris (line 420[3]) and in *Odyssey* books two and nineteen when describing the effect of Penelope's ruse (lines 106 and 151, respectively[4]). In all three latter cases, the presence of a goddess (Aphrodite with Helen and Athena with Penelope) enables the women to go unnoticed by mortals. By addressing Hera as a *daimon* whose notice he cannot escape, Zeus seems to acknowledge her power in their marital dynamic, power that he must acknowledge in order to maintain cosmic stability.

To reaffirm his own control, Zeus resorts to threatening Hera with violence by his 'invincible hands', and she yields to him:

> So he spoke, and ox-eyed mistress Hera was afraid,
> And she sat in silence, bending her dear heart,
> And the heavenly ones, the gods in Zeus' house, were moved with indignation.
>
> (Lines 568–570)

The Greek word used to describe the reaction of 'the heavenly ones' in line 570 is *ochtheo*, which P. Considine notes is used when the figures involved feel their wills or intentions have been thwarted, and their anger issues from feeling powerless to alter the situation.[5] The reaction of the gods mirrors that of Hera. In the moment, they submit, but the anger they feel at having to do so calls up an echo of their previous attempt to overthrow Zeus, in which Hera was implicated, and invites the possibility that they might, if pushed too far, attempt to do so again in the future. It is thus not in Zeus', or the cosmic order's, best interests to push his power too far.

It is neither the first nor the last time that Zeus threatens Hera (and others) in the epic, just as it is neither the first nor the last time that a man's brutalisation of a woman will leave, or threaten to leave, destructive effects in its wake. In the case of Helen, a massive expedition was undertaken to restore her to Sparta. In the case of Chryseis, her father appealed to Apollo, who sent a destructive plague that ravaged the Achaean camp, ultimately compelling Agamemnon to return her. In the case of Briseis, the quarrel over her between Achilles and Agamemnon leads to further destruction for Achaeans and Trojans alike. In the end, Agamemnon is again compelled to return the 'prize' he insists he is owed. Here, the conflict between Zeus and Hera threatens to spill over, causing strife among the gods over whom Zeus and Hera rule. Such a conflict could have cosmic implications that affect Zeus as well. If a group of weaker gods pooled their strengths, they might again attempt to challenge Zeus. Whether or not they were to succeed in unseating him, the attempt itself could provoke destructive instability for all involved.

In the moment, Hera's son, craft god Hephaestus, steps in to restore peace. Noting that gods should not quarrel over mortals, which will become a repeated refrain across the epic, he affirms Zeus' physical dominance over the Olympians and comforts his mother, urging her to be patient. Hephaestus, who has also been the victim of Zeus' violence, acknowledges his father's superior power, but the threat below the surface lingers: every leader, even Zeus, is subject to challenge. He may be the strongest, but even Zeus can be rendered vulnerable. No single being's power is inviolate, and when a leader is challenged, the escalation of conflict leaves no one untouched, as evidenced by events in the mortal realm at Troy. Peace and stability can only be maintained through mutual accommodation, under the guidance of strong but flexible leaders who can usher their communities expertly through the inevitable conflicts of interest that arise within them. Hera's response, 'bending her dear heart' to Zeus' will, provides a model for the other gods to follow, and they too submit, however uneasily. Whether their acceptance of his commands proves lasting will depend on whether he acknowledges their authority in turn.

Iliad book four opens during another counsel among the gods, this one at a crucial crossroads in the narrative. Aphrodite's intervention prevented the duel between Menelaos and Paris from achieving the outcome the heroes intended: to prevent further Achaean and Trojan deaths in battle. While Paris reunites with Helen, Menelaos is left alone on the field, leading his brother Agamemnon to declare him the *de facto* victor and issuing an ultimatum to the Trojans to return Helen and her treasure or forfeit the truce.

If the Achaeans and the Trojans are permitted to resolve their discord peaceably, and the war is brought to an end, Zeus' promise to Thetis will remain unfulfilled: there will be no battles in which the Achaeans will suffer from the absence of Achilles, and he will remain dishonoured. At the same time, the Olympians who wish to see Troy punished, each for his or her own reasons, will also be left unsatisfied. The gods' discrete goals converge in a common intention for the war to continue.

Yet Zeus here, for reasons that he keeps to himself, chooses to provoke Hera (and Athena). Noting that Menelaos was the clear victor in the duel, Zeus then invites the Olympians to deliberate whether to allow the war to end or rouse further enmity among the Achaeans and Trojans. As Zeus intended, his suggestion angers Hera:

> So Zeus spoke, and Athena and Hera murmured,
> Seated near each other, thinking of ills for the Trojans.
> Now Athena was silent, she did not say anything,
> Feeling indignant with her father, Zeus, and wild wrath took her,
> But Hera's chest could not contain her anger, and she spoke,
> 'Dread son of Cronus, what sort of words have you said?
> How can you wish my toil to be fruitless, without fulfilment?
> I who by toil has sweated sweat, my horses have toiled
> Bringing together the people, to be a bane for Priam and his children.
> Do it, but don't expect all the other gods will approve.'
>
> (Lines 20–29)

The formulaic construction of book one, line 568 above and line 20 here ('so he spoke') followed by the effects of these speeches ('and ox-eyed mistress Hera was afraid' and 'and Athena and Hera murmured' respectively) recurs repeatedly across the epic. The drumbeat of repetition attunes us to the dynamic interaction between speaker and receiver, cause and effect, endings and beginnings. All exist in a relationship of mutual dependence. Further resonances of these live in Hera's language and her name itself. Hera objecting to her labour being left 'fruitless' and 'without fulfilment' evokes the labour associated with farming, which revolves around the cyclically recurring seasons. The name *Hera* in Greek may be related to the words for both time (*hora*) and heroes (*heroes*), implicating the wife of Zeus in seasonality and timing, specifically as these pertain to heroes, who themselves are frequently compared to trees.[6] Her speech ends with the subtly ominous threat that the other gods will not approve of Zeus' decision. This leaves open the possibility that Zeus acting unilaterally could invite future rebellion since unilateral action could itself be understood as a transgression of the cosmic order. Ending the war abruptly would contravene the authority other gods have over their own domains.

Characteristically outraged, Zeus shifts the focus of the discussion, again calling Hera a *daimoni* and demanding to know what Priam and the Trojans have done to earn her enmity. As in the scene between Aphrodite and Helen, Hera intends to exert influence over the outcome of mortal events. Here, her will is in conflict with that of Zeus. Though he concedes that he will not pursue further conflict with her, he questions her violent hatred of Troy, which he refers to as the city dearest to him. He concludes his response to Hera with a bold challenge that he may choose to destroy one of her favourite cities in the future. She in turn concedes his right to do so but appeals for mutual compliance based on their shared genealogy and her status as his wife:

> Then the mistress ox-eyed Hera responded to him,
> 'Truly, there are to me three cities most beloved,
> Argos, Sparta, and Mycenae of wide streets.
> Destroy them when they are hateful to your heart.
> I will not make a stand against you. I will not even complain.
> For even if I bore ill-will and did not allow you to destroy them,
> Bearing ill-ill would not accomplish anything, since you are stronger by far,
> But it is necessary that my toil not be without fulfilment,
> For I too am a god, the family that bore me bore you too,
> And crooked Cronus brought me into the world most honoured
> On account of both being from the same family and being your wife,
> As I am called, you are the lord of all the immortals,
> But now, we will yield to each other,
> Me to you, and you to me, and the other gods will follow,
> The immortals. Command Athena swiftly
> To bring dread battle to the Trojans and Achaeans
> To endeavour for the Trojans against the far-famed Achaeans,
> To be the first to lay waste to the oaths.'
> So she spoke, and the father of men and gods did not disobey her.
> Straightaway, he addressed Athena with winged words,
> 'Go at once to the camps of the Trojans and Achaeans
> To endeavour for the Trojans against the far-famed Achaeans

> To be the first to lay waste to the oaths.'
> So having spoken, he sent forth Athena, who was yearning to go.
> She stepped down, swooping from the head of Olympus.
>
> (Lines 50–74)

Hera acknowledges that attempting to defy Zeus would be unproductive, since he ultimately has the greater physical strength, but she draws on their shared status to make an appeal for cooperation through mutual concession. In this way, Hera tells Zeus they will provide a model that 'the other gods will follow'. Hera is also providing Zeus himself a model to follow of how to concede to others' authority, which he will perhaps most notably observe in his conduct towards Thetis in book twenty-four.

Recognising the wisdom of Hera's suggestion, which also converges with his own intention to honour Achilles, Zeus obeys Hera's command. The words she speaks to him are the same words he speaks to Athena. This repetition of language, which also occurs elsewhere in the epic when instructions are issued, reflects Zeus' faithful adherence to his covenant with Hera, and it emphasises the convergence of their wills in the moment. To sustain this harmony of immortal wills proves fragile across the *Iliad*, as the immortals continue to challenge each other both directly and by proxy through their favourite heroes.

Determined to fulfil his promise to Thetis, Zeus drives the Trojans and Achaeans into battle and fuels the surging Trojans. At this time, he forbids the other immortals from interfering. An indignant Poseidon, who resents taking orders from the brother with whom he shares the same ancestry, secretly works to embolden the Achaeans. Pleased, Hera schemes to support his efforts by distracting Zeus with seduction, and an extended scene follows her as she plots her strategy and prepares to carry it out:

> Ox-eyed mistress Hera then pondered
> How she might deceive the intention of aegis-bearing Zeus,
> And this plan appeared best in her consciousness,
> To come to Ida having made herself beautiful,
> If in some way, he might then long to lie with her in love
> Beside her body, and over him, sleep, kindly and warm,
> She would pour upon his eyelids and his wise perceptions.
> Going, she stepped into an inner room, built for her by her dear son,
> Hephaestus, he fit compact doors in a standing post

And a secret bolt, which no other god could open.
There, going in, she closed the shining doors.
First, from the surface of her desirable body, with ambrosia
She washed away all dirt and anointed herself with rich oil,
Ambrosial, sweet, full of fragrant scents,
And when set in motion across the bronze-floored house of Zeus,
Its fragrance reached across the earth and sky.
Having anointed the surface of her beautiful body, and her flowing locks
Having combed, she plaited with her hands the shining hair
On her head, beautiful, ambrosial, immortal.
She put on her ambrosial robe, which Athena,
Having crafted it smoothly, had set into it many cunning designs.
She pinned it over her chest with golden clasps,
And she tied on a belt with a hundred tassels,[7]
And she put in her well-pierced ear lobes earrings,
Skilfully wrought with three drops, their great charm shone brightly.
The goddess of Zeus covered her head with a veil,
Beautiful, newly made, it was as bright as the sun.
And under her shining feet, she tied beautiful sandals.

(Lines 159–186)

The scene provides a striking variation on the many similar scenes in the *Iliad* of warriors dressing for battle. While the warriors cloak their bodies in protective armour, Hera purifies and beautifies her body with ambrosia, an armour of immortality. The repeated use of the word 'ambrosia' in this context of a goddess preparing to seduce Zeus with potentially cosmic repercussions at stake draws attention to its immortalising properties and association with immortal power: The same word is used in scenes of goddesses anointing heroes at crucial moments. Thetis anoints the body of Patroclus with ambrosia to prevent it from decomposing while Achilles nurses his grief and refuses to bury him. In book nineteen, Athena anoints Achilles with ambrosia to prevent him from losing strength when he refuses, from grief, to eat or drink. In the *Odyssey*, Athena anoints Penelope with ambrosia before she presents herself to the suitors to rebuke them for failing to bring her appropriate gifts. When the word is not translated consistently across its appearances, that heroes – whether Patroclus, Achilles or

Penelope – are receiving as a gift the very immortalising substance used by the gods themselves can be obscured.

Hera's seduction briefly achieves its end, as Zeus submits to her charms and to sleep, but when he awakes, Hera once again faces the threat of violence and finds herself compelled to assure Zeus of her willingness to align herself with him rather than against him with Poseidon. He responds that if she were to be 'equal in understanding' with him while seated among the other immortals, then Poseidon would follow her lead (line 50). If this is her intention, then she must carry back to Olympus his instructions that Poseidon remove himself from battle while Apollo rouses the Trojans. As Zeus obeyed her in the book four assembly, Hera here obeys him:

> So he spoke, and the shining-armed goddess Hera did not disobey him,
> She stepped from mount Ida to wide Olympus,
> As the understanding of a man who speeds across much
> Land, having arrived, thinks with his wise perceptions,
> 'Would that I were in this place or that', he ponders many things,
> So swiftly did Hera in her intentions wing her way.
>
> (Lines 78–83)

Seemee Ali notes that Hera first appears in the *Iliad* as a thought that impacts human outcomes (suggestive of a *daimon*): observing the Achaeans suffering and dying by Apollo's plague in book one, she inspires Achilles to call an assembly to address the problem.[8] At other times, when the Achaean army descends into panic in books two and eight, Hera inspires the restoration of order, associating her with political stability. Here in book fifteen, Hera returns to Olympus and is greeted deferentially by all the immortals. After accepting a cup from Themis, goddess of Good Order, whose presence acts as a signal that the cosmic order will be set right, Hera calls the gods to sit for a feast and hear Zeus' plans, noting,

> We were disconnected when we desired to be apart from Zeus in our intentions.
>
> (Line 104)

As earlier, the other immortals eventually follow her lead, some more reluctantly than others. Poseidon issues a warning to Zeus: he will comply only as long as Zeus does not attempt to alter Troy's destiny. If he prevents

Troy from falling, Poseidon will no longer cooperate with him. The threat of potentially devastating consequences hang over Zeus and all the immortals, who would be compelled to choose sides.

If the Olympians provide a paradigm for ancient (and modern) receivers of epic, perhaps it is the inevitability of conflict and the fragility of balance. Again and again across the *Iliad*, the wills of the various immortals clash. Zeus attempts to herd them, like the proverbial cats, repeatedly appealing to his superior strength as an incentive. They continue to challenge him but always yield just before their conflicts escalate into total war, demonstrating an ability to restrain themselves and concede to order that does not exist in the mortal world of Homer. Crucial to maintaining this balance is Hera, who, though at times resentful and antagonistic, is also the first to prioritise peace among the immortals by not only ceding to Zeus' authority when it is expedient for her to do so but also affirming the importance of her own authority. In this way, she provides Zeus a model for mutual concession and cooperation, which both he and the other immortals follow.

Hecuba and Anticleia

Homer's depiction of Hecuba, wife of Trojan leader Priam and mother of preeminent warrior Hector, suggests that mortal women participate in the preservation of a city through their relationship to the gods and/or through their roles as wives and mothers of warriors. To appreciate the significance of these roles requires the ability to suspend any disbelief one may have in the immortals. In the world of Homer, gods and goddesses are present and powerful, and their opposition or support turns the tides of battle across the *Iliad* and either subverts or preserves Odysseus' homecoming in the *Odyssey*.

The first time Hecuba is named occurs in book six, after her son Helenus, who serves as both warrior and seer, sends Hector to their mother with instructions to oversee prayers to Athena. He advises her 'to convene with the elder women' (line 87) at the temple of Athena and present the goddess with a beautiful garment of Hecuba's choice along with a sacrifice of twelve young cows. The gathering of women elders at the temple evokes the gathering of the elder men on the walls of Troy in *Iliad* book three, with a crucial variation: while the elder men oversee the duel that they hope will preserve the city, the elder women oversee the prayers to the immortals who they hope will protect the city. Both warfare and prayer are portrayed as essential to the survival of the city, both in the *Iliad* and in the historical period when the epics were performed at sacred festivals. Hecuba follows the instructions of Helenus, under the guidance of Theano, the priestess of Athena at Troy who offers the prayers and sacrifices. But unlike in classical Athens, where women of the city themselves wove the *peplos* that was presented to Athena under the direction of her priestess, Hecuba offers a beautiful garment woven not by Trojans but by captive women, perhaps a portent of the fate that awaits her after the city falls.

The *Iliad* does not depict the end of the war, the fall of Troy and the subsequent enslavement of Hecuba, but the death of Hecuba's son Hector signifies it. With its foremost defender defeated, the city can only fall and its surviving population, primarily women and children, captured and enslaved. Social status within Troy does not protect them in the post-Troy world, though it does impact to whom these women and children will be distributed. The higher their status, the more valuable they are as war prizes. The conditions of their enslavement remain unaffected, as expressed in Andromache's book six speech to Hector. As the wife of Priam, Troy's leader, Hecuba would presumably be among the most prized. Yet unlike Andromache, Hecuba mentions little about her own fate in the five speeches she gives in books twenty-two and twenty-four. Her concern instead is the fate of her city and the fate of her son, in life and after it.

Hecuba's first speech in book twenty-two is a plea to Hector. Following the death of Patroclus, Achilles' relentless and merciless rampage has driven the Trojans back toward the city, but while the rest of the warriors rush through the gates, Hector remains outside them, resolved to face Achilles in single combat. Priam begs him to relent and shelter in the city, describing in excruciating detail the horrors that await him after his son's death. The elder of Troy will be forced to witness the slaughter of his people; he will be murdered, and his corpse left as food for his own dogs. Hecuba follows Priam with a plea of her own, speaking first and foremost as a mother:

> Then in turn, his mother, pouring tears,
> Letting go the folds of her garment, she held up one of her breasts,
> And tears pouring, she spoke winged words,
> 'Hector, my child, have reverence and show pity for me,
> If ever I held this breast to you, to banish your cares,
> Remember this, dear child, and ward off this destructive man
> From inside the walls, and do not take a stand against this foremost fighter,
> Unwearying man, for if he were to kill you, I would not for you

> Weep on your death bed, dear child, who I myself bore,
> Nor would your richly dowered wife, but far away from us two,
> Beside the ships of the Argives, swift dogs would devour you.'
>
> (Lines 79–89)

Hecuba's actions and words can seem puzzling to modern readers who may not be conditioned to expect a queen to nurse her own child or to expose her body in a public space. Yet these acts draw stark attention to her loss as a mother who anticipates her son's body, the same body she nourished physically and emotionally, becoming disfigured, devoured, and left without a proper burial. Crucially, she includes Andromache, suggesting the sacred responsibility wives and mothers have to perform funeral rites, essential for the transition from life to afterlife.[9] Further, her concern over the state of Hector's body alludes to his status as a sacred hero, as becomes increasingly highlighted in her further speeches.

Priam and Hecuba's appeals fail to move Hector, who remains where he is as Achilles swiftly approaches:

> They two addressed their dear son in this way, weeping
> With many entreaties, but they did not persuade Hector's consciousness,
> But he stood fast for gigantic Achilles, coming closer.
>
> (Lines 90–92)

From the city walls, Hector's parents watch Achilles strike down their son, tie him to the wheels of his chariot and drag him through the dirt. Desperate to rush outside the gates and confront Achilles, Priam is forcibly restrained as he laments his most beloved son. Hecuba follows with her own lament:

> My child, I am wretched. Why should I now live through this grim suffering
> Of you having been killed, who was to me, night and day,
> My prayer, my pride throughout the city, a treasure in every way,
> For the Trojans and the Trojan women throughout the state, who you like a god
> They received, for truly, you were an exceedingly great prize for them,
> When you were alive, but now, death and your portion have reached you.
>
> (Lines 430–436)

Hecuba's language in Greek holds layers of meaning. On arguably the most transparent and relatable level for modern readers, she speaks as a mother who is proud of her cherished son, who fulfilled his responsibilities as a leader of the people and who earned their respect and admiration. Hecuba referring to Hector as her 'prayer' collapses her roles: she is the mother of a son who is the best defence for the city she leads, and the answer to her prayers. The words in the Greek text also subtly suggest Hector's status as a hero and future figure of worship. He was a prize, a *kudos*, for the people, and they received him as a god, a *theos*. The word *kudos* refers to the reputation, rewards and honours that heroes receive for their superhuman feats, which can lead to the *kleos* that immortalises them. Both *kudos* and *kleos* are frequently translated as 'glory' or 'renown'; more specifically, the former seems to imply the physical manifestations of glory and the latter the eternal breath of song. The emphasis on the material in this moment, via the use of *kudos*, underscores the magnitude of a mother's loss in the moment she is living through it, for which there is no compensation.

In her final lament for Hector delivered at the end of the *Iliad*, Hecuba is aware that the gods have favoured her son, since his body shows no sign of destruction or decay, but if this brings her comfort, it does not ease her grief:

> 'Hector, dearest in my consciousness of all my children,
> Truly, even though you were dear to the gods in life,
> They care also for your portion in death,
> For all my other children swift-footed Achilles
> Sold, who he took across the fruitless sea
> To Samos, to Imbros and inhospitable Lemnos.
> When he took out your mortal identity with sharp bronze,
> He dragged you many times around the tomb of his companion,
> Patroclus, who you struck down, though not even this could resurrect him.
> Now dewy and freshly slain, in the great room, by me
> You are laid out, resembling someone who Apollo of the silver bow,
> Having approached, has slain with his gentle arrows.'
> So she spoke, weeping in ceaseless lamentation.
>
> (Lines 747–760)

Significantly, Hecuba reflects on the futility of retribution; killing Hector and desecrating his corpse did not restore Patroclus to life. Once the hero crosses the boundary into Hades, nothing can bring him bodily back to the land of light and life. In observing this about Patroclus, Hecuba is also commenting on Hector's loss. Nothing can mitigate it; nothing can compensate for it. Hecuba thus never speaks of Hector receiving *kleos*, though he has received it by virtue of being woven into this song, this *Iliad*, and though she does apply this term to Priam.

Earlier in book twenty-four, spurred by the gods, who have commanded Achilles to return Hector's body to his father, Priam resolves to make his way to the Achaean camp and supplicate his son's killer. Hecuba opposes him emphatically:

> So he spoke, and his wife shrieked and responded with this speech,
> 'Ah me, your perceptions have gone, you who in times past
> Were made famous through song both among foreigners and those you rule over.
> How can you wish to go alone among the ships of the Achaeans,
> Into the vision of a man who of many and the best
> Of your sons has stripped you? Your heart now is made of iron,
> For if he sees you with his eyes and captures you,
> That treacherous eater of raw flesh will show no pity for you.
> Nor will he have any reverence. Now, let us weep from a distance
> Seated in the great room, as mighty Fate for him
> Spun this thread when he was born, when I brought him into the world,
> To satiate swift-footed dogs far away from his parents
> By a mighty man. I would have the middle of his liver,
> I would devour it, digesting it, then retributive acts would be born,
> For my son was not a coward when Achilles killed him,
> But before the men of Troy and the deep-girdled Trojan women,
> He made a stand, having no thought of fear or escape.'
> (Lines 200–216)

The violence of Hecuba's reply reflects her desire for retribution on a mortal level, the same kind of retribution that she will, in her final lament, recognise as futile. Here, though, she thinks not of recovering her son's body and performing funeral rites for him, seeming to accept its loss as fated, but of avenging her son. By contrast, Priam is concerned with attempting to recover the body at any cost, even if it means losing his life. The disconnect between them in this moment emerges not because one is right and the other wrong but because they approach the crisis from different points of view. Hecuba is thinking like a mother concerned not with honours for the hero Hector but with his loss as a mortal son and defender of the city, while Priam thinks as the warriors across the *Iliad* do, for whom protecting the bodies of their dearest companions is a primary responsibility.

What brings Hecuba and Priam into harmony once more is turning their attention to divining the gods' will. Hecuba's final appeal to Priam is to make an offering to and seek an omen from Zeus. If the response is favourable, only then should Priam travel to the Achaean encampment:

> Drawing near, Hecuba came to him, sorrowing in her consciousness,
> Having sweet wine in her right hand
> In a golden chalice, in order that he would go having poured an offering.
> Making a stand before the horses, she spoke these words to Priam by name,
> 'Here, pour a libation to father Zeus and pray that you will reach home,
> Back again from these hostile men, since your consciousness
> Urges you upon the ships, though I do not wish it,
> But pray then to the son of Cronus of the blood-dark clouds
> On Mount Ida, who looks down upon all Troy,
> Ask for a bird omen – a swift messenger, who to him are
> The dearest of birds and whose strength is greatest –
> On your right-hand side, so that, observing it with your eyes,
> You can go, trusting it, to the ships of the Danaans of the swift horses.
> If far-seeing Zeus does not give you his own messenger,
> I not would then urge you to be urged on,
> To go to the Argives' ships, even though you very much yearn to.'
>
> (Lines 283–298)

Hecuba here addresses Priam as she addressed Hector in her plea to him to seek shelter in the city: she is concerned about the consequences on the living man rather than with the legend he might become to future generations. This aligns her with another Trojan wife, Andromache, who begged Hector in book six not to pursue single combat with Achilles.

Hecuba and Andromache's concerns echo in a speech by Anticleia, mother of Odysseus and wife of Laertes, king of Ithaca, as reported by her son.

While narrating the story of his wanderings to the Phaeacians, Odysseus describes his visit to the land of the dead, which included an emotional reunion with his mother, who it is implied died during his protracted absence. In book eleven, Odysseus reports that he asked his mother about her manner of death and about his father, son and wife, and she gave this reply:

> Suffering exceedingly in her consciousness, Penelope remains there
> In your great rooms, always misery for her,
> Pouring tears, her nights and days wither away.
> Up to this time, no one as yet holds your great status but unmolested,
> Telemachus possesses your land and has an equal share of the feast.
> He feasts as is fitting to provide a dispenser of justice,
> For all call upon him. Your father himself remains
> In the fields, he neither returns to the city nor has a bed,
> A bedstead, nor a cloak and glittering blanket,
> But he lies down to sleep in winter where dwell slaves captured in war,
> In the ashes near the fire, and he wears rough clothes against his skin,
> But when the abundant harvest comes in late summer,
> Everywhere along the curves of his wind-producing orchards,
> Leaves are thrown on the ground, making a bed.
> There he lies, grieving, he strengthens the great sorrow in his perceptions,
> Longing for your return, difficult old age has come upon him.
> For in this way I too destroyed myself and pursued my destiny.
> The keen-eyed shooter of arrows[10] neither to me in the great rooms
> Approached and killed with her gentle arrows,
> Nor did some sickness come upon me, the kind which most
> Takes the consciousness from one's limbs in abominable wasting away.
> But longing for your counsels and schemes, shining Odysseus,
> Your gentleness, took away honey-sweet consciousness.
>
> (180–204)

In Greek, Anticleia's name means 'against kleos', which aligns with Odysseus' portrait of her through her speech that he reports. Anticleia makes no mention of Odysseus' fame, past, present or future. She shows no concern for any prizes he may have received at Troy nor with any songs that may be sung about him after the war. What she missed was his presence – his 'counsels', 'schemes' and 'gentleness'. Grieving the loss of her son, the man he had grown into, consumes and ultimately robs her of her life.

For the mothers (and wives) of heroes, there is no compensation for the loss of their sons (and husbands). In the lived moment, neither material nor eternal rewards can replace the man himself, nor can it save them from enslavement, nor comfort them in their old age. The wisdom of the epics lies in their ability to acknowledge their own limits, reflected in their sensitive depiction of women's grief and the weight and import it is given as a balance against the project of epic, *kleos*, for which their grief is both complementary and oppositional. While it cannot compensate a family for the loss of their loved one, memory is all that remains. Homer's 'songs of fame' immortalise not only the 'famous deeds' of heroes but also the grief of those who they left behind in life.

Arete

In the *Odyssey*, Odysseus' last stop before reaching Ithaca is the island of the Phaeacians, which is portrayed as a liminal space, an in-between place. It is neither the realm of the immortals nor fully integrated into the mortal world. Up to this point in Odysseus' journey, Athena has largely been advocating on his behalf out of scene. Though she will not reveal herself to him until he returns home, she does appear to him in the guise of a young woman to advise him, and he follows in her footsteps as she leads him to the dwelling place of Arete and her family. Its symmetry and abundance can be observed in both the heroes who dwell there and in the natural world they inhabit:

> Just as the Phaeacian men were skilled in all things to do with
> Quick ships to drive across the sea, so were its women
> Skilled with the loom, for Athena had given them
> Knowledge of beautiful works and noble perceptions.
> Outside the yard near the door was a great orchard of
> Four acres, and all around it a high wall was set.
> There, tall, luxuriant trees flourished,

> Bearing beautiful pears and pomegranates and apples,
> Sweet fig trees and olive trees flourished,
> Whose fruit neither perished nor failed to grow,
> Neither in winter nor summer, from year to year, but always
> Blowing Zephyr made some grow and others ripen,
> Pear upon pear ripened, apple upon apple,
> Grapes upon grapes, figs upon figs.
> (Lines 108–120)

The description of the Phaeacians' land evokes Hesiod's description in *Works and Days* of the Isles of the Blessed, where heroes dwell after their mortal deaths in the wars at Thebes and Troy:

> Then truly they were enfolded by the fulfilment of death,
> But for them, life and a place separate from mortals,
> Father Zeus, son of Cronus, settled them at the ends of the earth,
> And there they dwell, having a carefree consciousness,
> On the islands of the blessed near deep-eddying Ocean,
> Blessed heroes, the honey-sweet fruit
> The life-giving land brings forth, blooming three times a year.
> (Lines 166–172)

In this idealised land of the Phaeacians, Athena advises Odysseus, he can secure his return if he can secure the approval of Arete, wife of Alcinous and leader with him of the Phaeacians, whose name in Greek means *she who is prayed to*. Athena recounts the genealogy of Arete at length:

> The first person you reach in the great rooms is the queen of the house,
> Arete is her given name in the family line,
> The same one that also brought into the world the king, Alcinous.
> First Nausithous was a son of the earth-shaker Poseidon,
> And Periboea gave birth to him, the best in form among women,
> The youngest daughter of great-hearted Eurymedon,
> Who once ruled over the high-spirited Giants,
> But he destroyed the people with his recklessness, and he destroyed himself.
> Poseidon mingled with Periboea, and she birthed a child,
> Great-spirited Nausithous, who was lord over the Phaeacians.
> Nausithous brought into the world Alcinous and Rhexenor,

> Having no sons when Apollo of the silver bow struck him,
> Recently married in the great room, leaving behind one girl only,
> Arete, and Alcinous made her his wife,
> And he honours her, as no other woman is honoured upon the earth,
> As many as now have a home under their husbands.
> In this way, she was and is honoured from the heart,
> By both her dear children and Alcinous himself,
> And by the people, who look upon her as if she were a god.
> She receives their utterances when she walks through the city,
> For she is not lacking a noble way of understanding,
> Who possesses wise perception and solves the quarrels of men.
> If she has kindly thoughts about you in her consciousness,
> Then you may have hope to see your dear ones and to reach
> Your high-roofed home and the land of your fathers.
>
> (Lines 53–77)

Athena's extended attention to Arete's origins reveals that her lineage traces back to the god Poseidon, establishing Arete not only as the leadership counterpart of her husband but as a hero in her own right. She is descended from an immortal and regarded 'as if she were a god', as Hecuba describes Hector in Iliad book twenty-two (line 434). While Arete's ancestry confers status, she also possesses qualities that mark her as exceptional. According to Athena, Arete's nobility and wisdom have earned the trust of her husband and people, who seek her counsel to resolve their conflicts. Athena portrays Arete as a stabilising force, who enables the Phaeacians to achieve and maintain harmonious balance.

Odysseus heeds the disguised Athena's counsel and presents himself to Arete, who questions him in the traditional manner: she asks who he is and where he is from. Her third question, however, varies the formula slightly, as she has noticed that, though he claims to be a stranger, he is wearing a familiar garment:

> And speaking winged words, she addressed Odysseus,
> 'Guest-friend, first I will ask you this,
> Who among men are you, and from where do you come? Who gave you this garment?
> Did you not claim that you reached this place having wandered upon the sea?'
>
> (Lines 236–239)

The garment Odysseus is wearing has captured Arete's attention because it was crafted 'by she herself and her women servants' (line 235). Her daughter, Nausicaa, had given it to Odysseus earlier, when she discovered him after he had washed ashore. In addition to highlighting Arete's 'wise perception', as Athena noted in her speech, Arete's recognition of the garment also conveys that woven cloth carries the signature of its maker and/or designer. Upon seeing Odysseus' clothing, Arete immediately perceives that he has had contact with someone in her household. His clothing carries her signature, not because she has signed her name but by the mark of her unique craft.

Odysseus' response satisfies Arete, securing his journey home to Ithaca. Before sending him off, the Phaeacians treat him as a revered guest, observing the sacred laws of hospitality. In book eight, Odysseus is bathed, offered food and given valuable gifts, among them clothes:

> Arete came up to the stranger with a beautiful chest
> Brought from an inner room. She set in it beautiful gifts,
> Clothing and gold, which the Phaeacians gave.
> She herself set out for him a cloak and a beautiful tunic,
> And speaking winged words, she addressed him.
> 'Now, see to this lid for yourself. Quickly whip a knot on it,
> So that no one may make mischief during your journey, when again
> You lie in honey-sweet sleep, going in our ink-dark ships.'
> (Lines 433–445)

The land of the Phaeacians is Odysseus' final stop before arriving back in Ithaca, but it appears early in the narrative timeline of our *Odyssey*. Thus, a first-time modern reader may not yet know the nature of the trials Odysseus has faced on his long journey home. He has not yet narrated them for the Phaeacians, or for us. But for modern re-readers or ancient hearers well-acquainted with Odysseus' trials and errors, Arete's advice to carefully secure the chest containing his gifts so that 'no one may make mischief' can seem pointed. It is a proactive measure that Odysseus himself did not take: earlier in his journey, he failed to secure the bag of winds gifted to him by Aeolus to carry him and his companions back to Ithaca. With their home on the immediate horizon, while Odysseus slept, his curious and mistrustful companions released the winds too soon, resulting in his protracted journey and, ultimately, their own deaths. Implementing Arete's advice, Odysseus ties a cunning knot he learned from Circe, who he encountered after the incident with Aeolus' winds. If Odysseus had possessed Arete's advice and knowledge of Circe's knot, his journey could have been much shorter, and his *kleos* also likely forfeit.

PART 2
CAPTIVES

CAPTIVITY CAN TAKE many forms both in Homer and ancient Greek culture. In a sense, all mortals could be understood as captives of the immortals, as suggested in the dynamic between Helen and Aphrodite in the *Iliad* book three scene discussed earlier. In the historical ancient world, enslavement could result from war (as the Trojan women anticipate being enslaved following Hector's death), from abduction (as Chryseis and Briseis are captured in raids in the *Iliad* and Eumaeus by his own enslaved caretaker in the *Odyssey*) or from being born into it. For the purposes of our discussion, the women in this section are those whose captivity shapes or is foregrounded in their narratives.

As in the previous section, these women could align with other categories as well. Thetis, for example, is a goddess, and Helen is coded as both hero and goddess.[1] Placing these women alongside others whose captivity is more readily apparent to our modern perception – Briseis, Eurycleia, an unnamed barley grinder and Melantho – draws our attention to the dualities and permeable boundaries that preoccupied the ancient Greeks. They conducted their sacred festivals around transitions of the seasons, repeating them annually according to the eternally recurring rhythms of the natural world. The meanings of their myths are shaped around this seasonality and cyclicality, perhaps in the hope that, as the decay of winter eventually gives way to rebirth in spring, suffering too could be reborn into something generative and nourishing.

Yet the epics do not reduce this hope for purpose to a toxic positivity that obscures the depth of captive women's suffering, which is portrayed with heart-breaking clarity in Homer. Nor are these women undifferentiated props who exist solely to move the narrative and promote the fame of male heroes. Though they live as captives in a variety of forms, their conditions are not their identity in the epics. Each of these women is part of her own community who receives, recognises and amplifies her grief. Whether a leader of women facing certain enslavement after the death of her husband (Hecuba), a goddess mourning the mortality of her son (Thetis), or an enslaved labourer exhausted by her ceaseless toil (the barley grinder), Homer's epics give voice to these women's grief and pain, simultaneously recognising their place in a larger pattern of suffering associated with mortality, the unavoidable Fate which makes captives of all mortals.

Hesiod's depiction of the first woman's creation in *Works and Days*, his second, didactic epic, offers further insight into the interconnection of mortality and captivity as conceptualised in Homer. While *Theogony* narrates the lives and battles of immortals, *Works and Days* is concerned with mortal life during Hesiod's own time. Framed as advice for his brother, who is quarrelling with Hesiod, it provides advice for farming, sailing and lucky days for undertaking specific activities, and it offers an aetiology for human suffering, the same one offered in *Theogony*: Prometheus' attempts to help men, against Zeus' will, provoked Zeus to balance advantage with disadvantage:

> Against the fire, I will give to men a danger, with whom all
> Will delight in their consciousness while warmly embracing
>   his own harm.
>
> (Lines 57–58)

Zeus then calls on not only Athena and Hephaestus but also Aphrodite, Hermes, Persuasion, the Graces and the Hours to participate in the creation of woman, and Hermes gives her the name 'Pandora':

> Zeus ordered renowned Hephaestus as quickly as possible
> To mix water and earth and to put in human speech,
> Also strength, and a face in the likeness of the deathless
>   goddesses,
> A lovely maiden with a beautiful form, then Athena
> To teach her crafts, to weave cunningly wrought cloth,
> And for golden Aphrodite to pour charm over her head,
> Also painful longing and consuming sorrows,
> And to put in a shameless understanding and a wily nature,
> He commanded from Hermes, the messenger and slayer of Argus.
> So he spoke, and they obeyed the leader Zeus, son of Cronus.
> Straightaway, renowned Ambidexter moulded her from the earth
> Resembling a modest maiden, by the will of the son of Cronus.
> The goddess owl-eyed Athena dressed and adorned her,
> And the Graces and mistress Persuasion, goddesses,
> They set chains of gold on her skin, all around,

The beautiful-haired Hours crowned her with spring flowers.
Pallas Athena fitted all the adornments on her body,
And in her chest, the messenger, the slayer of Argus,
Falsehoods, flattering words and a wily nature
He furnished, by the will of loud-thundering Zeus, and in her a voice
The messenger of the gods put. He named this woman
Pandora because all those who have homes on Olympus
Gave her a gift, a bane for men who labour.
(Lines 60–82)

Appropriate to his theme of human life, Hesiod discusses the qualities with which the first woman is imbued in greater detail than he does when focused on the immortal realm in *Theogony*. Significantly, he emphasises that each of Pandora's attributes, which present such a 'bane for men who labour', is an immortal gift, an attribute shared and bestowed by gods and goddesses. The meaning of *Pandora* – *all the gifts* – holds a duality: it indicates both that she has received all the gifts and that she gives all the gifts, both beneficial and harmful. The two are inextricably interwoven in the 'unmanageable trap' Zeus devised (line 83). Hesiod concludes his narrative of Pandora's creation with the observation, 'In this way, no one can escape the intention of Zeus' (line 105).

In Homer, all mortals are likewise portrayed as captives to Fate and the gods. Each mortal is a thread in a cosmic web so much larger than him- or herself that she or he cannot perceive its full scope and cannot be sure what future awaits him or her. As queens can become captives, captives can become queens. Perhaps the hope for purpose through suffering is an insistence on agency in the face of all that lies beyond the control of mortals and the dictates of Fate, which not even immortals can circumvent. If these captive women cannot prevent the worst from happening in the moment, perhaps they can ensure that their grief is woven into the song that carries fame, the epic itself, which has immortalised them.

The barley grinder

Perhaps the most overlooked captive woman in Homer is the unnamed barley grinder who appears in book twenty of the *Odyssey*. She is heard once, on the day Penelope and Odysseus each wake up disoriented, having dreamt that the other was beside him and her. Ever mindful of the gods,

Odysseus utters a prayer to Zeus, asking for an omen. The god complies, sending a thunderbolt shooting down from Olympus. It is here the barley grinder enters the scene. She is one of twelve women responsible for grinding grains and the only one still at work, which enables her to witness the thunderbolt:

> She alone had not yet stopped, the most powerless one was still working,
> Making the millstone stand, she spoke a sign for her master.
> 'Father Zeus, you who rule gods and humans,
> You thundered loudly from the star-filled sky,
> Though no clouds are anywhere, you made this omen appear now for someone.
> Bring to pass now the words that, in my wretched state, I would say:
> Let this be the very last day that the suitors
> Take a lovely feast in the great room of Odysseus
> The suitors have loosened my knees with heart-grieving toil,
> Preparing barley for them, now let them have their last meal.'
>
> (Lines 110–119)

Notably, she is given neither a name nor a genealogy, two language features that attend heroes. She is described as the most powerless and the only one still labouring. Yet she utters the crucial omen that reassures Odysseus of his future success. As with 'the masses of men' who cannot all be named by the bard of the *Iliad*, the barley grinder's name is not recorded, but Homer does not allow us to forget that every mortal, from the humblest to the most exalted by mortals and immortals, is an essential thread woven into the cosmic fabric.

Eurycleia and Melantho

In contrast to the nameless barley grinder, Eurycleia's significance in the epic is announced by her name, which means *broad fame*. From the story perspective, she is a captive woman in the household of Odysseus who raised both him and his son, Telemachus. She functioned as a foster-mother to both men, and she has remained loyal to her former master and dedicated to his wife and son during his long absence. From the perspective of the epic project, Eurycleia, like Helen, is dually coded, in her case as both captive and hero.

When she is introduced at the end of book one, no speech is yet attributed to her. Rather, her genealogy unfolds as she tends to Telemachus, who is preparing for sleep:

> Kindling a torch, a trusted servant at once brought it to Telemachus, knowing
> Eurycleia, the daughter of Ops, the son of Pisenor.
> Laertes bought her with his own possessions,
> When she was in the prime of youth, he gave twenty oxen worth for her.
> He honoured her in the great room equivalent to his trusted wife,
> But he never mingled with her in bed, to avoid the anger of his wife.
> At once, she brought the kindled torch to Telemachus, and he most of all
> Was dear to the woman captured in war, and she nourished him when he was small.
> He opened the doors of the solidly made inner room,
> And he seated himself on the bed and took off his short tunic,
> And he put it in the hands of the elder, shrewd in counsel,
> And she folded the tunic with great care,
> Hanging it on a peg beside the carved bed.
> She stepped out of the inner room to go and pulled the door handle
> Of silver and stretched upon the bolt a leather strap.
> He was there all night long, covered with fine sheep's wool,
> Deliberating with his perceptions the journey that Athena had indicated for him.
>
> (Lines 428–444)

Several features of Eurycleia's introduction cohere with the introduction of heroes across both epics. In the *Iliad*, heroes who fall in battle are memorialised with the same formula: their genealogies (the names of their fathers and possibly grandfathers) are presented on one line, and ensuing lines provide a glimpse into their lives beyond the battlefield. Here, Eurycleia's genealogy is contained within its own line and ensuing lines add layers of information to her story. It is revealed that Laertes purchased Eurycleia with his own wealth and treated her with the respect due and paid to his own wife, though he did not touch her. In contrast to the violence that follows the introduction of warrior heroes in the *Iliad*, the rest of this scene is quiet, showing Eurycleia and Telemachus wordlessly cycling through the daily task of preparing for bed. When viewed through the lens of pattern and variation, the interactions between Telemachus and Eurycleia, heroes in a domestic scene, seem to provide contrast to and complement with the interactions of heroes on the battlefield.

The word used to describe Eurycleia in the final line of the first stanza is *dmoee,* whose broadest definition is 'enslaved woman' but which more specifically can be used to refer to those captured in war. The presence of this word seems significant for the beginning of this post-war epic. The fall of Troy is not portrayed in Homer, but the inevitability of the women's enslavement is implied in the laments of Andromache, Priam and Hecuba. Though it does not tell the stories of what the Trojan women endured, the *Odyssey* remembers them; their experiences reverberate through the presence of 'enslaved women captured in war' across the epic.

Eurycleia's potential status as a hero and her role as Telemachus' foster-mother is signalled also by the epithet she shares in common with Penelope: *periphron,* which literally translates to *thinking all around* and is rendered below (and elsewhere) as *circumspect.* Her speech in the following passage from book twenty is addressed to Telemachus, who has questioned whether his mother is adequately looking after their guest, who both he and Eurycleia know is Odysseus in disguise:

> Circumspect Eurycleia again addressed him,
> 'You must not assign causation to her now, child, for she is not the cause,
> For the man drank his wine, seated, as long as he himself wished to be,
> And he said that he was not hungry for food, for she asked him,
> But when he was reminded of a place to lie down and sleep,
> She commanded that a bed be spread out by enslaved women captured in war,
> But he, as one altogether woeful and unhappy,
> Did not want to lie down on a bed or rug,
> But on an untamed ox hide and fleece.
> He slept in the forecourt, and we put a cloak on him.'
> So she said, and Telemachus stepped out through the great room.
> (Lines 134–144)

As expressed in the description of her at line 438 of book one, Eurycleia does not refrain from advising either Telemachus or Penelope, with the intention of promoting harmony and reconciliation. When Telemachus discloses his intention to sail to Pylos and Sparta in book two, Eurycleia begs him to reconsider, presciently anticipating that the suitors will plot to destroy him, which they do:

> So he spoke, and his dear nurse Eurycleia shrieked,
> And wailing, she spoke winged words,
> 'Dear child, why this thought in your perception
> Has come? How can you wish to go across so much land
> Alone, being beloved as you are? He has perished far from his fatherland,
> Among unknown people, Odysseus, born from Zeus.
> You having gone, the suitors will plan a future harm against you straightaway.
> You might decay in their trap, and they will all divide these things among themselves,
> But be seated here on this spot. It is not necessary for you
> To suffer ills or to wander across the fruitless sea.'
>
> (Lines 361–370)

Her recognition of the suitors' intentions exemplifies her attentiveness, perception and insight. She is consulting with Telemachus for his benefit, which Telemachus understands. In his response, he assures her that the plan is not his own invention but immortal intention and directs her to swear that she will not reveal his departure to his mother until questioned directly:

> 'Be of good courage, foster-mother, since this plan is not without the will of a god,
> But swear to say nothing of this to my dear mother
> Until the eleventh or twelfth day has come to pass,
> Taking your cue either from my mother missing me or having heard of my departure,
> So that her weeping does not spoil her beautiful skin.'
> So he spoke, and the old woman spoke a great oath by the gods,
> But when she had sworn and brought her oath to fulfilment,
> Then straightaway, she drew the wine into amphorae,
> And she poured barley into well-stitched leather bags.
> Going through the house, Telemachus joined the company of the suitors.
>
> (Lines 372–381)

Eurycleia fulfils her oath, keeping Telemachus' journey to herself until Penelope raises the subject at the end of book four. When Eurycleia then reveals all, Penelope's instinct is to send the news to Laertes, Telemachus' grandfather:

> If weaving some cunning among his perceptions,
> And coming here, he might make a grievance against those
>   who are eager
> To see his people and those of Odysseus, equal to a god, wither
>   on the vine.
>
> (Lines 739–741).

Eurycleia again shows her wisdom in counsel. She advises Penelope against troubling the elder. Instead of appealing to a mortal, masculine authority, she instructs Penelope to appeal instead to Athena, the immortal authority who moves through both masculine and feminine domains:

> But using water to clean your skin and choosing a garment,
> Going to the upper part of the house with your trusted women
> Pray to Athena, daughter of aegis-bearing Zeus,
> For she may yet save Telemachus from death,
> Without distressing a distressed elderly man, for I do not
>   suppose
> The people of the son of Arcisius[2] are by the blessed gods
>   altogether
> Hated, but someone in the future will be there who will hold
> His high-roofed rooms and fertile fields beyond.
>
> (Lines 750–757)

Penelope immediately sets Eurycleia's advice in motion, ascending to her rooms to pray to Athena. In turn, the goddess responds by appearing to Penelope in a dream disguised as one of her sisters. Though she reveals nothing about Odysseus, she assures Penelope that Athena herself is escorting Telemachus on his journey. Eurycleia's insight and guidance are again shown to have merit as they bring Penelope the assurance she craves and soothe her fears.

Eurycleia's role in Odysseus' household is advisory and restorative. She functioned as the 'foster-mother' of Odysseus and Telemachus and provides advice and comfort to Penelope. When she realises Odysseus has returned, she is filled with joy and wants immediately to share the news with Penelope, but Odysseus threatens her with violence to remain silent. Eurycleia's characterisation throughout the epic shows that he need not have since she follows his orders and keeps his identity secret out of her own loyalty and care for him and his family. When Telemachus criticises his mother, Eurycleia steps in to smooth things over, and when Odysseus defeats the suitors, she is the first to deliver the news to Penelope.

Seeing herself as part of the social fabric of the household, she works to recover for Odysseus his former place in the community, to achieve the reunion of Penelope and Odysseus and to resolve tension between mother and son. Her masculine counterpart in the epic is Eumaeus, the enslaved swineherd in Odysseus' household who shows him proper hospitality when he is disguised as a beggar and who helps him defeat the suitors after he reveals his identity. Both are integral to the successful reunion of Odysseus and Penelope. As masculine and feminine forms of leadership and authority must work together for a community, whether an immortal or mortal one, to function harmoniously, so must all parties within that household work in communion, whatever their place in the social hierarchy. This harmonious balance can only be achieved through mutual respect and consideration: Eumaeus and Eurycleia, along with other members of Odysseus' household, repeatedly recall how he treated all under his authority as a father to his children.

The loyalty and integration of Eurycleia (and Eumaeus) have a foil in Melantho (and her masculine counterpart, Melanthius), who is likewise enslaved in Odysseus' household but who aligns herself with the suitors. Melantho is described in a book eighteen interaction with a disguised Odysseus:

> Beautiful-cheeked Melantho abusively rebuked Odysseus.
> Dolios brought her into the world, but Penelope took care of her.
> She reared her as her own child, giving her toys to delight her consciousness,
> But she did not have grief in her perceptions for Penelope,
> But she mingled with Eurymachus and held him dear.
> She rebuked Odysseus with reproachful words,
> 'Wretched stranger, you are bereft of sense in your perceptions,
> Coming into this house, you don't wish either to sleep among the bronze,[3]
> Or in some place where men exchange news, but you harangue many men in assembly here,
> Audacious among many men, not even in your consciousness

> Are you afraid. Truly, wine has gotten hold of your perceptions,
>   now or always for you
> Your understanding is like this, and either you speak in vain
> Or you wander in your understanding, having defeated Irus.
> Do not be rash. Another man stronger than Irus might make a
>   stand against you,
> Striking you about your head with sturdy hands.
> He might send you out of the house, defiled with much blood.'
>
> (Lines 321–336)

Having been raised by Penelope, Melantho is likely still a young woman who has not, as Eurycleia has, had an opportunity to integrate herself into the community as a matured adult. Notably, Penelope, a leader of the household, assumed the role of foster-mother for the enslaved young girl, as the enslaved Eurycleia assumed the role of foster-mother over future household leader Telemachus. Though she was treated as a daughter by Penelope, Melantho is disengaged from her concerns and in love with one of her suitors. When she interacts with the 'beggar', she follows the lead of the suitors and verbally abuses him rather than following the lead of Penelope and Telemachus and treating him with hospitality. Like the suitors and the companions of Odysseus, Melantho is disconnected from the social fabric that is held together by sacred laws, preoccupied more with the concerns of the moment (finding favour with the suitors) than with the past (her upbringing by Penelope) or the future (what will happen if Odysseus achieves his return).

After Odysseus threatens to report her to Telemachus and to cut her into pieces, Melantho is subdued in the moment, but she later delivers a second rebuke in book nineteen:

> Melantho reproached Odysseus for a second time,
> 'Stranger, are you still here? Will you torment us throughout
>   the night?
> Whirling throughout the house, will you ogle all the women?
> But go out the door, wretch, and benefit the feast,
> Or presently, someone throwing a torch will send you out the
>   door.'
>
> (Lines 65–69)

This time, Odysseus, still in his disguise, responds with a story of having once been prosperous and now being reduced to beggary, and he warns Melantho that anyone's condition can be reversed. Now she is beautiful and desirable, but both conditions are fleeting. Now Odysseus is away, but tomorrow, he could return. Telemachus has been young and unsure, but he is growing into his authority and could take exception to her behaviour. Material conditions are mutable. Eurycleia has learned this and survives, but Melantho in contrast has not and does not.

After Odysseus has slaughtered the suitors, twelve enslaved women judged to be disloyal, Melantho presumably among them, are ordered to clean the site and carry out the bodies, after which they are herded into a 'narrow space from which there was no escape' (line 460). Angry at what he calls the abuse of his mother by these women, Telemachus orders a painful death for them:

> So Telemachus spoke, and the steel-dark cable of a ship
> He threw over the vaulted roof, having fastened it around a tall pillar,
> Stretching it up high so their feet would not reach the ground.
> As when wide-winged thrushes or wild doves
> Rush into a trap made to stand in a shrub
> Sending them into a roosting-place, but it is a dreaded rest that receives them,
> Like so were the maidens, their heads lined up in a row. Around all
> Their necks a noose was tied so that their deaths would be most pitiable.
> They struggled for a short while, their feet convulsing, but not for very long.
>
> (Lines 465–473)

While the previous lines voice Telemachus' point of view, those following line 465 narrate from that of the enslaved women. They have been led into a trap. In the moment, the courtyard holds the trap. In the past, it was the suitors' beds. And these traps have cut the women off from a potential future. In the allusive grammar of Homer, the 'most pitiable' death the women suffer could refer not only to their being hanged but also to the inescapability of their circumstances.

Briseis

Among the captive women in Homer, Briseis' story perhaps most immediately embodies the notion of mutable circumstances in the mortal world. When she is first mentioned in the *Iliad*, it is as an enslaved woman, a war prize given to and subsequently confiscated from Achilles. In their quarrel, Agamemnon and Achilles speak of her as a symbol of masculine status and honour, an object to be given as a reward and taken away as a punishment. She appears briefly in book one, being led reluctantly away from Achilles, and she speaks only once in the epic, in book nineteen, to deliver a lament for Patroclus after Hector kills him. If we were to measure Briseis' importance in the *Iliad* by how often she appears and how much she speaks, we might conclude that she is the most minor of characters. Yet the quarrel over her between Agamemnon and Achilles prompts the latter to appeal to his mother, Thetis, to seek redress from Zeus, which sets in motion the events of the epic. In this sense, Briseis within the *Iliad* serves the role of Helen within the larger Trojan war myth in which the *Iliad* is set.

The lament of Briseis, ostensibly delivered for Patroclus, provides a compressed narrative of her reversal from wife to war prize, revealing that she witnessed Achilles murder her husband and brothers. The verbal art of lament in ancient Greece was generally associated with and sung by women,[4] though in the *Iliad*, both men and women perform them. Its traditional structure begins with an address to the dead, continues by revisiting a past memory and/or alluding to the grim future that awaits the speaker and concludes with a second address to the dead. Briseis' lament for Patroclus follows this traditional structure:

> Then Briseis, resembling golden Aphrodite,
> As she saw Patroclus torn apart by sharp bronze,
> She shrieked loudly, pouring herself around him, and tore with
>   her hands
> Her chest and her tender cheeks and her beautiful face.
> So she spoke, the woman equal to a goddess,
> 'Patroclus, most obliging of my wretched consciousness,
> Leaving this shelter, I left you alive.
> Now, leader of men, I reach you having been killed,
> Reaching back again, as I receive ills from ills always.
> My father and mistress mother gave me to a man who
> I saw torn apart by sharp bronze.
> Three brothers my same mother bore,
> Cared for, all were pursued to their day of destruction.
> You never permitted me – when swift Achilles my husband
> Killed, or when he ravaged the city of godlike Myntos –
> To weep, but you asserted to me that godlike Achilles

> Would set me as his wedded wife and lead me in the ships
> To Pythia and give a wedding feast among the Myrmidons.
> I weep incessantly for you having died, who was always gentle.'
> So she spoke, weeping, and the women wailed in response,
> For Patroclus as the cause, but each for her own cares.
>
> (Lines 282–302)

The memory Briseis shares of Patroclus is his attention to both her grief and her status, but it invokes the fullness of her life – a childhood with three brothers and attentive parents, marriage, then having to witness the destruction of her world. With no men left to defend her city, she became a captive, but Patroclus acted as a father-figure by promising to arrange a lawful marriage for her, one that would restore her social status by rendering her the legal wife of Achilles.[5] With Patroclus gone, the cycle continues to turn, 'reaching back' and stretching forward, evoking the eternal cyclicality expressed in nature through the seasons.

Briseis' change of status also foreshadows the fate of Andromache and all the Trojan women. While Briseis' lament expresses grief over her own now uncertain future, what has happened to her has happened to countless other women before and will happen to countless more in the future. Thus, it is both personal and collective. The death of Patroclus provides the occasion for the women to express their personal griefs. 'The women wailed in response' is a formulaic structure that repeats across laments in the *Iliad*, but it is not empty formula. It is an expression of the pattern of loss and grief repeating, endlessly, up from the past and forward into the future. It is an invocation of countless 'famous deeds' and songs of grief, yoked together and made eternal in our *Iliad*.

Thetis

The story of Thetis starkly illuminates the mutability of boundaries. She is at once a captive woman, an immortal goddess and a grieving mother. As her speeches in the *Iliad* convey, these identities mutually inform each other. As a sea nymph, one of the fifty daughters of the sea god Nereus, Thetis can change her form at will, but this does not enable her to escape the fate imposed on her, one the *Iliad* references as very much essential to the stability of the cosmic order.

In book eighteen of the *Iliad*, Thetis arrives at the workshop of Hephaestus, who credits Thetis with saving him after Hera threw him off Olympus, to request that he craft new armour for Achilles. When Hephaestus asks what has brought her to his door, Thetis replies,

> Truly, Hephaestus, as many goddesses as there are on Olympus, are there any
> Who have endured upon their perceptions as many baneful sorrows
> As Zeus, the son of Cronus, has given to me from among all others?
>
> (Lines 429–431)

She then describes being forced to marry the mortal king Peleus 'very exceedingly against my will' (line 434). The *Iliad* offers no further explanation as to why Zeus forced her to marry Peleus, but an ode by Theban poet Pindar, who was active in the fifth century BC, provides a narrative that can shape how one reads Thetis' place in the *Iliad*. According to Pindar's *Isthmian* 8, Zeus and Poseidon both desired marriage with Thetis, but Themis, the goddess of good order, revealed that the sea nymph was fated to bear a son greater than his father. If Thetis were to marry either, she could bear a son who could be powerful enough to challenge and overthrow his father, evoking the succession wars that led to the ascension of Zeus. The potential threat to the Olympian order could not be permitted. Themis advised the powerful gods to abandon their intentions to marry Thetis and instead give her in marriage to the hero Peleus. She gave birth to his son Achilles, who she 'nourished like a tree in an orchard on a hill' and sent off to Troy but who she will 'never receive back again' (line 438, 440). Being forced to marry a mortal means Thetis is forced to bear a mortal son who she will love, lose and grieve for eternally.

In book one, after Agamemnon's heralds have led Briseis out of the encampment of Achilles, he prays to his mother at the seashore, and Thetis comes to him, asking, 'what grief has reached your perceptions?' (line 362). Revealing how Agamemnon has dishonoured him, Achilles begs his mother to appeal to Zeus on his behalf. The basis for her appeal, Achilles reminds her, is her own claim to have been the immortal who saved Zeus from being overthrown. Within the *Iliad*, this plot against Zeus is attributed to Poseidon, Hera and Athena. Pindar's *Isthmian* 8 offers an alternate but complementary story of Thetis preventing Zeus from being unseated: being forced to marry a mortal and bear a mortal son ensured that she would not give birth to a son who could challenge the leader of the gods. While the narrative details differ, the narrative themes converge to portray Thetis as a figure of cosmic significance, as the scholar Laura Slatkin has compellingly argued.[6] Thetis has secured the stability of Zeus' reign, which is achieved at the price of Thetis' son.

After Achilles explains to his mother what Agamemnon has done and makes his request, Thetis delivers a speech that has the contours of a lament:

> Then Thetis responded, pouring tears,
> 'Oh child of mine, why, bringing you into this world, did
>   I nourish the grim events of this time?
> If only you could be by the ship, without tears and unharmed,
> To be seated, now and for a long while, since your share of life
>   is short, not very long at all.
> Now, swift-fated and miserable in all things, you
> Have become. In a great room, I brought you into the world for
>   a bad share of life,
> This word I will say for you to Zeus who delights in the
>   thunderbolt.
> I myself will go to snow-covered Olympus to see whether he
>   can be persuaded.
> But you now remain here by the swift-fated ships,
> With anger against the Achaeans, and stop fighting altogether,
> For Zeus is across the Ocean with the noble Ethiopians.
> Yesterday, he stepped through a feast, and the other gods
>   followed him.
> In twelve days, he will return to Olympus again. For you,
> At that time, I will go to Zeus' home, heavy with bronze, for you,
> I will clasp him by the knees, and I think I will persuade him.'
>   (Lines 413–426)

One of Thetis' gifts as a sea nymph is prophecy. Later, in book nine, Achilles will reveal a prophecy told to him by his mother which offers him one of two options: either to die at Troy but achieve imperishable fame in song, or to return home and live a long mortal life but lose his fame in song. In her speech above, the grief Thetis expresses over Achilles' sorrows and short life seems to imply that she knows he will choose to remain at Troy. Pindar's narrative in the *Isthmian 8* offers an additional, complementary cause for her grief: Had Thetis not been forced to marry a mortal, she would not have had to bear a mortal son who would suffer and die as he has and will. Thetis' references to Achilles' 'bad portion' and 'short life' highlight the grief of an immortal mother for her mortal son. However long his life is by mortal standards, it will still be heartbreakingly short by the standards of a goddess who will live forever.

Unlike Hecuba and Andromache, Thetis does not urge Achilles to choose either option, neither impeding nor encouraging his *kleos*, but she fulfils her promise to him by asking Zeus to honour her son:

> She found the far-seeing son of Cronus seated without others
> At the furthest, highest point of Olympus with many ridges.
> She seated herself in his presence and took his knees
> With her left hand, with her right, taking his chin,
> Beseeching, she addressed Lord Zeus, son of Cronus,
> 'Father Zeus, if ever I helped you among the immortals,
> With word or deed, bring to fulfilment this wish of mine.
> Honour my son, earliest to die among others
> He was. But now, lord of men Agamemnon
> Has dishonoured him, for having taken his prize, he holds it for himself, robbing him,
> But you, pay him honour, oh Zeus, councillor who dwells on Olympus,
> Put the might with Troy, in order that the Achaeans
> Pay a price to my son and increase his value.'
>
> (Lines 498–510)

When Thetis goes to Zeus, she performs the traditional gesture of supplication, grasping the knees and chin of the one being supplicated, here Zeus, who is himself the god who protects suppliants. The gesture initiates a contract between the two parties, suggesting Zeus cannot deny her without violating his own laws. Moreover, Thetis' request aligns with Zeus' own larger plan. According to the *Cypria*, an archaic Trojan war epic known only through fragments and summaries, Earth was overburdened by an excess of heroes, and Zeus planned the Trojan war to relieve her. Thetis' request to punish the Achaeans and Zeus' intention to relieve earth of the burden of heroes converge across the epic, as Achilles' absence from battle leads to the loss of more lives. Pindar's *Isthmian* 8 adds an additional layer of perspective to Thetis' reference to having 'helped [Zeus] among the immortals' and her description of Achilles as 'earliest to die among others' (line 505). The latter can seem puzzling given that Achilles is far from the first to die at Troy. If, however, he was denied immortality to preserve the cosmic order, then his death can be seen as 'earliest' in that he must die at all. As unfolds repeatedly across the two epics, narratives and themes within them both contrast with and complement narratives and themes beyond them, the totality of which we call 'the oral tradition', consistent not in their narrative details but their thematic meaning.

Zeus delivers his promise. The Trojans surge to the fringes of victory, penning the Achaeans against their ships and threatening to burn them down, which would mean certain destruction since it would rob them of their transport home. The threat of total destruction for his Achaean comrades compels 'gentle' Patroclus to rebuke Achilles for his inaction. Though moved, Achilles cannot bring himself to re-enter battle but allows Patroclus to serve as his substitute. Going into battle dressed in Achilles' armour, Patroclus is killed. The plan that Thetis and Achilles so carefully orchestrated to give victory to the Trojans has become the source of the most acute grief for Achilles, who mourns the loss of his dearest companion.

At the beginning of book eighteen, when Achilles first learns of Patroclus' death and cries out in grief, Thetis in the depths of the sea hears her son, immediately begins lamenting the grief he has endured, then rushes to his side.

> Hear me, sisters, daughters of Nereus, in order that you all well
> Know, hearing the cares upon my consciousness.
> Ah me, I am wretched, ah me, the unhappy mother of a noble son,
> He who, when I brought him into the world, was a blameless and mighty son,
> Standing out among heroes, he shot up like a young sprout.
> I nourished him like a tree in an orchard on a hill.
> I sent him forth in the crooked ships to Ilium
> To fight at Troy, but I will never receive him back again,
> Returning home to Peleus and his house.
> As long as he lives and sees the light of the sun with me,
> He grieves, not even I can ward this off for him,
> But I go to him, in order that I may see my dear child and hear
> Whatever grief has come over him from remaining at the war.
> (Lines 52–64)

> His mistress mother took her stand beside Achilles, groaning heavily,
> She took her son's head, wailing sharply,
> And she spoke winged words, lamenting,
> 'Child, why do you weep? What grief has reached your perceptions?
> Speak, don't hide it. Things for you have come to fulfilment

> From Zeus, as you prayed for before, holding up your hands,
> For the sons of the Achaeans to be packed against the sterns of the ships,
> To suffer disgraceful works, being in want of you.'
>
> (Lines 70–77)

Notably, Thetis does not understand why her son is grieving since his prayer has been granted. While she is connected to her son and his grief, she is not, as her son is, integrated into a mortal community and capable of understanding the loss Achilles is experiencing. The Achaeans have suffered from his absence in battle and experienced in a most excruciating fashion the folly of having dishonoured him. But too late, Achilles has realised that his insistence on compensation has resulted in the loss of the one person who is dearest to him. He must explain to his mother, 'I have destroyed [Patroclus]', and he no longer cares whether he lives or dies (line 82). As before, Thetis neither encourages nor dissuades Achilles from his choice but reflects on its consequences, for if he chooses to remain and die at Troy then, she tells him, 'my child, you will indeed be short-lived' (line 95).

Once Achilles makes his choice, Thetis again draws on her immortal status to help him achieve his objectives. She secures new arms and armour from Hephaestus to replace those which Hector tore from Patroclus' body, and she presents them to Achilles in book nineteen. He praises the immortal craftsmanship of the armour but worries about the impact of time on Patroclus' body; the longer he lies unburied, the more likely his corpse will become a feast for flies. Promising to protect Patroclus' body, Thetis breaths strength into her son:

> Then, the goddess, silver-footed Thetis responded to him,
> 'My child, do not let these things be concerns upon your perceptions.
> I myself will attempt to ward off these cruel tribes from him,
> Flies, which devour men slain by Ares,
> For if he were laid out for a full year to come to fulfilment,
> The surface of his skin would be forever unblemished or even more excellent.
> But calling the Achaean heroes to an assembly,
> And renouncing your godlike wrath against Agamemnon, shepherd of the people,
> Arm yourself for battle with a breastplate and cloak yourself in valour.'

> So having spoken, she fuelled him with intrepid might,
> For Patroclus again, ambrosia and ruddy nectar,
> She let it fall through his nostrils, in order that the surface of his skin should be unblemished.
>
> (Lines 28–39)

Thetis' immortal gifts of arms, armour and physical strength will fuel Achilles' destruction of men and with them their families and communities. With his mother's gifts, Achilles will deliver grief to countless women who will eventually become captives. Disconnected from this human cycle, eternally outside of time, Thetis thinks only of easing her short-lived son's grief. Yet the portrait of Thetis in the *Iliad* is not one of a heartless goddess but suggests the danger of eternal beings being tethered to mortal lives. An immortal so deeply invested in a single mortal life endangers the stability of both the immortal and mortal realms, invoking Hephaestus' observation in book one of the *Iliad*, which is repeated across the epic: immortals should not allow mortals to become a source of conflict among them. Zeus' plan to end the age of heroes, referenced in the *Cypria*, may have as much to do with stabilising the cosmic order as it does with relieving the burden on Earth.

The *Iliad*'s final scene of the immortals in assembly occurs at the beginning of book twenty-four. Achilles' rampage against the Trojans has failed to dispel his wrath against Hector, and he continues to disfigure Hector's corpse, offending the gods who have supported Troy and will have to stand aside as it is destroyed by the dictates of Fate. Speaking on these gods' behalf, Apollo rebukes the ones who continue to allow an impious man (Achilles) to defile a pious one (Hector). When Hera angrily responds that the men cannot be compared, since Achilles was nursed by a goddess and Hector by a mortal, a quarrel threatens to erupt, until Zeus intervenes. He affirms Hera's point that Hector cannot receive the honours due to Achilles but concedes that he must be ordered to stop his impious behaviour. But Zeus insists that Thetis be the one to deliver the message and sends Iris to fetch her. Thetis is due this respect: that nothing with regard to her son be done without her consent and cooperation.

> So Zeus spoke, and storm-footed Iris rose to carry his message
> In between Samos and rugged Imbros,
> She dove into the ink-dark sea, and the water roared.
> She dropped into the depths of the sea like a piece of lead
> On the horn of an oxen who dwells in the field.
> It comes bearing death upon flesh-eating fish.

She found Thetis in a hollow cave. Around her, others,
Goddesses of the sea, were seated, and at the centre among them she
Was weeping over the portion of her noble son, who was intended
To decay in fertile Troy far from his fatherland.
Making a stand near Thetis, swift-footed Iris addressed her,
'Stand up, Thetis, knowing Zeus whose plans are imperishable summons you.'
Then the goddess, silver-footed Thetis, responded to her,
'Why does that great god command me? I am restrained by reverence
To mingle with the deathless ones. I have ceaseless pain in my consciousness.
Nevertheless, I go, so that the words he spoke will not be fruitless.'
So having spoken, the goddess of Zeus took her head covering,
Dark as steel, no garment is darker than this.
She stepped to go, fast as the wind, swift-footed Iris before her,
She led her, and the waves of the sea bent around them.
Reaching the promontory, they two darted up to the sky.
They found the far-seeing son of Cronus, around whom all the others,
The blessed gods who are eternal, were assembled and seated.
She took her seat beside father Zeus. Athena gave way.
Hera placed in her hand a beautiful chalice of gold
And cheered her with words. Having drank, Thetis stretched out.
The father of gods and men began speaking these words among them,
'You came to Olympus, goddess Thetis, even though you are distressed,
Having unceasing grief through your perceptions, I also know this,
But even so, I will tell you on what account I have summoned you here.
For nine days a quarrel has been brewing among the immortals
Over both the body of Hector and city-sacking Achilles.
They are encouraging the keen-sighted slayer of Argus to steal the body,
But I grant this glory to Achilles,

> Warding off shame and out of affection for you from times past.
> Go very quickly to the army's encampment and command your son.
> Tell him the gods are angry, myself among all others.
> He has angered the immortals with his enraged perceptions.
> He holds Hector by the crooked-beaked ships, not letting him loose –
> If in some way he fears me and sets Hector loose.
> But I will send Iris to great-hearted Priam
> To release his dear son from the Achaean ships
> And to bring gifts to Achilles, such as will warm his heart.'
> So he spoke, and silver-footed goddess Thetis did not disobey him.
>
> (Lines 77–120)

Despite her grief, Thetis assents to Zeus' summons, following Iris to Olympus. The community of goddesses greet her solicitously, comforting her materially and emotionally, and Zeus offers her the rarest of his offerings: transparency. Revealing the full scope of the quarrel and its causes to Thetis, he affirms his intention to honour her son by forbidding the gods from intervening without the knowledge and consent of Thetis and Achilles. Achilles must release the body of Hector, but it will be done through the intervention of Thetis herself.

A paradox of the Homeric epics is that they are complete in themselves and suffused with reminders that they are pieces of a larger fabric, the oral tradition of retelling stories. The final portrait the *Iliad* leaves of Thetis is of a paragon of this paradox, a figure whose form shifts depending on the vantage point from which one views her. She is a grieving mother who will spend eternity lamenting her only son. She is a powerful goddess, whose story shapes the cosmic order. She is a captive woman, yoked to a mortal against her will and sentenced to eternal grieving. She is unable to relate to mortal concerns, but the contours of her eternity are shaped by them. She helps her son visit unfathomable destruction but is a gentle and conciliatory figure within her own immortal community.

Helen

Helen is one of a handful of figures who appear in both the *Iliad* and the *Odyssey*, along with, most notably, Athena, Odysseus and Zeus. Popular contemporary retellings and anthologies have tended to portray Helen's genealogy as it is known largely through first-century Roman poet Ovid, in whose work she is portrayed as the daughter of Zeus/Jupiter and the mortal Leda. A fragment from the archaic Greek *Cypria*, however, names the goddess Nemesis as Helen's mother. Zeus pursued her, and she tried desperately to escape him, transforming herself into different creatures as she fled, but she could not escape him. Helen is born from this act of sexual violence, echoing the conception of Achilles from the likewise unwilling Thetis. Viewed through this lens, Helen and Achilles could be understood as masculine and feminine counterparts, both brought into the world through violence and both instrumental in generating and escalating the Trojan war that would bring Hesiod's age of heroes to a catastrophic end.

As noted earlier, our *Iliad* finds Helen in book three narrating the story of the Trojan war with thread and cloth. Iris has been sent to bring Helen to the walls of Troy to witness the duel between Spartan Menelaos (her past husband) and Trojan Paris (her current husband); its outcome is intended to determine who her future husband will be. Paris suggested the duel after Hector rebuked him for running away from Menelaos in the midst of battle, leaving the fighting to Achaean and Trojan men who were not responsible for the conflict. Mindful that his comrades were dying on his behalf and eager to save them from future strife, Menelaos accepted. But the duel runs contrary to the war narrative Helen is weaving. As the men strive to end the war with the duel, Iris pulls Helen away from her work. She set the war in motion, but now the heroes have brought the war to an abrupt halt. They are striving to avoid more battles and deaths, contrary to the plans (plural potential) of Zeus. Without battle, Achilles cannot be honoured, and the age of heroes will grind on.

> Iris found Helen in the large room weaving on a great loom,
> A dark, gleaming, double-folded mantle. She was sprinkling
>   into it the many contests
> Of the Trojans, tamers of horses, and the Achaeans, clad in
>   bronze,
> Who on account of her were suffering at the hands of Ares.
> 'Come now, dear bride, so that you can see the wondrous
>   works
> Of the Trojans, tamers of horses, and the Achaeans, clad in
>   bronze,
> Who before brought many tears upon each other by Ares
> On the plain, longing for destructive battle.

> Now they have ceased fighting and are seated in silence,
> Reclining against their shields alongside their long spears which are planted firmly,
> But Alexander and Menelaos, dear to Ares
> Will fight with their long spears over you.
> You will be summoned as the dear wedded wife of whoever prevails.'
> So having spoken, the goddess threw honey-sweet longing into her consciousness
> For her former husband and her city and her parents.
>
> (Lines 125–140)

Led once again by a goddess, Helen ceases her weaving and hurries to the walls. Watching her approach, the Trojan elders seated there to witness the duel remark that no mortal is ultimately the cause of the war and recognise the presence of an immortal in Helen:

> In her face, she looks dreadfully like a deathless goddess,
> But as she looks this way, she should go away in the ships,
> So that she will not be a source of calamity for our future children.
>
> (Lines 158–160)

Helen's appearance marks her as preeminent, something more than human, but the Trojan elders recognise that for mortals to possess the superhuman is dangerous. Like Achilles and his godlike wrath (*menis*), Helen and her immortal beauty have brought destruction to the Achaeans and Trojans. Paris bringing Helen to Troy was the occasion for the war, but she is not ultimately the cause. That lies with Zeus and the Fates. Yet the intermingling of immortal and mortal breeds instability. Priam nevertheless welcomes Helen kindly and invites her to tell him who the Achaean leaders are, a request that can seem curious when the *Iliad* is approached purely as a story: the epic's events are set in the ninth year of the war, at which point the Trojans would know against whom they are fighting. But the request results in Helen delivering a second, more compressed 'catalogue of the ships', the first having famously been delivered by the bard of our *Iliad* in book two. For the second time in book three, Helen is cast in the role of myth maker.[7] The first time with cloth and thread, the second with spoken words.

After the formalities are observed, the duel commences, and Menelaos surges toward victory, prompting Aphrodite to remove Paris from the field 'very easily, as a god can do' and deposit him in his bedchamber (line 381). Aphrodite entrusts no messenger to the task of delivering Helen to Paris. In disguise as a woman from Sparta dear to Helen, the goddess fetches her personally, and the two wrangle:

> Aphrodite herself went to call Helen. She reached the
> High-raised tower, and around her Trojan women were swarming.
> Seizing Helen's nectar-scented, enveloping clothing with her hand, she shook it.
> She addressed her looking like an old woman born long ago,
> A wool dresser, dwelling in Lacedaemon.
> She worked beautiful wool, and Helen regarded her most affectionately,
> Appearing as her, Aphrodite called Helen.
> 'Come here. Alexander[8] is calling you to return home.
> He is there in the inner room on the rounded bed,
> Gleaming in his beauty and garments. No one would say
> The man had come from battling, but to a round dance
> He goes, or from a round dance he has returned to rest.'
> So she spoke and roused the consciousness in Helen's chest
> And when she perceived with her eyes the goddess' very beautiful neck,
> Breasts that provoke desire and her sparkling eyes,
> She was amazed, then spoke a word from out of her and named her,
> '*Daimoni*, why do you long to deceive me with these things?
> Is it to a former city, well populated, that
> You will lead me, Phrygia or charming Maeonia?
> Perhaps there is in that place a certain other mortal man, someone dear to you?
> Or now is it on account of Menelaus over Alexander
> Prevailing, and he wishes to lead hateful me home?
> For this reason, now, you make your stand here, being wily-minded.
> Sit beside him yourself, withdraw from the way of the gods,
> Turn your feet back, never again toward Olympus,
> But always for him suffer and protect him
> Until he makes you into either a spouse or a slave.
> I will not go there. It would cause indignation,
> Preparing a bed for him, the Trojan women hereafter,

> All of them will find fault with me. I have endless pain in my consciousness.'
> Provoked to anger, Aphrodite born of Zeus addressed her,
> 'Do not provoke me, perverse woman. Don't make me angry and let you go,
> Or I would hate you as terribly as I now love you.
> And I would devise baneful enmity among the two sides,
> Trojan and Danaan, and you would be destroyed by destructive doom.'
> So she spoke, and Helen born of Zeus was afraid.
> She walked, covering her face with her bright, radiant robe
> In silence and escaped the notice of all the Trojan women; a *daimon* led her.
>
> (Lines 383–420)

The full passage dramatises to chilling effect Helen's captivity: her captor is Aphrodite, and her captivity is carried out by the hands of Paris and the Trojans.[9] Aphrodite has attempted to lure her to Paris in the guise of a benign and beloved old acquaintance, but Helen is not fooled. She perceives that she is in the presence of the goddess of seduction and attempts to resist, reflecting back at Aphrodite the position her schemes have put Helen in. If Aphrodite decides to send her to another man's bed, will Helen have a choice? Is she a lawful wife or a slave? Perhaps the distinction is a matter of semantics since Helen here has no choice. The dispute between these women, both 'born of Zeus', is settled with Aphrodite's grim warning, and Helen silently obeys. She cannot be permitted to disobey Aphrodite, just as the duel between Menelaos and Paris cannot be permitted to determine the winner of the war. Helen is at once the maker of the war, the weaver of the story and powerless to stop its forward motion.

In a book six conversation with Hector, Helen seems to acknowledge this paradox as a convergence of mortal and immortal, and to understand its purpose:

> Zeus has set a bad portion upon us so that in time to come,
> We may become famous songs for future generations.
>
> (Lines 357–358)

At two pivotal moments in the *Iliad*, Achilles swears a solemn oath by a sceptre crafted by Hephaestus. Formed from wood cut from a tree on a mountaintop, it is set with bronze. In his *The Best of the Achaeans*, Gregory Nagy describes this sceptre as 'a thing of nature that had been transformed into a thing of culture'. Perhaps heroes, who are frequently compared to trees which are cut down to become ship timber or chariot wheels, can also be thought of as 'things of nature' that become 'things of culture': through their worship in cult, heroes become foundational institutions that bring communities together. The songs of these heroes' fame are recited in the sacred rituals that honour them, and these songs are frequently rooted in the heroes' suffering, which finds expression in songs of lament.[10]

Helen, the cause and object of the war, delivers the final lament in our *Iliad*. Hers is the last woman's voice heard in the epic as, following Andromache then Hecuba, she laments Hector:

> Third and next, Helen began her lament,
> 'Hector, of all my husband's brothers most dear in my consciousness,
> Truly Alexander, godlike in form, is my husband,
> Who led me here to Troy, though I ought to have been destroyed before,
> For now already the twentieth year is upon me
> Since I stepped out of that place and departed from my native land,
> But up to this time, I never heard from you a harmful or degrading word,
> But if someone or another in the great room rebuked me –
> My husband's brother or sister or beautiful-robed sisters-in-law,
> Or my mother-in-law; my father-in-law was always a gentle father –
> You held them back with words, advising them
> With your gentle words and your kindliness.
> Therefore, grieving in my heart, I weep for you and for my luckless self,
> For no one else in wide Troy to me
> Is gentle and dear. All shudder at me.'
> So she spoke, weeping, and the boundless people burst forth their grief in response.
>
> (Lines 761–776)

Her lament observes the familiar structure. Helen begins with a direct address to her brother-in-law, then recalls his kind regard for her, his protective response to the censure levelled at her by Troy's women – the mothers and wives for whom, as noted earlier, *kleos* offers no comfort or compensation for the men they have lost. That Helen delivers the last of the women's laments, following both Hector's wife and mother, who one might expect to have the final word as his closest relatives, underscores, according to Maria C. Pantelia, Helen's connection to *kleos* and the project of epic.[11] In response to Andromache, 'the women wailed in response' (line 746); within the story, Hector is the occasion for these grieving women to express emotion in a socially sanctioned public forum. Hecuba's lament roused 'unforgettable lamentation' (line 759), suggesting the enduring power of grief and the songs it generates as well as the incorporation of lament in hero cult rituals. After Helen performs, 'the boundless people burst forth their grief in response' (line 776). This image of heroes becoming the focal point that brings together 'boundless' communities of people invites associations with the incorporation of lament and epic in public rituals. Collectively, the laments of Andromache, Hecuba and Helen seem to move from the story world of myth to the ritual world of cult.

The events that bring our *Iliad* to a close reinforce this shift from myth to cult. After Helen concludes her lament, Priam orders a funeral pyre to be constructed for Hector. When his body has been burned and his bones collected and placed in a container, a funeral mound is built, and a feast held in his honour. The final line of the epic concludes, 'So they moved through the funeral rites for Hector, tamer of horses.' The fulfilment of the funeral rites for Hector suggests the initiation of hero worship and the place of epic within it. Helen's is the voice that ushers the transition from lament to epic.

When we next encounter her, it is in book four of the *Odyssey* where she is ensconced back in Sparta with Menelaos. Their home is the last stop on Telemachus' travels, instigated by Athena so that he might seek information about his missing father. Menelaos has just recounted in brief the trials he endured returning home from Troy, concluding that the comrade he misses above all others is Odysseus, because he toiled and contributed more than all others. Menelaos grieves that Odysseus' whereabouts are unknown and acknowledges the grief this must cause for his family in Ithaca – Penelope, Laertes and Telemachus. Menelaos' story provokes Telemachus to weep, which the Spartan leader notices, and he weighs whether to wait for Telemachus to mention who his father is or prompt the information by questioning and testing him.

As he deliberates, Helen arrives in the great room flanked by attendants carrying the apparatus of weaving and the gifts she has received from friends in Egypt:

> As Menelaos pondered these things in his consciousness,
> From the high-roofed inner room that smelled of incense, Helen
> Came looking like Artemis of the golden distaff,

> And with her came Adrasti, who placed a well-made chair,
> And Alcippe brought a coverlet of soft wool,
> Phyllo brought a silver basket, the one given to Helen
> By Alcandre, wife of Polybius, who dwelled in Thebes,
> In Egypt, where many possessions were kept in their houses.
> Polybius gave Menelaus two silver bathing tubs
> Two tripods, ten gold talents.
> Separately, his wife offered Helen beautiful gifts.
> She sent a golden distaff and a basket on wheels
> Made of silver, finished with gold around the rims.
> Now bearing this basket, her attendant Phyllo placed it by her
> Stuffed full of curiously wrought spun items, and upon this
> A distaff having dark-hued wool stretched over it.
> She seated herself on a couch, the footstool under her feet.
> Straight away, she asked her husband these things with these words,
> 'Menelaus, nourished by Zeus, do we know these men,
> The men who have come into our house, who they declare themselves?
> Shall I lie or shall I speak the truth, my consciousness urges me.
> For I say, up to this time, I have not seen anyone
> Neither man nor woman – reverence holds me beholding
> How this one looks like the son of great-hearted Odysseus,
> Telemachus, who he left newly born in his house
> That man, who on account of dog-eyed me, the Achaeans
> Went unto Troy, eager for audacious war.'
>
> (Lines 120–146)

The passage is threaded with resonances. Popular narratives about Helen have tended to emphasise her preeminent beauty and overlooked that ancient sources also cite her weaving – which is connected to storytelling – as a source of her fame.[12] Helen arrives with the implements that in the *Iliad* marked her as a maker of the Trojan war story. The dark-hued wool stretched over her distaff invites association with the 'dark gleaming double-folded mantle' on which she wove that story in *Iliad* book three. The references to the gifts she received from Alcandre may allude to an alternate narrative, memorably dramatised in Euripides' *Helen* and mentioned in Herodotus' *Histories*, in which she was never at Troy but waited out the war in Egypt. The exchange of gifts establishes women as participants in hospitality rituals and highlights the role of woven garments within these rituals. Gazing at Telemachus, Helen declares that he looks not like his father but like his father's son. This wording recalls warriors on the battlefield in Troy being exhorted to live up to the skill and might of their fathers. Telemachus has come to Sparta hoping to discover news about his father and has heard Menelaos praise him. Now, Helen is subtly laying down a gauntlet. Telemachus resembles his father, but whether he will live up to him or make a lie of the resemblance remains to be written.

Helen's final appearance in Homer occurs in *Odyssey* book fifteen. Telemachus is anxious to depart for Ithaca, and Menelaos insists on sending off the son of his dear comrade with the proper rituals. Gifts are assembled. Menelaos offers a silver mixing vessel and Helen a shining garment that she herself crafted:

> But when they came to where treasures had been placed
> The son of Atreus then took a double-cupped chalice.
> He commanded his son Megapenthes to bring a mixing vessel
> Of silver. Helen stood beside a chest.
> It held richly worked garments that she herself had toiled over.
> Lifting them, Helen, godlike among women, bore
> The most beautifully crafted and the greatest,
> It shone as brightly as a star and had been placed beneath the others.
> Going back through the house, they walked until they reached Telemachus, then fair-haired Menelaos addressed him:
> 'Telemachus, let me tell you truly about your return, as you desire in your consciousness,
> So may Zeus, the loud-thundering husband of Hera, bring it to fulfilment.
> As for gifts, as many treasures lie in my house,
> I will give to you the most beautiful and honoured among them.
> I will give you a mixing vessel cunningly wrought of silver,
> The whole of it, it is completed with gold around the rim,
> A work of Hephaestus. It was given to Phaedimus, the hero,
> King of the Sidonians, when his house enfolded me,
> When I passed through on my return home. I wish to send you with this.'
> So speaking, he placed in his hands the double-cupped chalice,
> The son of Atreus, the hero. Then, the shining mixing vessel –

> Bearing it, Megapethnes placed before Telemachus the mixing vessel
> Of silver. Helen of the beautiful cheeks stood,
> Holding in her hands the woven garment, she addressed him and said this word:
> 'I have a gift for you too, dear child. This I give,
> A memory by Helen's hands, for the time of your very lovely marriage
> To bear to your wife. Until such time, beside your dear mother
> In the great room let it lie. I would have you arrive rejoicing
> To your well-built household and to the land of your father.'
> So speaking, she placed it in his hands, and he received it, rejoicing.
>
> (Lines 101–130)

As Polybius and Alcandre bestowed to Menelaos and Helen gifts associated with the two craft gods, Hephaestus and Athena, metals and cloth respectively, so are the gifts they bestow on Telemachus. Under the auspices of the gods, divinely crafted objects passed from hand to hand are depicted in Homer forging bonds among mortal communities across vast stretches of land and across cultures, here Sparta, Sidon and Egypt, from one generation to the next. These objects hold memories of the responsibilities that mortals have to each other and to the gods.

Once again, Helen has the final word as she bestows the final gift, the exemplar of her weaving. When viewed through the modern focus on Helen's 'fidelity', or lack thereof, it can seem puzzling, perhaps even questionable, that she would be the one to give Telemachus a wedding gift for his future wife. But viewing this gift through the lens of Helen as the weaver of the story of Troy offers an alternative reading. Perhaps Helen here anticipates Telemachus marrying and bringing a new generation into the post-Trojan war, post-heroic world, a generation that will be responsible for carrying the memory of Troy forward. The woven garment she gifts him is meant to rest with Penelope until such time as it is passed on to Telemachus' future wife. Does the cloth hold a message for Penelope from Helen? Is it the cloth that she wove in the *Iliad*, which narrated the struggles of the Trojan war heroes, whose song future generations will sing? The text does not say, but perhaps the ancients who received the epic would know the answer.

GODDESSES

PART 3

IN BOTH THE *Iliad* and the *Odyssey*, goddesses are more powerful than mortal men. This bears mentioning because when figures in the Homeric epics are approached as characters in a fictional story, the power dynamics between goddesses and mortal men as portrayed in Homer can become obscured. Within the narratives of the *Iliad* and the *Odyssey*, mortal men can trick or wound a goddess (or god) only when authorised and assisted by another immortal. The *Iliad* is saturated with examples of goddesses working their will through mortals, preserving the lives of their favourites and advocating for them with Zeus, notably Aphrodite with Paris and Aeneas, Athena with Diomedes and Odysseus, and Thetis (and Hera in book twenty-four) with Achilles. In the *Odyssey*, the scope narrows to one family's attempt to reunite after the war, and the attention shifts to Athena's patronage of a family unit: Penelope, Odysseus, Telemachus and Laertes.

Even given the narrower scope, the Olympian gods and goddesses noticeably recede from view in the *Odyssey*. Fewer major immortals are personally involved in mortal quarrels and challenges, and they are careful not to confront each other directly, deferring or conceding to Zeus in matters of disagreement. The *Odyssey* has no contentious assemblies of gods scheming and squabbling amongst themselves and no parallel of the battlefield scene in *Iliad* book twenty-one, in which the gods face off against each other in hand-to-hand combat, some more reluctantly than others.

Viewed through this lens, the *Odyssey* seems to pick up where the *Iliad* left off, not necessarily in a narrative sense but in a thematic sense. In the final assembly at Olympus in the *Iliad*'s book twenty-four, Thetis heeds Zeus' summons, despite her grief, and he makes a point of noticing and honouring her for this. Their exchange contrasts sharply with another archaic Greek song depicting an interaction between Zeus and a grieving immortal mother, Demeter, goddess of the harvest. The *Homeric Hymn to Demeter* recounts the abduction of her daughter, Persephone, and Demeter's enraged destruction in response. While she grieves, the crops that nourish mortals wither and die, threatening the existence of the morals whose offerings the gods enjoy.

Zeus summons her to Olympus, but Demeter refuses to return until her daughter is restored to her, forcing him to reach a compromise with Hades.

On Homer's Olympus, gods and goddesses challenge Zeus but consistently back off before the conflict escalates. By the end of the *Iliad*, they seem to have reconciled themselves that, however imperfect Zeus' reign, it remains preferable to war. Zeus too recognises the need to balance the contributions and authorities of the other gods. At the *Iliad*'s final assembly of the gods, in addition to affirming his intention to honour Thetis, Zeus also concedes to Apollo's concern for Hector and Hera's for Achilles, negotiating a compromise between them. In the *Odyssey*, this mood of conciliation is manifested in Calypso's grudging concession to Zeus' demand that Odysseus be released, despite her irritation, and Athena's persistent concern not to challenge Poseidon, who is angry at Odysseus, directly. She waits until he has landed on his home soil in Ithaca before appearing to him undisguised.

When placed alongside Homer, Hesiod's epics provide a complementary narrative to explain this shift in the dynamic between immortals and mortals. Together, his *Theogony* and *Works and Days* usher the reader or listener through transitions of the cosmic order, from the origins of the universe in the former to the historical present of Hesiod's time in the latter. Hesiod envisions the conditions of his present as an unfortunate consequence of transgressions from times past. Prometheus' scheme to benefit mortal men violated Zeus' command, and his response was to balance the benefit with a danger: the creation of Pandora. Hesiod immediately follows his discussion of the creation of woman with a narrative about the origins and ages of mortals: the 'deathless ones who dwell on Olympus' created them, in five stages, the fourth of which is the age of heroes, or demigods, as Hesiod refers to them (line 110).

According to Hesiod, the destruction of the age of heroes in the Trojan and Theban wars ushered in a new age, the 'age of iron', the bard's own time. The gods did not vanish. They could still be felt and communicated with, but they became more inscrutable and distant. With regard to the creation of man and women, Hesiod offers no clear timeline of events which can subsequently be mapped onto recorded historical events. Rather, he portrays a shift from the age of myth, when heroes were alive in the world, to the age of cult, when they were thought to have transitioned to the eternal realm and were worshipped in sacred rituals. It is this transition that Homer's epics can be understood to explore.

In the texts of Hesiod and Homer that have survived, the two 'bards' do not agree on all points about the immortals. Homer, for example, depicts Aphrodite as a daughter of Zeus and Dione while Hesiod names her as part of an earlier generation of gods. Yet both are concerned with the transitional period between the end of the mythic age and the beginning of historic time. Hesiod's texts are more sweeping in scope when set alongside Homer's, which remain rooted in narratives about Trojan war heroes. Yet both sets of texts convey cosmological knowledge about the immortal forces who were worshipped in the historical present, when the *Iliad* and *Odyssey* were incorporated into a city's sacred rituals to honour their gods and heroes.

As ever in Homer, the transition from myth to history is felt through the intimate and personal. In our *Iliad*, this new age feels present in the moments when the immortals agree, in *Iliad* book twenty-four, that Achilles and Hector will both be honoured, each in a way appropriate to his status, and when Achilles returns the body of Hector to his father. Our *Odyssey* does not speak directly to its historical listeners as Hesiod does in *Work and Days*, narrating the stages of man, the creation of woman and offering practical advice. But when Athena intervenes to order an end to hostilities between Odysseus and the suitors' families, it seems an age has come to an end, and a new order will emerge from the remains. Both epics end with retributive justice being revealed to foment social instability and new systems for reconciliation of differences needing to be conceived. To move forward into the new age, mortals will need to know what is worth remembering about the goddesses (and gods) they worship, and the epics convey this knowledge.

The Muses

The invocations of the 'goddess' at the beginning of the *Iliad* and 'Muse' at the beginning of the *Odyssey* are formulaic features, invitations and prayers for immortal memory to preside over the occasion of retelling a sacred story. In the *Iliad*, the *goddess* is invoked at the beginning of the whole and the *Muses* at a critical moment in book two when the bard will introduce the leaders of the entire Achaean contingent. As discussed earlier, the invocation suggests that these daughters of Zeus and Mnemosyne hold the eternal memory of 'famous deeds'. All that needs to be remembered about heroes and gods can reach the present moment through the bards who become conduits of their eternal breath:

> Tell me now Muses who have homes on Olympus,
> For you are goddesses, you are present, and you know all things.
> We hear only the song that brings fame but know nothing.

> Who were the leaders and rulers of the Danaans?
> I could neither speak of nor name the masses of men,
> Not even if I had ten tongues and ten mouths,
> An unbreakable voice and a heart of bronze, would it be possible,
> If not for the Olympian Muses of aegis-bearing Zeus
> His daughters, who can recall to memory how many came upon Ilium.
>
> (Lines 484–493)

The bard's invocation indicates that his authority comes not from his own skill but from his receptivity to channel their eternal memory. As Athena repeatedly breathes courage through heroes, then, the Muses breathe knowledge through the bard. In contrast to the opening invocation, which asks the goddess to 'sing' (*aoido*), in the book two passage above, the bard asks the Muse to 'tell' (*ennepo*), the same verb used to invoke the Muse at the beginning of the *Odyssey*. Exploring the place of bards and rhapsodes in the transitional period when literacy was introduced during the archaic period may reflect a shift of meaning enfolded in the shift of language.

In the earliest ancient sources that mention Homer, the epics attributed to him are not referred to as poems whose medium of transmission is texts but as songs whose medium of transmission is breath. In the popular imagination, the epics are often described as being sung by bards at feasts to entertain guests. This portrait owes some debt to the *Odyssey*, in which bards, called *aoidoi*, are described singing at social gatherings to the accompaniment of a lyre. Phemius, the bard at Ithaca, which in the epic is located within the flow of mortal time, sings under compulsion at the feasts of the suitors and is spared in the slaughter Odysseus later inflicts upon them. Phemius is described singing the newest songs being passed from mouth to mouth. In contrast, Demodocus, the bard at the Phaeacian palace, which is portrayed as a liminal place, sings the 'famous deeds of men' that have already reached the 'wide sky'. Having travelled far and wide and presumably been deemed worthy of the eternal memory of the Muses, these songs then reach the timeless land of the Phaeacians.

As noted, both Phemius and Demodocus sing at social gatherings, which modern readers are inclined to assume are entertainment events. While events such as these may indeed provide entertainment, that outcome may be consequential rather than the purpose itself.[1] The difference can pass unobserved within a modern culture that has created discrete categories for 'secular' and 'sacred'. In the mythical framework of Homer, however, the sacred suffuses all things. It is ever-present. Every emotion, every experience, every object in nature has an eternal manifestation. As the Trojan elders remark among themselves in *Iliad* book three while they observe Helen, acknowledging this is not a matter of finding someone or something to blame – though some heroes within the epics may do just that. Rather, it is a matter of recognising causality, reconciling with what *is* and moving forward in the understanding that mortals are not always in control and do not have vision into the totality of the cosmos, at least not in the ways that they would like.

To return to the feasts of the *Odyssey*, in book three, Athena and Telemachus arrive in Pylos as a feast for the god Poseidon is underway. The final feast depicted, at which Odysseus slaughters the suitors with his bow, is held on a sacred day in honour of Apollo, god of the bow. The god is not present as a character in the story, but a mind trained to attend to the sacred in all things could be expected to recognise the significance of Penelope holding her contest of the bow on his day. Whether every feast in the epic is held on a god's day of honour is not specified, but the gods are honoured at every feast with libations and sacrifices, portions of meals offered to them and invocations of them.

Whether bards were viewed as entertainers or mouthpieces of the Muses by the pre-literate historical people who heard them is not recoverable and will inevitably be debated. Perhaps there is some truth in both versions. When Phemius sings his song in book one, the song that distresses Penelope and provokes her to confront him, there is no mention of a goddess or Muse prompting him, other than as contained in his standard epithet, 'god-inspired'. Conversely, when Demodocus is brought out to sing for the Phaeacians and their guests in book eight, it is a Muse who sets his song in motion:

> They sent forth their hands for all the good things set before them,
> But when they had satisfied their desire for food and drink, then
> The Muse prompted the bard to sing the famous deeds of men,
> A song whose fame had reached the wide sky,
> About a quarrel between Odysseus and Achilles, son of Peleus,
> The time they quarrelled at a bountiful feast of the gods
> With terrible words, but the lord of men Agamemnon
> Rejoiced in his understanding that the best of the Achaeans were contending,

> For so had Phoebus Apollo described through an oracle
> In sacred Python, when he had stepped over the stone threshold
> In search of an oracle, for that was the beginning of the calamities that rolled across
> The Trojans and the Danaans by the plan of great Zeus.
>
> (Lines 71–83)

Notably, there is no surviving myth in which Agamemnon and Achilles quarrel. While this does not prove that one did not exist, it is also notable that at this sacred occasion, initiated by a Muse as Odysseus is so close to achieving his return to Ithaca, the story offered is of a quarrel between the two central figures of Homer's epics who represent oppositional (and complementary) forms of fame. Achilles' is that of might and Odysseus' of cunning. Achilles ends his epic mourning the loss of his dearest companion and anticipating his own death soon to follow, Odysseus with his reunion with his dearest family. Our *Odyssey* frames their quarrel as one that launches the war which will end one age and usher in another.

Whoever historical bards were and whatever function they served in the pre-literate ancient Greek world, by the time epic material attributed to Homer appears in the historical record, this material was not sung by bards but recited by rhapsodes. These recitations were held at religious festivals, which notably included competitive events and public feasts. If these rhapsodes worked from texts, these texts were apparently not deemed important enough to mention. Their coherence within the system rather than the specific words recorded on papyrus or tablets seems to be what made them 'Homeric'. And for this, the Muses are portrayed as essential, for they possess the memory of everything that mattered, and they can distil the totality (of what needs to be remembered about heroes) through the particular (Achilles and Odysseus), as exhibited in the opening lines of our *Iliad* and *Odyssey*:

> The divine wrath of Achilles, son of Peleus, sing, goddess,
> Of its destructiveness, which set in motion
> The countless agonies of the Achaeans
> Sending forth to Hades many mighty breaths of life,
> Of heroes, rendering them the spoils of dogs
> And all birds of prey, bringing to fulfilment the will of Zeus,
> From whom these two were first set apart, quarrelling,
> The son of Atreus, leader of men, and Achilles, born of Zeus.
> Who brought these two together in strife to fight?

The son of Leto and Zeus,[2] for his anger was provoked by the king,
And he launched devastating plague upon the encampment, destroying the people
On account of the priest Chryses, who he dishonoured,
The son of Atreus, for the priest had come to the swift ships of the Achaeans
To release his daughter bearing an immense ransom.
Holding in his hands the garland of far-shooting Apollo
Upon a golden staff, and he beseeched all the Achaeans.
(*Iliad*, lines 1–15)

A husband, a versatile man with many plots and schemes,
relate to me, Muse, of him who very much
Was made to wander, after sacking the sacred citadel of Troy.
He saw many people and cities and came to know their way of understanding.
He experienced at sea many sorrows upon his consciousness,
Striving to recover his mortal identity and the return home of his companions,
But not even he could rescue his companions, having very much desired to
For they destroyed themselves by their own recklessness,
Being disconnected, the sacred cattle of Hyperion, the Sun,
They devoured them, and the god took away their day of returning.
From any point whatever, goddess, daughter of Zeus, tell us too.
(*Odyssey*, lines 1–10)

Whether singing or telling, the essential function of the Muses within the epics remains stable through the transition and variation of wording. In both, the Muse can enable the bard or rhapsode to encapsulate the entirety of the mythical past within a paradigmatic story. The opening lines of each locate the totality within a particular. The story of the Trojan war can be accessed through the quarrel of Achilles and Agamemnon over Briseis. This quarrel which frames the *Iliad* replicates on a smaller scale the quarrel between the Achaeans and the Trojans over Helen that launches the Trojan war. Odysseus' journey home in the *Odyssey* is one iteration of homecoming hero narratives, each of which plays out in its own way. Menelaos returns home having recovered his wife, while his brother Agamemnon is murdered by his wife and her lover. Each narrative can be spun with its own variations, but these variations belong to a cosmic whole over whose memory the Muses preside.

During a conversation between the shades of Agamemnon and Achilles in Hades in the final book of our *Odyssey*, Agamemnon recounts the funeral of his former antagonist:

> All nine Muses in beautiful antiphonal voice
> Sang the funeral song. You observed no one there without tears
> Among the Argives, for so did the clear voice of the Muse
>   move them.
>
> (Lines 60–62)

The funeral song sung by the Muses complements the lament sung by Thetis and her sisters. The phrase 'sang the funeral song' is expressed in the Greek text through the verb *threneo* (its noun form is *threnos*), which is associated with professional mourners, and the latter is *goos*, which is associated with personal mourners. At Achilles' funeral, the Muses represent the 'professional' mourners, Thetis and her sisters his personal ones. By reaching back to the funeral of Achilles, the end of the *Odyssey* brings the role of the Muses in sacred memory full circle. By singing the funeral song of 'the best of the Achaeans', as Achilles is described in Homer, the Muses oversee the transformation of a personal expression of grief (*goos*) into a social institution (*threnodies* sung as part of cult worship). If Achilles' death represents a compressed narrative signifying the transition from the age of myth to the age of cult, then perhaps the Muses singing his funeral song can be understood as a compressed narrative signifying the evolution of lament into epic, recited at sacred community festivals.

Ino

Ino's one brief appearance in the *Odyssey* can seem insignificant when the epic is examined through the lens of narrative cohesion. We might read past her seemingly decorative speech and scene, feeling that it has nothing to add to the story. If we approach her through the lens of thematic patterning, however, seeking to access what the epic suggests needs to be remembered about goddesses, the scene becomes vital.

> The daughter of Cadmus saw Odysseus then, Ino with the
>   beautiful ankles,

> The luminous goddess, who before was mortal, speaking with a human voice,
> But now, dwelling in the sea, she receives her portion of honour, as a goddess of the sea.
> In her way, she felt pity for Odysseus, wandering and suffering.
> She ascended, looking like a gull rising from a lake,
> And sat upon his raft with its many fastenings, and spoke these words:
> 'Man of destiny, why has the earth-shaker Poseidon
> Worked so fearfully against you that he has seeded countless ills against you?
> Even so, he will not destroy you, though he desires to very greatly.
> Now, do exactly as I advise, for you do not seem to lack understanding.
> Strip off your clothes, and let the wind bear the raft away,
> Leave it behind, and strive to obtain your return swimming with your hands
> To the land of the Phaeacians, where it is your portion to flee.
> Here now, stretch this veil across your chest.
> It is immortal, you need not fear either suffering or destruction,
> But when your hands feel land beneath them,
> Loosen the veil, and throw it back into the wine-dark sea
> Far from the land, then yourself turn away.'
> So having spoken, the goddess gave Odysseus her veil,
> And herself sank down beneath the waves,
> Resembling a gull, and a dense, ink-dark wave covered her.
>
> (Lines 333–353)

Her entire story is compressed in the first six lines, which describe her noticing Odysseus battling Poseidon's storm and struggling to survive. In the first line, 'The daughter of Cadmus' identifies her genealogy. Her father was the founder of Thebes and father of four daughters: Ino, Semele (mother of Dionysus), Agave (mother of Pentheus) and Autonoe (mother of Actaeon). The story of Agave and Pentheus, as portrayed in Euripides' *Bacchae*, is especially resonant in this scene. After Pentheus dishonours Dionysus, the god inflicts his mother, Agave, with bacchic frenzy, and she dismembers her son, having mistaken him for a lion. When the madness passes, she and her surviving family members are consigned to exile and wandering. Other surviving ancient sources from classical Athens to the Roman Empire, spanning hundreds of years, offer variations and interpretations of these myths. In one version, Ino invoked Hera's ire by helping to raise Dionysus. Hera then hounded Ino into madness until she finally threw herself into the sea to escape. However the stories are told, in all three cases, a pattern unfolds: these women and the heroes they give birth to experience 'wandering and suffering', what Ino observes Odysseus experiencing and which provokes her to pity him.

The phrase 'who before was mortal' in the second line picks up a thread of her story: as Ino threw herself into the sea, Zeus took pity on her and transformed her into a goddess. This iteration of her story follows the pattern of her nephew Dionysus'. In one traditional version of his story, he too began his life as a hero and was transformed into a god. In a larger sense, Ino's story maps onto the pattern of heroes, who begin their lives as mortals and, at the moment of their deaths, are immortalised and subsequently honoured in cult. In two lines, our bard offers a condensed narrative that speaks to the cult worship of gods and heroes without ever overtly referencing them. But for those who recognise the signs, these lines reinforce the meaning of heroes that must be remembered.

Odysseus is initially wary of Ino's advice, since immortals are not always transparent about their intentions for mortals. In the *Iliad*, Hector presses forward attacking the Achaeans because he believes that Zeus' favour is with him, and he will be the saviour of Troy. And he is not entirely wrong. Zeus does favour him, but Hector does not realise that this favour is temporary, part of a larger plan of Zeus, within the *Iliad*, to fulfil his promise to Thetis and beyond it to relieve Earth's burden by eliminating the heroes who are exhausting her resources. When Hector stands firm to face Achilles, Athena appears in the guise of Hector's brother, deceiving him into believing that he is not facing Achilles alone. When the ruse is revealed, Hector understands that death has arrived for him and charges forward to attack Achilles. Since he must die, he will do so with valour.

Whether Odysseus knows of specific occurrences of immortal deception is not as important as recognising that he does not, in the moment, know the reason behind Ino's gift. He recognises the limitations of his knowledge and is cautious, attempting to survive by his own hands alone. When this proves impossible, he accepts the gifts, which can be said to represent accepting the cosmic plan, whatever it may be. In Hector's case, it resulted in his death. For Odysseus, it delivers him safely to the shores of Ithaca.

Observing the pattern behind Ino's story illuminates its purpose and meaning. We now have an explanation for why this story is here and what it reminds historical hearers about what they need to remember: A goddess who had once been mortal and can relate to and empathise with the suffering of mortals may be inclined to use her power to benefit them. The purpose of Ino's presence in our *Odyssey* is not to add to the narrative but to reinforce its meaning.

Aphrodite

If a goddess can deploy her power to be helpful, it is also possible for her to deploy it to be harmful. Dualities of this kind suffuse ancient Greek language but can feel especially challenging for contemporary readers because they run counter to modern moral concepts of 'good' and 'evil' as discrete categories, whether these categories are religious or secular. If we think of Aphrodite as 'the goddess of love', and love is a universal good, then her coercion of and violent threat against Helen in book three of our *Iliad* can seem shocking. If we think of her as 'the goddess of sexuality', then we might celebrate or critique her depending on the assumptions we bring to our understanding of sexuality. Perhaps we are not accustomed to thinking of her as a generative goddess, a creative goddess, with love and sexuality being subsets of this, who can deploy this power in ways that can seem either helpful or harmful to the mortals under her sway.

In our *Iliad*, Aphrodite is the mother of the Trojan prince Aeneas, who Homer tells us is fated to survive the war. The son of the generative goddess will not be destroyed in the fall of the city but live on to bear future generations who will carry its memory. Through Aphrodite's son, the destruction of Troy will not be total. The *Homeric Hymn to Aphrodite* provides a narrative of Aeneas' birth. The hymn begins by qualifying Aphrodite's power among the gods. Three goddesses are immune to her charms: Hestia, Artemis and Athena. These three aside, no other mortals or immortals can resist her power, including Zeus, who Aphrodite beguiled at will, causing him to forget his 'glorious' wife Hera and unite with mortal women. The hymn notes that mating gods with mortal women and goddesses with mortal men was a favourite trick of Aphrodite's, but Zeus turned the game back on her. He threw 'honey-sweet longing' for the mortal Anchises into her consciousness, and she went to him in the guise of a young woman.

When Anchises realised Aphrodite's true identity, he was terrified and begged for mercy, but Aphrodite assured him that she would not harm him. Citing the grief of Ganymede's father after Zeus swept him away, and the unfortunate end of Dawn's mortal lover Tithonus, who was granted immortality but not endless youth, Aphrodite pledged neither to remove Anchises from his human community nor bestow immortality upon him. But she would give him a son whose line would never die.

In *Iliad* book five, this destiny of Aeneas' is challenged. Under Athena's patronage, Achaean hero Diomedes has established his dominance on the battlefield. With Athena guiding his spear, Diomedes strikes and kills Trojan ally Pandarus. In response, Aeneas leaps off his chariot to protect the dead man's body, and Diomedes aspires to make Aphrodite's son his next victim. Noticing him in danger, Aphrodite rushes to Aeneas' side:

> And now, lord of men Aeneas would have perished there
> Had not keen Aphrodite perceived him,
> His mother, she brought him upon Anchises, who tended cattle.
> She wrapped her two shining arms around her beloved son,
> Then she wrapped him in her shining, folded garment,
> To be a wall against arrows, lest some swift-horsed Danaans
> Throw bronze into his chest and take out his consciousness.
> She carried her own beloved son away from the battle.
> (Lines 311–318)

One of the qualities that makes this image so striking is its dissonance. In the midst of bloody battle and gruesome injuries, a mother swoops in to save her son. Moreover, she has the power to protect him. The folds of her immortal garment can defend him against spears and swords, and her 'shining arms' are large and strong enough to lift him out of danger. We might imagine any mother wishing she could wrap her fully grown son in her dress and carrying him out of danger, armour and weapons included, as easily as she would a small child. The familiar and the strange live together in this image: the devotion of a mother and the power to save loved ones from brutal injury or death.

When Athena granted her patronage to Diomedes, she revealed herself to him and removed the mist from his eyes, enabling him to distinguish immortals from mortals. She warned him that he must not fight any of the gods, with one exception. If he encountered Aphrodite, Athena gave him permission to wound her. Recalling Athena's instructions, when Aphrodite took Aeneas in her arms, Diomedes pursued, struck and wounded her, causing her to drop Aeneas and run away weeping:

> Eager one, Diomedes went toward Cyprus with his pitiless bronze,
> Knowing how un-valorous a goddess she was, not a goddess
> Who is lord over men in battle,
> Not like Athena or Enyo, sacker of cities,

But when he reached her, having followed her through the throng of warriors,
There, the great-hearted son of Tydeus, having lunged
At the furthest point, leaping with his sharp spear, he wounded her hand,
Which was soft. At once, his spear bore right through the surface of her skin,
Through her ambrosial garment, which the Graces made for her.
The ambrosial blood of the goddess flowed over the palm of her hand,
Ichor, of such a kind as flows through the blessed gods,
For she neither eats food nor drinks fiery-looking wine,
For this reason, gods are without blood and are called immortal.
Letting out a great shout, she dropped her son,
And Phoebus Apollo protected him with his great hands
With a steel-dark cloud, lest the swift-horsed Danaans
Throw bronze into his chest and take out his consciousness.
And noble Diomedes shouted a great shout,
'Give way, daughter of Zeus, to battle and the strife of battle.
Truly, is it not enough that you lead feeble women astray?
If you go up and down in battle, truly I think you
Will shiver at the war, even at what you may hear about it.'
So he spoke, and she stepped away, dreadfully distressed,
And taking her, wind-swift Iris led her away from the throng of warriors,
Afflicted with pain in her body, her beautiful skin was darkening.
To the left of the battle, she found impetuous Ares
Who was seated. His spear and swift horses were resting against a cloud.
On bended knee, throwing herself at her beloved brother,
With many entreaties, she begged for his horses banded in gold,
'Beloved brother, provide for me and give me your horses.
In order that I can reach Olympus, where the immortals have their resting place.
I am exceedingly afflicted with a wound which a mortal man gave me,
The son of Tydeus, who now would fight even father Zeus.'

(Lines 330–362)

The description of Aphrodite as 'un-valorous' and 'not a goddess / Who is lord over men in battle' is not as straightforward as suggesting that goddesses do not belong in battle or that a mother's protection is ultimately futile. Two goddesses are named lording 'over men in battle', Athena and Enya, and several times in Homer, similes compare warriors defending their comrades to mothers defending their children. Some goddesses do belong in battle, but not Aphrodite, not the generative goddess. Her works can provoke the longing that causes conflicts that lead to war, as she did by leading Helen to Troy, but facing off against Athena in battle, who is also her antagonist in this moment, Aphrodite will not prevail. A scene in book twenty-one, in which Zeus invites the other immortals to enter the field of battle, will reinforce the point. After Athena defeats Ares, Aphrodite will rush to his aid, and Athena will knock her out with a punch to the chest, then mock her and Ares as they lie in the dirt. Here, shocked and in pain, Aphrodite drops Aeneas, who is protected by Apollo, and rushes to Ares, who is reclining near a cloud. Athena had led him there earlier to prevent him from throwing his support behind the Trojans.

The antagonisms and quarrels among the gods can feel almost like comic relief – Aphrodite wrapping Aeneas, armour and all, in her dress and carrying him off the battlefield but dropping him when she is injured, Apollo picking up the relay with a 'steel-dark cloud' as Aphrodite nurses her pain, thoughts of her son's safety forgotten. These moments can feel comical because they seem to have no immediate stakes for the gods themselves. Diomedes can wound Aphrodite, but she will heal. The quarrels that flare up among the gods eventually disperse when they prioritise peace and stability. For the warriors of our *Iliad*, the stakes are always high. The quarrels among the gods determine whether heroes live or die. As such, they are deadly serious all the time.

Revisiting the scene between Aphrodite and Helen through this lens, we might notice that the benign guise Aphrodite adopts to lure Helen to Paris' side belies her destructive potential. When Aphrodite had her own injury to occupy her, thoughts of her son's safety fled from her mind. Helen's feelings towards Paris similarly carry no weight against Aphrodite's plans. Though she may not be suited for warfare, Aphrodite's power is fearsome and not to be toyed with, as seen in their exchange, explored previously from Helen's point of view:

> Aphrodite herself went to call Helen. She reached the
> High-raised tower, around her Trojan women were swarming.
> Seizing Helen's nectar-scented, enveloping clothing with her
>   hand, she shook it.

Goddesses

She addressed her looking like an old woman born long ago,
A wool dresser, dwelling in Lacedaemon.
She worked beautiful wool, and Helen regarded her most affectionately.
Appearing as her, Aphrodite called Helen.
'Come here. Alexander is calling you to return home.
He is there in the inner room on the rounded bed,
Gleaming in his beauty and garments. No one would say
The man had come from battling, but to a round dance
He goes, or from a round dance he has returned to rest.'
So she spoke and roused the consciousness in Helen's chest
And when she perceived with her eyes the goddess's very beautiful neck,
Breasts that provoke desire and her sparkling eyes,
She was amazed, then spoke a word from out of her and named her,
'*Daimoni*, why do you long to deceive me with these things?
Is it to a former city, well populated, that
You will lead me, Phrygia or charming Maeonia?
Perhaps there is in that place a certain other mortal man, someone dear to you?
Or now is it on account of Menelaus over Alexander
Prevailing, and he wishes to lead hateful me home?
For this reason, now, you make your stand here, being wily-minded.
Sit beside him yourself. Withdraw from the way of the gods.
Turn your feet back, never again toward Olympus.
But always for him suffer and protect him
Until he makes you into either a spouse or a slave.
I will not go there. It would cause indignation,
Preparing a bed for him, the Trojan women hereafter,
All of them will find fault with me. I have endless pain in my consciousness.'
Provoked to anger, godlike Aphrodite addressed her,
'Do not provoke me, perverse woman. Don't make me angry and let you go,
Or I would hate you as terribly as I now love you.
And I would devise baneful enmity among the two sides,
Trojan and Danaan, and you would be destroyed by destructive doom.'
So she spoke, and Helen born of Zeus was afraid.

> She walked, covering her face with her bright, radiant robe,
> In silence and escaped the notice of all the Trojan women.
> A *daimoni* led her.'
>
> (Lines 383–420)

According to the *Homeric Hymn to Aphrodite*, before Aphrodite's experience with Anchises, her powers had invoked fear in the other gods, and she delighted in being able to bend their minds. After having experienced it herself, she can no longer make light of leading them astray. But Aphrodite does not know what it is like to be mortal and cannot use her power any way other than to achieve her ends. If her affair with Anchises has taught Aphrodite not to inflict her powers on gods, compelling them to desire mortals, perhaps the *Homeric Hymn to Aphrodite* provides a complementary explanation for why demigods stop being born. The examples of Ganymede and Tithonus speak to the grief mortals suffer when they mix with gods. The gods are ever-present, but as the Trojan elders express, perhaps it is best to preserve a boundary between god and mortal.

Athena

Uniquely among the Olympian goddesses, Athena is a central figure in both the *Iliad* and *Odyssey*. She performs the same function in both, as a patron of heroes. At times, her fulfilment of this role is at her father's bidding; other times, she prompts her father to send her forth to a hero's side. In the *Iliad*, she ranges across the Achaean lines, picking favourites to infuse with courage and might and targeting Trojans and their allies to deceive into fatal errors. Her role in the *Odyssey* does not change, but the targets of her patronage and the works they perform do: in addition to Odysseus, who is an established favourite, Penelope, Telemachus and Nausicaa all receive Athena's immortal gifts, which include both might and cunning.

Perhaps Athena's most remarked-upon feature is the striking manner of her birth. Two ancient Greek sources for it can be found in Hesiod's *Theogony* and a *Homeric Hymn to Athena*. In Hesiod's version, Athena's mother is Metis, the first wife of Zeus whose name can mean 'cunning', 'clever' or 'crafty'. But Zeus was forewarned of a prophecy that Metis would give birth first to a daughter, 'owl-eyed Athena', who would be her father's equal in 'might and sound counsel' (line 896), then to a son who would rule over gods and men, 'having a heart of overwhelming strength' (line 898). Before his first child can be born, Zeus puts Metis into his belly to be his adviser of what is 'noble and ignoble' and births Athena himself from his head (line 900). The *Homeric Hymn* describes her leaping out 'shaking her spear'. The power in her 'owl-eyes' causes Olympus to tremble, the earth to shriek and the sea to froth, producing dark waves. Beholding her, 'crafty Zeus' rejoices.

Her birth provides an origin story for her close connection to her father across myth retellings. In ancient (and modern) versions, Metis has at times been elided from Athena's genealogy. In Aeschylus' tragedy *Eumenides*, for example, Athena herself claims that she has no mother. Hesiod's alternate account suggests instead that Zeus has subdued Metis' cunning and wisdom, putting it under his control and using it to maintain his authority. As Ann Bergren explores, Zeus then himself births his and Metis' daughter, who holds the power of her father and mother but, as an eternal maiden, remains under her father's authority.[3] Viewed through the system of oral tradition, in which the part can stand in for the whole, the narrative of Athena's birth complements at a micro level Hesiod's macro narrative of cosmic history, which ends with Zeus having successfully overthrown the previous generation of gods, subduing all others and assuming control of the cosmos.

In our *Iliad*, Athena obeys her father's commands, but she is not merely his instrument. In the book four assembly, in which Zeus intentionally provokes the gods by suggesting that Menelaos and Paris' duel be allowed to bring the war to a peaceful end, contrary to the wishes of his wife and daughter, Athena is wise enough not to provoke him in the moment as Hera does, but silently, she nurses her rage:

> So he spoke, and Athena and Hera murmured,
> Seated near each other, thinking of ills for the Trojans.
> Truly, Athena was silent. She did not say anything,
> Feeling indignant with her father, Zeus, and wild wrath took her.
> (Lines 20–24)

In book eight, when Zeus has thrown his might behind the Trojans to fulfil his promise to Thetis, Athena complains bitterly to Hera:

> But this father of mine is raging in his ignoble perceptions,
> Perverse, always offensive, thwarter of my might.
> He remembers none of the very many times his son,[4]
> Worn away by his trials under Eurystheus, was saved by me.
> Truly, he wailed toward the sky, but Zeus sent me
> To defend him, sending me forth from heaven.
> (Lines 360–365)

Athena's anger at her father acknowledges her power. This finds resonance in the story Achilles relates in his book one conversation with Thetis that Hera, Athena and Poseidon bound Zeus in an attempt to overthrow him. In the wake of the plan's failure, all three gods are shown deferring to Zeus' supremacy, to varying degrees. Athena's description of Zeus thwarting her might similarly can refer both to Zeus in the moment and to his having subdued her in the past. Though angry when Zeus opposes her, Athena channels that anger into cunning. She does not challenge Zeus publicly, as Hera does, but schemes in opposition to his will. In book five, for example, noting Ares rousing the Trojans and their allies, she cleverly leads him away from battle on the pretence that they should not be opposing Zeus' command:

> The consciousness of all the gods were agitated, but owl-eyed Athena
> Taking the hand of impetuous Ares, spoke these words,
> 'Ares, plague of man Ares, blood-stained sacker of walls,
> We should not allow the Trojans and Achaeans
> To do battle, father Zeus should decide which of the two achieve glory.
> We two should withdraw and avoid the godlike wrath of Zeus.'
> So having spoken, she led impetuous Ares out of the battle.
>
> (Lines 28–35)

It is there that Aphrodite later finds him resting with his spear propped against a cloud. Athena's strategic approach with her father is also expertly deployed at the beginning of the *Odyssey*. Following the invocation of the Muse, the narrative opens at an assembly of the gods on Olympus, in which Zeus complains that mortals assign causation to the gods for their suffering when it is their own recklessness that causes them to suffer beyond their allotted fates. The man on his mind is Aegisthus, the lover of Clytemnestra who murdered her husband Agamemnon upon his return home from Troy and who was subsequently killed by their son Orestes. The family of Agamemnon provides a clear parallel to the family of Odysseus, another Trojan war hero on his way home whose wife could choose a new husband, in her case from a large contingent of eager suitors. But Odysseus' return at this moment has stalled; Calypso is holding him captive. The example of Aegisthus provides Athena an opportunity to provoke her father into securing her favourite's release by drawing his attention to the contrast between the two men.

In their extended ensuing exchange, Athena disguises a scolding of her father as a question. She concedes the appropriateness of impious Aegisthus' death, then notes that a pious man, Odysseus, is being held captive in despair, concluding that Zeus must, inexplicably, hate him. Zeus reveals that it is not he who is angry with Odysseus but Poseidon, whose son Odysseus blinded. Zeus alone would not want to leave his powerful brother feeling dishonoured by intervening on Odysseus' behalf, since this could provide destabilising strife between the brothers. But since *all* the gods agree that Odysseus must be allowed to return home, Athena's scheme succeeds. She is able to manoeuvre her father into acting for Odysseus' benefit while presenting herself as his devoted helper:

> Then owl-eyed Athena responded to him,
> 'Our father, son of Cronus, supreme ruler,
> That one[5] has been destroyed, as was exceedingly fitting,
> And as any other man too should be destroyed, who behaves as he did,
> But my heart burns at both ends for fiery-hearted Odysseus,
> Ill-fated man, who has been suffering for a long while, far from his people,
> On an island surrounded by flowing waters, the navel of the sea,
> A wooded island, which a goddess has made her home.
> The daughter of destructive-intentioned Atlas, who of the sea,
> Of all its depths, he knows, and he himself holds the pillar,
> The long one that holds the earth and sky apart.
> His daughter holds back the wretched, lamenting man,
> Always with soft and wily words,
> She bewitches him, to cause him to forget Ithaca, but Odysseus
> Longs to perceive the smoke leaping up
> From his land. He longs to die,[6] but even now, in you,
> Your dear heart turns away, Olympian. Now, did not Odysseus
> Please you with sacred acts beside the ships of the Argives,
> In wide Troy? Why do you now hate him so much, Zeus?'
> In response, Zeus, the cloud-gatherer, spoke to her,
> 'My child, what sort of words have escaped the barrier of your teeth?
> How could I fail to notice godlike Odysseus,
> Who is above and beyond mortal men in his way of understanding,
> above and beyond in sacred acts for the gods

That he gives to the immortals, who hold wide heaven.
But earth-holding Poseidon persists unceasingly
Angry on behalf of a Cyclops, who Odysseus blinded,
Equal to the gods Polyphemus, whose might is greatest
Of all the Cyclops, Thoosa, a nymph, brought him into the world,
Daughter of Phorcys, lord of the unfruitful sea.
She mingled with Poseidon in a hollow cave.
Since then, the Earth-Shaker Poseidon is against Odysseus,
But he does not kill him. He makes him wander far from the land of his father,
But come, let all of us here consider carefully the whole
Of his homecoming, in order that he can return. Poseidon will release
His anger, for he will not have the power to oppose all,
To contest alone against the will of the immortal gods.'
Then the goddess, owl-eyed Athena, replied to him,
'Our father, son of Cronus, supreme ruler,
If now this is dear to the blessed gods,
For much-thinking Odysseus to return home,
Then Hermes, the messenger, the slayer of Argus,
Let us rouse him to Ogygia, so that quickly
He can tell the nymph with the beautiful hair our infallible will,
That forbearing Odysseus must return to light and life.
But I will go to Ithaca in order that his son
I can urge on and put courage in his consciousness
To summon the long-haired Achaeans to an assembly
To forbid the suitors who forever
Slaughter his thick sheep and curve-horned cows who roll as they walk.
I will send him to Sparta and sandy Pylos
To learn about the homecomings of the men dear to his father, and if he can hear any news,
In order that he may have a good report among men.'
So having spoken, she tied under her feet her beautiful sandals,
Ambrosial and golden, they bore her upon the flowing water,
And upon the boundless earth, at the same pace as a breath of wind.
She took her stout spear, tipped with sharp bronze,
Massive, matchless, mighty, with which she subdues ranks of men,

Heroes, who the daughter of a mighty father is angry with.
She descended from Olympus, swooping down from the summit.
She made her stand in the land of Ithaca, at the front door of Odysseus,
At the threshold of the courtyard, holding in the palm of her hand a spear of bronze,
In the likeness of a guest-friend, Mentes, leader of the Taphians.

(Lines 44–105)

In both epics, Athena achieves her ends not by challenging her father's authority directly or conspiring to overthrow him but through strategic planning. She thinks ahead, weighing how he might respond and shaping her plans accordingly. In her patronage of heroes, Athena deploys both, as the situation demands, deceiving and tricking the opponents of her favourite heroes and fuelling those favourites with whatever ability the situation calls for in the moment. In the process of doing so in the above passage, she plots the courses of Telemachus and Odysseus, determining how their stories will unfold and converge across our *Odyssey*.

In the *Iliad*'s book four, when Zeus grants her permission to provoke the Trojans into breaking the truce that was in place during the duel of Menelaos and Paris, she goads Lycaon by offering what he longs for, gratitude, admiration and material rewards:

Standing near him, she spoke winged words,
'You would be persuaded by me, warlike son of Lycaon,
To take it upon yourself to send forth a swift arrow at Menelaos.
You would receive gratitude and renown, from all the Trojans,
And most of all from prince Alexander.
From him, first of all, you would carry shining gifts
If he were to see Menelaos, warlike son of Atreus
Overpowered by your arrow, going upon the painful funeral pyre,
But shoot an arrow at glorious Menelaos,
Pray to Lycian-born Apollo, famous for the bow,
Offer a renowned sacrifice of firstborn lambs,
When you return home to the sacred city of Zeleia.'
So Athena spoke, and she persuaded his consciousness, being without understanding.

(Lines 92–104)

Seduced by the vision of wealth and fame that Athena provides him, Lycaon shoots the arrow that breaks the truce. In the ensuing battles, Athena brings her double-edged skills to Diomedes, who has prayed to her, infusing him with the might of his father and enabling him to distinguish mortal from immortal, a formidable gift:

> So he spoke, offering prayers, and Pallas Athena heard him.
> She made his limbs light, above his hands and his feet.
> She took her stand beside him and spoke words with wings,
> 'Be of good courage now Diomedes, to bring the fight to the
>   Trojans.
> For I have put into your chest the might of your father,
> Dauntless, of such a kind as shield-wielding, horse-driving
>   Tydeus had.
> I have taken the mist from your eyes that was there previously,
> So that you can perceive gods from men.
> Now, if a god attempts to approach you here,
> Do not fight against immortal gods,
> The others, but if Aphrodite, daughter of Zeus,
> Comes into the war, wound her with your sharp bronze.'
> So having spoken, owl-eyed Athena stepped away.
>
> (Lines 121–132)

On one level, Athena is rewarding Diomedes for praying to her; the prayers of mortals please her, as they please all the gods. On an additional level, Athena is calculating how best to achieve her ends in contradiction to her father without seeming to challenge him directly. Granting Diomedes the authority to overpower Aphrodite would remove her, and her support of the Trojans, from the fight. This is precisely what Athena achieves, and she does so at an opportune moment when Aphrodite is attempting to save Aeneas. Though Apollo is present to preserve Aeneas' destiny, through her support of Diomedes, Athena is able to remove Aphrodite and her interference from the battlefield. Crucially, Athena's patronage is not a matter of either/or: either she cares about Diomedes, or she is using him. In Homer, the two exist in a conceptual Möbius strip. They are so interdependent that it is impossible to distinguish where one ends and the other begins. Diomedes' native strength, courage and piety please Athena, and she offers him support in ways that also benefit her. The dynamic parallels the complementarity of Zeus' plan to end the age of heroes and his plan to fulfil his promise to Thetis: The two converge in common purpose.

One telling simile in *Iliad* book four portrays Athena as a maternal figure, evoking Aphrodite protecting Aeneas, her son, or lifting Paris, one of her favourites, out of danger:

> The blessed gods did not fail to notice you, Menelaos,
> The deathless ones, first among them the daughter of Zeus, bringer of spoils.
> Taking her stand beside you, she warded off the sharp arrow.
> She brushed it away from the surface of your skin, just as a mother
> Brushes a fly away from her child when he lies down in honey-sweet sleep.
> She herself guided it straight to where his belt buckles
> Of gold were held together, and the two parts of his breastplate met.
>
> (Lines 127–133)

Athena's protection here has the immediate effect of preserving his life. In other places, her protection is implied through an omen that communicates her approval. In book ten, for example, as Odysseus and Diomedes set out for a night raid, Odysseus prays to Athena before setting out, and pleased that he has appealed to her, she sends a heron to fly alongside him on the right, an omen of future success. Perceiving it prompts Odysseus to offer a second prayer in response:

> She set in motion a heron near their path on the right,
> Pallas Athena. They[7] did not see it with their eyes
> In the dusky night, but they heard its sharp cry.
> Odysseus rejoiced at the bird, and he prayed to Athena,
> 'Hear me, child of aegis-bearing Zeus, who is with me always.
> Stand with me in all my toils. I am not unseen by you,
> Moving, now most of all, hold me dear, Athena.
> Give us to return to the ships with glorious report
> Having done a great deed, that is of concern to the Trojans.'
>
> (Lines 274–282)

Odysseus consistently acknowledges Athena through prayer as a necessary ally. When he feels her absence in the *Odyssey*, he strives to draw her back to him through toil and endurance. The relationship between him and Athena suggests that the hero's success is not through either his skills and efforts or the work of the goddess. It is both. This is perhaps most explicitly evident in book twenty-two, in which Andromache, unaware that Hector has died, continues to work at her weaving:

> Andromache was disconnected. She did not perceive
> that he was far away from baths.
> Owl-eyed Athena had subdued him at the hands of Achilles.
> (Lines 445–446)

The image of Athena defeating Hector through Achilles' hands suggests a fusion of goddess and hero in this moment. Athena has the intention, Achilles the skill. As with Aphrodite and Helen, the goddess is the agent and the hero the instrument. But to be the instrument, the hero must possess both will and skill. The potential must already lie within the heroes in order for the gods to channel their intentions through them. The *Odyssey* depicts this dynamic in a non-martial context through the relationship of Athena and Nausicaa, the Phaeacian princess. When Odysseus appears suddenly where Nausicaa and her handmaids have gathered to wash their clothes, the young women are frightened and scatter. Nausicaa alone stands firm, through the intention of Athena:

> Odysseus appeared terrifying to the girls, all caked in brine.
> They fled in a panic, each in different directions along the
>   jutting shore
> But only the daughter of Alcinous remained, for Athena in her
> Breathed courage, into her heart and understanding, and stole
>   fear from her limbs.
> She made her stand face-to-face with Odysseus, holding her
>   ground, and he pondered.
> (Lines 137–144)

As in the case of warrior heroes, Athena's patronage does not necessarily bestow qualities on Nausicaa that she does not innately possess already; rather, the goddess amplifies them. The same can be said for Penelope's cunning and skill. They are gifts of Athena's, but the recipient must know how to deploy them.

In the *Iliad*, the notion of amplification appears in a critical scene in book eighteen. Hector has killed Patroclus, and a fight is raging over possession of his corpse. If Achilles appeared in battle, the Trojans would flee in fear, but his armour is now in the possession of Hector, who has stripped it from

Patroclus' body. Unable to re-enter battle to protect Patroclus, Achilles finds another way to terrify the Trojans into abandoning the fight, with Athena's patronage:

> But Achilles, dear to Zeus, rose up, around him, Athena,
> She threw on his stalwart shoulders the tasselled aegis,
> And around his head, the goddess born of Zeus put a cloud
> Of gold, and from it burned a beaming flame –
> As when smoke coming from a city reaches the ether,
> From a faraway island, hostile men fight around each other,
> And all day long their contesting is decided by Ares
> From out of their own city, but when the sun sinks,
> The closely woven beacons burn, their brightness aloft
> Is borne, shooting around for their neighbours to see
> That in some way, protectors from Ares might come in their
>   ships –
> So from Achilles' head, a bright flame reached the ether.
> Coming from the ditch, he made his stand on the wall. With
>   the Achaeans,
> He did not mix, for he regarded with awe and dread his
>   mother's wise counsel.
> There, making his stand, he roared aloud, and Pallas Athena
>   from afar
> Spoke out, and roused unutterable confusion among the
>   Trojans –
> As when a trumpet shrieks, and the clear sound
> Life-destroying enemies spread through the city,
> Just such a sound the grandson of Aeacus[8] made.
> When they perceived the voice of bronze-clad Aeacus'
>   grandson,
> The consciousness of all was agitated, but the horses with
>   beautiful manes
> Turned their chariots around, for they foresaw pain with their
>   consciousness.
> The charioteers were astonished when they saw the effortless
>   fire,
> Dreadful, around the head of the great-hearted son of Peleus
> Burning, which the goddess owl-eyed Athena kindled.
> Three times godlike Achilles roared aloud across the ditch,
> Three times the Trojans and their renowned allies were stirred up.

> Then and there, twelve of the best men were destroyed
> By their own chariots and spears, but the Achaeans,
> They were glad, dragging Patroclus away from the arrows.
> They placed him on a bed, his beloved companions around him,
> Running, swift-footed Achilles followed after them,
> Pouring hot tears when he beheld his trusted companion,
> Lying on the litter, torn apart by sharp bronze.
> Truly, he had sent him out with his horses and carriages
> Into battle, never would he receive him, returning home.
> Ox-eyed mistress Hera untiring Helios
> Sent, against his will, to go into the streams of Ocean.
> The sun sank, and the godlike Achaeans brought to an end
> The mighty din of battle and distressing war.
>
> (Lines 203–242)

Achilles is already the most fearsome Achaean warrior. Athena's presence and her gifts magnify his, creating a terrifying image. Without any armour or weapons, Achilles' presence has caused the deaths of twelve of the best warriors on the Trojan side from a combination of his own reputation and Athena's favour. The relationship between the goddess and heroes is portrayed as a dynamic that feeds itself, an eternally spinning cycle of reciprocal effect. When they secure the support of Athena, 'first among [the deathless ones]', the heroes achieve superhuman feats.

Because the scene of Athena's work in the *Iliad* is war and her patronage of Odysseus in the *Odyssey* evokes that war, it can be tempting to overemphasise her role as a war goddess. However, the most notable elements of Athena's characterisation, her cunning and forethought, are consistently connected to her signature craft of weaving. When she finally reveals herself, as herself, to Odysseus in book thirteen, she tells him, 'Now, I have come here again in order that I may weave a *metis* along with you' (line 303). Later in the same book, Odysseus asks her to 'weave a *metis*' so that he can 'repay' the suitors for their impious disregard of proper custom (line 386). Athena is mighty because she knows how to set and execute a plan, and these skills are as useful in peacetime as they are in war. *Iliad* book five provides a potential reference to this when she is described dressing for battle:

> However Athena, daughter of aegis-bearing Zeus,
> She poured down upon her father's floor her fine peplos,

Many-coloured, that she had crafted and toiled over with her
  own hands.
Donning the chiton of Zeus the cloud-gatherer,
She armed herself with a breastplate, the apparatus of war,
  bringer of tears.
She threw across her two shoulders the tasselled aegis,
Terrifying, which all around was crowned with Fear
And with it Strife, and with it Courage, and with it chilling
  Rout,
And with it, the head of the terrifying monster, the Gorgon,
Full of terror, terrible to behold, a portent of Zeus the Aegis-
  bearer.
She placed on her head the double-sided helmet with four
  crests,
Golden, Blazing, fitted with foot soldiers from a hundred
  cities.
She stepped with her feet into a flaming chariot, seized her
  spear,
Massive, matchless, mighty, with which she subdues ranks of
  men,
Heroes, who the daughter of a mighty father is angry with.

(Lines 733–747)

In the third line, she removes her peplos, or dress, of many colours. The word used in the Greek text, *poikilon*, can also be translated as *intricately embroidered*. The suggestion is that this could be a story cloth[9] – what we might recognise as a tapestry – of the kind that Helen is weaving in *Iliad* book three. To weave such a dress would require planning, skill and, as the bard reports, toil. The image contains the duality of Athena: her skills are not only for warriors, not only for men trying to get home by sea, but also for women who nurture those dear to them and protect their households, as is explored through Athena's relationship with Penelope.

Calypso

The role of Calypso in the *Odyssey* is contained within her name, which in Greek means 'to conceal'. The opening ten lines introduce the epic's theme. It will develop a variation on the Trojan war hero who is striving to return home and recover his mortal identity, which John Miles Foley notes begins with the hero having gone away to war and being held captive for a substantial period of time.[10] Immediately after this theme is introduced, the bard explains that the husband and man of this epic – only later named as Odysseus, husband of Penelope – is the only surviving hero who has not yet achieved his return. He is being held back, concealed, by Calypso.

> A husband, a versatile man with many plots and schemes,
>   relate to me, Muse, of him who very much
> Was made to wander, after sacking the sacred citadel of Troy.
> He saw many people and cities and came to know their way of
>   understanding.
> He experienced at sea many sorrows upon his consciousness,
> Striving to recover his mortal identity and the return home of
>   his companions.
> But not even he could rescue his companions, having very
>   much desired to
> For they destroyed themselves by their own recklessness,
> Being disconnected. The sacred cattle of Hyperion, the Sun,
> They devoured them, and the god took away their day of
>   returning.
> From any point whatever, goddess, daughter of Zeus, tell us
>   too.
> All the others, as many as had escaped steep destruction,
> Were home, having escaped the war and the sea,
> One man alone, needing to return to life and light and to his
>   wife,
> The mistress nymph, Calypso, goddess of Zeus, held him
>   back
> In her hollow caves, longing to make him her husband.
>   (Lines 1–15)

The Greek word that is translated as 'mortal identity' in the above passage is *psyche*, which eventually comes to mean soul. Translations of Homer tend to render it as *spirit* or *shade*. Gregory Nagy describes the *psyche* as the life force of heroes which animates them while they are alive and carries their identities through the underworld after their mortal bodies have died. When we encounter heroes in the underworld in Homer, as we do in *Odyssey* books ten and twenty-four, they are conscious of their mortal identities. Odysseus speaks with his mother. Achilles asks about his son. Agamemnon discusses the treachery of his wife. My choice to render *psyche* as mortal identity in line five above is intended to convey that Odysseus, while he is with Calypso, has been removed from the flow of time, in which mortals live and die. While on Calypso's Island, he is neither living nor dead. If he chooses to remain with her and become her husband, as she desires, however, his mortal identity will be forfeit. He will no longer be Odysseus of Ithaca, husband of Penelope. The broadest definition of *nostos* is *return*. In the context of Odysseus in this moment, he needs to return to the flow of time, the land of 'light and life'.[11] Only then can he continue his quest to return to Ithaca and his family.

As noted earlier, after introducing Odysseus' dilemma, the narrative turns its attention to the council of the gods, where Athena successfully manoeuvres her father into ordering Odysseus' release. Hermes is sent to deliver the message to Calypso, and she responds resentfully:

> 'Now, you gods are indignant that a mortal man is present for me,
> A man who I myself saved, who was wrapped around his ship's keel
> Alone, after his nimble ship with a glancing thunderbolt
> Zeus split apart in the middle of the wine-dark sea.
> There, all his good companions perished,
> But he came here, carried by the wind and the waves,
> And I held him dear and nourished him, and I promised
> To make him deathless and ageless for all days.
> But since there is no way for another god to go against
> the intention of aegis-bearing Zeus,
> Neither to evade it nor to frustrate it,
> If Odysseus himself urges and commands it, let him go
> Upon the fruitless sea, but I will in no way send him myself,
> For I have neither oared ships nor companions,
> Who can send him across the broad back of the sea.
> But I will earnestly advise him, not concealing anything,
> So that he can reach his native land very much unharmed.'
>   (Lines 129–144)

Calypso's speech reinforces the implication that the reign of Zeus will not be challenged. She resents his order but will not subvert it. It also reinforces that Odysseus now has a choice to make whether to remain with Calypso or pursue his return, regardless of the suffering it may cause him. Though Calypso will no longer be permitted to hold him captive, he could still choose to stay with her, though it is clear that he will not.

The Epic Women of Homer

After her meeting with Hermes, Calypso finds Odysseus in his usual place, seated at the seashore staring out at the water and 'pouring tears', evoking the lamenting women of our *Iliad*. When Calypso reveals her intention to release him, Odysseus distrusts her, fearing that he is being tricked by the goddess, as he fears with Ino as well. His suspicion and caution delight her, as they also delight Athena. They are a sign of his forethought and prudence, and she swears an oath by the river Styx that she intends him no harm. Later, after they dine, Calypso offers Odysseus one more warning:

> And after they had satisfied themselves with food and drink,
> Then Calypso, goddess of Zeus, began, sending forth these words:
> 'Son of Laertes, sprung from Zeus
> Odysseus, full of resources,
> So, homeward to the dear land of your father,
> Do you wish to go now, straightaway? Fare you well then, despite everything.
> Anyway, if you knew, in your heart and understanding, the portion
> Of sorrows that will fill you before reaching the land of your father,
> You would keep watch over this house, remaining with me here on this spot.
> You would be immortal, even though you are longing to see
> Your wife, who you are forever wishing for, every day.
> But surely, I vow that I am not inferior.
> Neither in body nor in stature, since it is not likely in any way
> For mortals to contend with immortals in body or form.'
>
> (Lines 200–213)

After this speech, Odysseus concedes the point, asking the goddess not to be angry with him. Calypso indeed outdoes Penelope in beauty and form, but for all that, he longs to return to her and to Ithaca. He longs to recover his mortal identity, and he will accept whatever suffering is part of the bargain. As an immortal goddess, Calypso cannot understand Odysseus' choices any more than he can bear to live at ease for eternity, cut off from the land of the living and from his mortal community. From her perspective, she is providing and caring for him; from his, she is holding him captive.

Circe

Everything the reader or listener knows about Circe within the *Odyssey* comes through the reported speech of Odysseus. She appears only in the story of his wanderings, which he recites to the Phaeacians while stranded on their island. By telling his story, he hopes to persuade them to provide him safe passage back to Ithaca. Everything we understand about Circe must then be filtered through this net: Odysseus has been on an exceedingly long and wearying journey, and he wants to return home. The Phaeacians are his best hope. He must convince them to help him, and his representation of his encounter with Circe is part of this persuasive project. A question we can ask of his encounter with Circe, then, is what he has to gain by presenting it as he does.

According to Odysseus, he and his men arrived on Circe's Island, Aeaea, traumatised and grieving following their encounter with the Laestrygonians. These cannibal giants destroyed the ships and men travelling with Odysseus from Troy. Only his own ship, and the men on it, escaped the slaughter, since he alone had the foresight to anchor outside the harbour, facilitating a quick escape. Before the disastrous Laestrygonian encounter, Odysseus and his men had come tantalisingly close to Ithaca through the help of Aeolus, who gifted Odysseus a sack of the winds he rules over. But suspicion and jealousy overran his men. Believing the sack contained expensive gifts for Odysseus, they opened it while he slept, prematurely releasing the winds. Just as they were close enough to see the smoke rising from Ithacan fires, the winds bore them away again, back to the island of Aeolus. But the lord of the winds refused to help them a second time, believing that their reappearance, despite his assistance, must mean they had 'incurred the hatred of the gods'. Which Odysseus had, during his disastrous stay on the island of Polyphemus, a Cyclops and son of Poseidon. Polyphemus had consumed six of Odysseus' companions, but he and his surviving men managed to escape by plying Polyphemus with strong wine, waiting for him to fall asleep and then blinding him. Before the Cyclops, Odysseus and his men had faced down the Lotus-Eaters, who tempted them with the plant of forgetting, and prior to that, they had battled the Cicones. From their first stop to the moment they land on Aeaea, Odysseus and his men have had to battle for their survival against foes both internal (their errors of judgement) and external.

When Odysseus and his men first arrived on Aeaea, he surveyed the island from a high point. Noticing fire and smoke from a distant dwelling, he sent out a group of men, led by Eurylochus, to find its source, and they discovered the dwelling of Circe. The tame wolves and lions around it astonished and frightened the men, who were unaware that Circe had enchanted them. From inside the house, they heard her singing as she wove:

> The beautiful-haired goddess had made her stand near the front entrance.
> They heard from within Circe's house a beautiful voice singing,
> While plying a great immortal loom, of such a kind on which goddesses
> Set in motion subtle, graceful and shining works.
>
> (Lines 220–224)

According to Odysseus' account, the men called her, and she invited them in, fed them a drug that transformed them into pigs and drove them into the pigsty. Only Eurylochus escaped because he hung back, 'suspecting a trap' (line 232). He rushed back to deliver the news to Odysseus, who promptly strapped on his sword and marched off to confront Circe. On his way, he encountered the god Hermes in the guise of a young man, who informed Odysseus that Circe had enchanted his men and warned that she would try to do the same to him. As Athena enabled Diomedes to wound Ares and Aphrodite, Hermes authorised Odysseus to remain unaffected by Circe's enchantments and meet her on his own terms. He provided for Odysseus a drug that would prevent those of Circe from transforming him and instructed him, when struck with Circe's wand, to pull out his sword as if intending to strike her. She would be startled perform the traditional role of both suppliant and host, and invite him into her bed. Hermes warned Odysseus not to refuse her, since she is a goddess, but he must make her swear an oath, as Calypso did, that she would not harm him further.

Arriving at Circe's dwelling, Odysseus followed Hermes' instructions, surprising Circe, and all transpired as the god forewarned, as Odysseus recites to the Phaeacians in book ten:

> 'Now go to the pigsty and lie down with your other companions!'
> So Circe spoke, and drawing my sharp sword from alongside my thigh,
> I rushed at Circe, as if earnestly desiring to kill her.
> She let out a great shout and ducked, taking my knees
> And weeping, she addressed winged words to me,
> 'Who among men are you? From what city do you come, and who is your father?

Goddesses

> Astonishment holds me that drinking this drug, you are not bewitched,
> For no other man, not one, endured against this drug,
> Once they drank and it first passed the barrier of their teeth.
> The way of understanding in your chest cannot be beguiled.
> Surely you are Odysseus of the many plots and schemes, who always to me
> The god of the golden wand, the slayer of Argus, said would come
> From Troy in a swift, ink-dark ship.
> But come, set your sword in its sheath, then us two will go to our bed
> in order that mingling
> In bed and love we will persuade each other.'
> (Lines 320–335)

As forewarned, Odysseus complied only after extracting an oath from her not to harm him, as he does from Calypso. After, Odysseus was bathed and offered food, but he was unable to partake, prompting Circe to question him:

> Seating herself, Circe perceived me not for the bread
> Sending forth my hands, having a mighty grief.
> Making a stand beside me, she addressed winged words,
> 'Odysseus, why do you sit silently in this way,
> Consuming your consciousness, touching neither food nor drink?
> Truly you suspect some sort of trap. It is not necessary
> To be afraid, for already I have sworn a strong oath.'
> (Lines 375–391)

Odysseus replied with a gentle reproach, asking Circe how a man could eat and drink while his companions remained under an enchantment. According to Odysseus, when he then requested that she lift it, Circe promptly complied with his request:

> So I spoke, and Circe stepped through the great room,
> Holding her wand in her hand, she opened the door to the pigsty,
> And she drove out the pigs, looking like they were in their ninth year,

> And they made a stand across from her, and she among them
> Went and rubbed another drug on each one.
> The bristles fell from their limbs, which previously were brought forth
> By the baneful drug, the one mistress Circe had offered them.
> Once again, they became men, more youthful than they had been before,
> And much more handsome, and greater to behold.
> They perceived me there, and each one took me by the hand, and
> Passionate lamentation dove into all, and throughout the house
> The clamour was fearful to behold, even the goddess took pity on them.
> Making a stand beside me, the goddess born of Zeus addressed me,
> 'Son of Laertes, born from Zeus, Odysseus of the many plots and schemes,
> Go now to the swift ships and the seashore.
> First drag your ship to the land,
> Bring all your provisions and possessions into the caves,
> Then return yourself and lead your trusty companions.'
>
> (388–405)

Odysseus recounts that he and his surviving men spent a full year with Circe, feasting on her endless supplies of meat and wine. He admits that it was only at the prompting of his companions that Odysseus was reminded to resume his journey home and to request assistance from Circe to do so. Her instructions were for the men to travel to the underworld and seek advice from Tiresias. Despite his and his men's fears, Odysseus obeyed the goddess. After his trip to the underworld, he returned to Circe, who provided him parting instructions. Odysseus carefully observed them, but his men did not. They consumed the sacred cattle of Helios, the sun god, and were destroyed while Odysseus himself endured his further trials until Ino finally guided him safely to the shores of the Phaeacians.

Odysseus offers the Phaeacians no further explanation for Circe's abrupt shift from ominous to magnanimous, nor does he provide a reason why Circe turned men (his or others) into pigs. As an immortal goddess, her intentions and plans remain inscrutable to mortals, perhaps enfolded in a larger plan spun by the Fates. According to Odysseus, Circe herself recognises the identity of the man who can resist her enchantments and pursues no further mischief against him, for it is not his own plots and schemes – though they are many and formidable – that ensure his invulnerability to her enchantments, but the protections provided by Hermes. By Odysseus' own account, immortal, not mortal, power propelled Odysseus safely through his encounter with Circe because he heeded the council and edicts of the gods, which his comrades foolishly neglected.

For Odysseus to persuade the Phaeacians to help him, he must explain why he has washed up alone, without a ship and without his men, without giving them reason to determine, as Aeolus did, that helping him would incur the gods' displeasure. Each episode Odysseus recounts demonstrates his patience, acceptance of whatever suffering the gods deliver and his ingenuity and inventiveness to survive every hardship. As he tells it, his story shows, too, that, though he made mistakes, Odysseus alone among his men exhibited these qualities to the highest degree. While the others lacked forethought and allowed themselves to be lured into impiety by the needs of the moment, Odysseus repeatedly exhibited a willingness to suffer in the short term in order to achieve his long-term goal. Thus Odysseus portrays himself as having earned his survival through hardship and skill.

To consider the extent to which Odysseus' portrayal of Circe can be trusted, we can look to other stories he recites about himself: his 'lying tales', which he shares after the Phaeacians have returned him to Ithaca. In his disguise as a beggar, Odysseus claims to be a man from Crete. This identity is a construct that he shapes and reshapes as suits the needs of the moment. Depending on who his audience is and how he intends to influence that audience, Odysseus presents the man from Crete as the son of a noble father who was cheated by a family member, a resourceful soldier who received the favour of Odysseus, a wealthy man who lost everything and serves as a cautionary tale. The stories take whatever shape the interaction demands. But while the identity of the man from Crete is false, the stories themselves draw from Odysseus' real-life experiences. Odysseus is the son of a noble father. He served at Troy. He was a wealthy man who has lost everything, though he hopes to regain it.

The reader or listener of the *Odyssey* has no complete bardic account of Odysseus' travels to which to compare his own version of them. The closest approximation is the summary of Odysseus' travels which he recites to Penelope in book twenty-three. Unlike the narrative structure of the

Odyssey, which weaves backwards and forwards through time, the bard's summary unfolds in chronological order, and it features one line on Circe:

> And Odysseus recounted to Penelope the trickery of Circe and
> of her many resources.
>
> (Line 321)

Even here, the bard reports Odysseus' speech. What 'really' happened with Circe – as with all of Odysseus' travels – remains concealed beneath a cloak of context and point of view. The episode with Circe being known only through the narrative of Odysseus draws our attention to the perspectival nature of storytelling. Narratives are provisional, shaped in the interaction between teller and receiver. For us as modern readers of the Homeric epics, Odysseus' story about Circe reminds us too of all that we do not know about the Homeric epics, including the context in which they were recited (or sung) and how this context impacts the shape of the story that we have received.

One of the islands closely associated with Homer is 'rocky Chios', as Nestor describes it in *Odyssey* book three. (Author)

Located in the north Aegean off the coast of modern-day Turkey, the colour of the water around the island can appear to change depending on the angle from which it is viewed, the time of day and the amount of cloud cover. (Author)

Viewed from above, the water can seem lighter on the top than the bottom, a possible explanation for the phrase 'the wine-coloured sea'. (Author)

Viewed at eye level, the play of light on the surface of the sea creates the effect of twinkling lights. (Author)

The sea spray caused by the tide hitting the rocky coast can resemble the diaphanous quality of clouds. (Author)

Terracotta kylix (drinking cup), ca. 550 BC, portrays the birth of Athena from Zeus' head. (Metropolitan Museum of Art)

Above left and above right: The craft of weaving is associated with poetry, both in Homer and in visual images, as in this image of a young man singing and playing a kithara (an instrument associated with the performance of epic poetry). The image on the reverse of the amphora is believed to depict a judge. Terracotta amphora, ca. 490 BC. (Metropolitan Museum of Art)

The stages of weaving, an esteemed and essential craft, are depicted in detail. Marie-Louise Nosch notes the resonance with images of ships: the fabric across the top of the loom resembles an unfurled sail. Terracotta lekythos (oil flask), ca. 550–530. (Metropolitan Museum of Art)

Additional images on the oil flask, reproduced here with the permission of the artist, include the measuring of wool, weighing of wool and women folding woven cloth.

Weaving implements included leg guards with a rough surface across the top used for carding wool. The scene portrayed in this sample is of women working wool. Others feature bridal and battle scenes. Terracotta onos, ca. 510–500 BC. (Metropolitan Museum of Art)

Above left and above right: The scene on this vase depicts Athena Pollias before a burning altar with a woman playing the flute across from her and a woman possibly holding a peplos offering above her head. The image on the reverse may depict a king or god, possibly Zeus while awaiting Athena's birth from his head. Terracotta neck amphora of Panathenaic shape, ca. 550–540 BC. (Metropolitan Museum of Art)

Athena depicted being venerated by a man. Terracotta oinochoe: olpe (jug), ca. 470–460 BC. (Metropolitan Museum of Art)

Athena is also depicted alongside mythical heroes and participants in athletic games. Here, she is believed to be leading Heracles to Olympus. Terracotta amphora, ca. 530–520 BC. (Metropolitan Museum of Art)

Above left and above right: One side of this amphora features Athena in her armour, the other a chariot racer. Terracotta Panathenaic prize amphora, ca. 525–500 BC. (Metropolitan Museum of Art)

Athena standing between Hera and Zeus. Homer depicts both Hera and Zeus sending Athena forth to execute their intentions. Terracotta stamnos, ca. 490 BC. (Metropolitan Museum of Art)

Above: This image of a youth pursuing a woman may represent Peleus pursuing Thetis, a narrative woven into the *Iliad*. Terracotta hydria: kalpis (water jar), ca. 450–440 BC. (Metropolitan Museum of Art)

Left: Terracotta calyx-krater depicting Paris' abduction of Helen, one of the inciting events for the Trojan war, early fourth century BC. (Metropolitan Museum of Art)

The body of this jar depicts Menelaos reclaiming Helen at the end of the Trojan war. Terracotta neck-amphora, ca. 540 BC. (Metropolitan Museum of Art)

Left and below: Terracotta lekythos (oil flask), ca. 420 BC, featuring three zones, each of which portrays women and warriors. The scene in the top panel is unclear but seems to include men and women surrounding a chariot. The middle panel in white depicts the Nereids bringing a grieving Achilles new armour, a scene depicted in the *Iliad*. The bottom panel portrays the Amazonomachy. (Metropolitan Museum of Art)

Above left and above right: Vase images provide insight into women's roles in ancient life. Here, a woman and a departing warrior pour libations. Terracotta pelike (jar), ca. 470 BC. (Metropolitan Museum of Art)

Right: Terracotta loutrophoros, late sixth century BC, depicting funeral rites: grieving women with shorn hair making gestures associated with ritual lamentation surround the body of a youth laid on a high couch. (Metropolitan Museum of Art)

Terracotta kylix (drinking cup), ca. 460–450 BC, of two young girls. The one to the left holds writing tablets and stylus. (Metropolitan Museum of Art)

Terracotta kylix (drinking cup), ca. 460 BC, portrays women in what has been interpreted as a domestic scene. (Metropolitan Museum of Art)

HEROES

PART 4

ONE OF OUR challenges approaching the ancient Greek hero generally is that our word *hero* is essentially a transliteration of the Greek word *heros*. The term has thus become so familiar that we struggle to untangle the familiar from the strange so that we can hold both simultaneously. Doing so enables us to approach the hero not only in our cultural context, which we will inevitably do, but also its own, to the extent that we can access it. A broad definition of the hero in ancient Greek culture that enfolds familiar and strange could be understood as follows: the hero was not only a role model (of both beneficial and harmful behaviour) or a figure from a story – as we might apply the term today – but also an eternal force who could be invoked in the present moment by faithfully and precisely observing ritual steps. The hero of the myth and the hero of the ritual informed each other, to paraphrase Nagy.

Thousands of cult heroes existed across the ancient Greek world, established in localised spaces associated with them, and they enter the historical record contemporaneously with the appearance of 'Homer'. As noted, Homer does not explicitly reference hero cult, but signals of it are threaded across his epics, not only through the presence of the word *heroes* but also through allusions embedded in language, image and action. While the practice of hero cult lies beyond the scope of this project, recognising the women in this section as heroes in the ancient Greek sense depends upon how we define 'hero' and recognising how our definition might depart from that of the ancients.

For our purposes here, we are working from an understanding of the hero as dual: the heroes of myth – of the heroic age described by Hesiod, about whom songs of fame were sung – are the heroes who had once walked the earth in mortal bodies. During their mortal lives, they performed remarkable deeds (again both harmful and beneficial). After those mortal bodies died, the life force of heroes transitioned[1] through Hades and became immortalised, which is conceptualised in a variety of ways in ancient myth narratives. In the age of cult, what we might call the 'historical' age or Hesiod his own 'age of iron', the power of the hero's life force to impact events in the mortal world was acknowledged and honoured in seasonally recurring ritual events intended to invoke the hero's power to benefit the social unit. The myths tell us what needs to be remembered about heroes, and the ritual manifests them in the moment.

Heroes who were recipients of cult in ancient Greece included men, women and children (even babies), yet when we think of and talk about ancient Greek heroes, the names Achilles, Odysseus or Hector perhaps come more readily to mind than the names Penelope, Andromache or Nausicaa. And when male heroes are invoked, it may be alongside debates about the degree to which they were 'really' heroic and whether they should be held up as 'heroes' at all. Such debates generally emerge from the expectation or assumption that heroes hold – or should hold – a moral value. How can we call Achilles a hero when he stands mercilessly by watching his fellow Achaeans die? How can we call Odysseus a hero when he repeatedly lies to achieve his own ends? Today, we may not associate these behaviours with heroes, based on our moral qualifications, but for the ancient Greeks, heroes hold the title based on their status as figures of myth who are eternal in the song that never dies, the song that carries the memory of the hero and why he or she is important, and eternally honoured in cult.

As discussed earlier, one way the epics seem to signal the eternal power of the hero's life force is through the application of the word *daimon*, which can most broadly be translated as *superhuman force* and which is applied to both men and women, immortals and mortals in Homer. As the absence of overt references to cult in Homer may contribute to our challenge connecting his women to cult heroes, so too that the epics do not apply the term *heros* to women. The word itself is used sparingly in Homer and only in reference to men, though the feminine form of *heros* is used to describe women of myth in classical Greek texts. Still another complication may derive from Hesiod's narratives about the creation of Pandora. Hesiod may be (and has been) interpreted as marking women as a separate race from heroes. Yet while Hesiod does describe men being created separately from women, and the age of heroes preceding his own age of iron, he does not specify precisely when women came into existence. After discussing Pandora and her effect at length in *Works and Days*, Hesiod continues,

> In this way, there is no way to escape the intention of Zeus.
> If you wish, I will sum up for you another tale,
> Well and skilfully, and you must cast it into your perceptions,
> How the gods and mortals liable to death were born from the same place.
>
> (Lines 105–108)

From this starting point, he launches into the five ages of mortals, the last of which is his own. The word I have been rendering as *mortals* is *anthropoi*, the plural of *anthropos*. The grammatical gender of *anthropos* is masculine, but the word can be used metonymically to refer to humans in general, in the way the word *man* (and *men*) has in the past been used as a stand-in for humans in general. In his discussion of these ages of mortals, Hesiod uses a variety of words, the aforementioned *anthropos* as well as *thnetois* (meaning *liable to death*) and *andra* (meaning *man* or *husband*).

When he describes the five ages, does Hesiod specifically mean men only? The answer to this question will inevitably be debated with recourse to various, and sometimes conflicting, forms of evidence. But however the question is answered, we can nonetheless notice that Hesiod presents the narrative of woman's creation and the narrative of mortals' – or men's – creation side-by-side without imposing a timeline of events, other than that men already existed when Pandora was created. Within myth narratives of heroes, mortal women exist as seers, priestesses, leaders, captives, mothers, wives, sisters and daughters. Thus, while men and women were apparently understood to have two distinct creation stories, their lives converge and are woven together through their unions and offspring.

The unions of men and women in the heroic age speak also to their unity, their inextricable interconnection. Given that Homer neither references cult heroes nor uses the feminine form of *heros*, which might enable us more readily to identify women as heroes of myth, how does that unity manifest? One way is in the harmony of language around heroic figures, masculine and feminine. Another is in their mutual dependence. The song of fame that transmits the stories of heroes down the ages, breath to breath, depends first and foremost on survivors and descendants. Without them, there is no one to sing or tell the story, no one to hear it, no one to pass it on, and the story dies. Women heroes are those survivors and creators or protectors of descendants, and they are the composers and conveyers of songs of fame. Because of them, the story need never die but can live eternally in each succeeding generation that enfolds the discrete into the totality.

Nausicaa

The daughter of Phaeacian leaders Alcinous and Arete, Nausicaa is introduced into the narrative of the *Odyssey* in book six. The first four books followed Telemachus as he travelled to gather news of his father. His journey is framed as a compressed *nostos*, a return story and initiation ritual that will prepare him to be his father's son, meaning to have confidence speaking in public assemblies and to possess the might to back up his words with actions in defence of his home and family, if and when necessary. In book five, the narrative finally turns to Odysseus himself as he grieves his captivity on Ogygia. But the gods have not forgotten him: Hermes is sent to secure his release, and Odysseus crafts a raft with a mast (*histos*) and sail (*histion*). After successfully battling a storm of Poseidon aided by the immortal intervention of Ino, he washes ashore on the island of the Phaeacians and falls into an exhausted sleep. While he rests, Athena sets a plan in motion that will enable his return, and Nausicaa is a crucial part of it:

> Athena stepped to go into the richly appointed inner room in which the maiden
> Was sleeping, equal to the deathless ones in stature and appearance,
> Nausicaa, daughter of great-hearted Alcinous.
>
> (Lines 15–17)

As with the warrior heroes of the *Iliad*, a line of verse is devoted to identifying Nausicaa both by her name and the name of her father, and her appearance and stature are likened to those of immortals. Entering Nausicaa's dreams in the guise of a dear friend, Athena chides her for neglecting her work:

> Nausicaa, why has your mother born a girl so careless? At this time
> Shining garments lie uncared for by you,
> But your wedding feast is growing near, for which it is necessary that you have beautiful things
> To wear yourself and to provide for others, those who lead,
> For I tell you truly, your reputation circulates among the people,
> A good one brings delight to your father and mistress mother.
>
> (Lines 25–30)

Athena's speech suggests that Nausicaa is at a transitional stage of life, much like Odysseus' son, Telemachus, for whom she functions as a counterpart and complement. Both are adolescents preparing to step into adult leadership roles. For Telemachus, this will entail being prepared to stand by his father upon his return or, if necessary, avenge and succeed him, all of which require authoritative public speaking and the ability to project might. For Nausicaa, an adult role will mean marriage to a prominent man and a community to lead and care for, as Athena suggests in her ensuing speech when she notes, 'you will not be a maiden for very long' (line 33):

> For already they are mindful of wooing you, the best men in the land
> Among all the Phaeacians, to which your family also belongs.
> (Lines 34–35)

Leaders of the city, both men and women, would be expected to project authority and provide a positive model for those who follow in their footsteps, as the gods of Olympus follow Hera and Zeus, as heroes follow their immortal patrons and as the mortals who heroes lead follow them. As a daughter of the leaders of the city who will marry one of its 'best men', Nausicaa too will assume the responsibilities associated with leadership, including ensuring that she and her family members project an inspiring public vision. Accordingly, Athena advises Nausicaa to take her washing to the river where, unbeknownst to her, Odysseus is sleeping. Acting on the goddess' instructions the following day, Nausicaa requests a wagon from her father so that she can oversee the washing of the family's clothes, pointing out that he himself needs to be well dressed when he deliberates in assemblies among leaders of the city. This exchange with her father suggests that Athena's counsel is, as it did with Telemachus, moving Nausicaa through her transition into adulthood: she is proactively taking responsibility for a core task that is essential to the productive functioning of her household and community.

Having contrived to bring Odysseus and Nausicaa together, Athena presumably recognised that Nausicaa possesses a heroic mentality that could also benefit Odysseus, and this is precisely what she displays when they finally meet. After she and her handmaidens wash the clothes and set them out to dry, Nausicaa keeps time while the other girls play with a ball. Their shouts wake Odysseus, and as he bursts out of his hiding place naked, he is compared to 'a mountain-bred lion who prevails in might' (line 130). The simile here evokes the many appearances of lion similes in the *Iliad* to describe warriors. However, Odysseus is not confronting an armed antagonist on a battlefield but a group of young girls who are unsurprisingly frightened, with the exception of Nausicaa:

> Odysseus appeared terrifying to the girls, all caked in brine.
> They fled in a panic, each in different directions along the jutting shore

> But only the daughter of Alcinous remained, for Athena in her
> Breathed courage into her perceptions and stole fear from her limbs.
> She made her stand face-to-face with Odysseus, holding her
>   ground, and he pondered.
>
> (Lines 137–144)

The lion simile and Odysseus' nudity charge the mood of the scene, framing him as a predator, which is how he would presumably have appeared from Nausicaa's perspective. He is a man who has apparently washed up alone, without a boat, companions or even clothing, and he seems to have snuck up on the unsuspecting girls. Yet while the others run, Nausicaa 'stands her ground' (the verb is *histemi*), as do warrior heroes in the *Iliad*'s battle scenes. Also as with warrior heroes, Athena has amplified her power: She 'breathed courage into [Nausicaa's] perceptions'. Nausicaa in turn behaves as a leader is expected to: she stands at the front line to confront the threat, here Odysseus, and her behaviour shapes his response. Rather than grasping her knees in a typical gesture of supplication, which could be received as a threat, he supplicates her with reverent words:

> I clasp you by the knees, leader. Are you some god or a mortal?
> If you are one of the gods who dwell in the wide sky,
> It is to Artemis, the daughter of great Zeus, I to you
> Compare as nearest in stature and form,
> If you are a mortal, those who dwell upon the earth,
> Thrice blessed are your father and mistress mother,
> Thrice blessed your brothers, I very much imagine their
>   consciousnesses
> Always warm with merriment on account of you,
> Looking at such a young person entering the dance,
> But blessed among others is that man in heart
> Who leads you home weighed down with wedding gifts,
> For up to this time, I have not seen a mortal such as this with
>   my eyes,
> Neither man nor woman, reverence holds me beholding you.
> In Delos once, alongside the altar of Apollo, this quality
> I perceived with my eyes in the young sprout of a date palm.
>
> (Lines 149–163)

Questioning whether Nausicaa is a goddess and, if so, suggesting that she must be Artemis signals his reverence both for the gods and for her youth and innocence, communicating immediately that he does not intend to harm her. His ensuing remarks build on this message. If she is mortal, he continues, then she is a blessing to her family, and she inspires reverence in him, of such a kind as he felt when beholding the sacred date palm at Delos. A parallel to Telemachus is evoked through the repetition of the phrase 'reverence holds me beholding', the same phrase Helen speaks while looking at Odysseus' son in book four (line 142). Considered together, Odysseus' opening remarks frames his meeting with Nausicaa as a sacred occasion, binding them to the laws of the gods. The remainder of his speech leads to his request; he explains the hardships he has experienced and begs for her assistance:

> Show me where the city is, and give me a garment to wrap around myself,
> If you have some piece of cloth that you brought here,
> May the gods grant you what you most desire with your perceptions,
> And may they join you with a husband and home in unity of mind and feeling,[2]
> In noble unity, for nothing is mightier or more excellent
> Than when they two have unity of mind and feeling in their understanding,
> Husband and wife, many pains for those who are hostile to them,
> And a source of joy for those who wish them well, as they themselves most willingly hear.
>
> (Lines 178–185)

Nausicaa in turn receives the intended message and treats him as the laws of hospitality dictate a suppliant should be treated. She provides him with clothes and guidance to secure the assistance of her parents:

> You will come upon a shining glade near a grove of Athena's
> Poplars. A spring flows through it there surrounded by meadow.
> My father's land and blooming orchard are there,
> As far from the city as the shout of a man carries.
> There, taking a seat, remain for a time, until I
> Come to the city and approach my father's house,
> But when you expect that we have arrived at the house,
> At that time, go to the Phaeacians' city and inquire

> About the house of my father, great-hearted Alcinous.
> It is easy to know, even a child could lead you there,
> One who is disconnected, for it is built such that it does not resemble the others,
> The houses of the Phaeacians, of such a kind is the house of Alcinous
> The hero, but when the house and the courtyard have hidden you,
> Very swiftly pass through the great room, in order that you can supplicate
> My mother, she sits by the hearth in the light of the fire,
> Constantly spinning the dark, gleaming wool on her distaff, a wonder to behold,
> Reclining against a pillar, enslaved women captured in war seated behind her.
> There my father's chair is placed beside her.
> Seated there, he drinks wine like an immortal.
> Passing him by, around my mother's knees your hands
> Throw, in order that you can see your day of return,
> Rejoicing swiftly, from however far away you may be.
> If she has kindly thoughts about you in her consciousness,
> Then you may have hope to see your dear ones and to reach
> Your well-built home and the land of your fathers.
>
> (Lines 291–315)

According to Nausicaa, then, the key to Odysseus achieving his return lies not with her father but with her mother. At the hearth, Arete spins 'dark, gleaming wool', evoking the 'dark, gleaming, double-folded mantle' referenced two times only in the *Iliad*, both at cosmically significant moments. Helen weaves the story of the Trojan war onto a 'dark, gleaming mantle' in book three as Menelaos and Paris prepare to duel over her, and Andromache weaves prayers for Hector on a 'dark, gleaming mantle' in book twenty-two, unaware that he has already died, portending the fall of Troy and her future enslavement. That Arete is spinning 'dark, gleaming wool' seems to signal the cosmic significance of Odysseus' future meeting with her. Though his return is fated, this does not absolve him from activating the heroic mentality that will lead to its fulfilment, and Nausicaa's advice (which Athena will later reaffirm) ensures that he is prepared to meet the moment.

Further, the sight of Arete spinning is described as 'a wonder to behold', a phrase that repeats at significant moments in Homer and that is also mentioned repeatedly in Hesiod as the effect of Pandora being god-created.

In *Iliad* book twenty-four, it is the word used when Priam appears suddenly at the feet of Achilles, his son's killer, to offer a ransom for Hector's body, and the word used to describe the effect of each man on the other after they weep together over their shared grief, experiencing a moment of unity. The Greek word for *wonder* is *thauma*; the verb form is *thaumazo*. Jessica Lightfoot notes that archaic Greek poetry associates *thauma* with 'divine epiphany' or presence.[3] Here, it seems to suggest Arete's close connection to the gods, her importance to Athena's plan for Odysseus and her heroic status: immortal power is flowing through the work of her hands, which continually spin wool for the cosmic fabric. As repeats across Odysseus' journey, his survival depends equally on his strength, endurance and cunning and on the support and assistance of women, both immortal and mortal. And when he does return to Ithaca, recovering his mortal identity cannot be achieved without the consent and cooperation of Penelope.

But just as Nausicaa can benefit Odysseus, she also poses a threat. Her youth and marriageability could tempt Odysseus off course, inviting him to remain with the Phaeacians and become the honoured son-in-law of the illustrious leader of the city, and the husband of the young girl who he proclaims inspires him with reverence. An offer is implied by Nausicaa, who expresses a desire to have a man like Odysseus for a husband, and by Alcinous, who expresses a desire to have a man like Odysseus for a son-in-law. As in his conversation with Calypso, Odysseus politely redirects in both instances. He never mentions Penelope while among the Phaeacians, but his focus never wavers from his intention to return to Ithaca.

In Nausicaa's charged final exchange with Odysseus, she herself affirms her heroic status:

> Now Nausicaa, who had beauty bestowed by the gods,
> She made her stand beside the post that held up the solidly made roof.
> Seeing Odysseus with her eyes, wondering at him,
> She spoke, uttering words with wings,
> 'Fare well, guest-friend, as ever, when you are in the land of your father,
> Remember me, for to me first you owe a reward for saving your life.'
>
> (Lines 457–462)

As she makes a stand (*histemi* again) against an upright post, signalling her authority in the house, the bard again likens her beauty to that of immortals. This comparison to immortal beauty brings her final scene with Odysseus full circle: he began his speech by comparing her to Artemis. Her 'wondering' likewise recognises the presence of immortal power present in him. Her final dictate displays awareness of authority, of being the daughter of Arete, 'she who is prayed to', as she reminds Odysseus that she herself set in motion his meeting with her mother and the Phaeacians, which has led to his imminent departure for home. Odysseus' response affirms her request, acknowledging his debt to her:

> Nausicaa, daughter of great-hearted Alcinous,
> So may loud-thundering Zeus, spouse of Hera, set in place
> For me to come home and see my day of return,
> That there I may pray to you as to a goddess
> For all my days, for you, maiden, have kept me alive.
> (Lines 464–469)

Odysseus' mode of address affirms Nausicaa's heroic stature. His response echoes her request to be remembered but framed in the form of a prayer to Zeus, who is identified as the spouse of Hera. The memory of her excellence is co-dependent with his survival. He prays that he will reach Ithaca and achieve his 'day of return' (his *nostos*) so that can pray to Nausicaa 'as to a goddess' whose kindly intervention participated in preserving his life, language that resonates with cult significance. In the epic, the reward promised Nausicaa is to be remembered eternally within the 'song of fame'. Each time the story of Odysseus is recounted, his wandering and suffering and the people and ways of understanding that he encountered along the way, the story of Nausicaa will be told. In this way, their fates can be understood as bound together: by achieving his return to Ithaca and recovering his mortal identity, the memory of Odysseus will ensure the memory of Nausicaa.

If we approach Nausicaa's scenes only through the lens of Odysseus' journey, she can seem to function merely as a prop that moves his narrative. Viewing the same scene through the lens of story patterns that repeat with variations, each conveying a story about the heroic age that must be remembered, she has her own arc that intersects with but is no less significant than Odysseus'. Both are in a transitional state, Nausicaa between adolescence and adulthood, Odysseus between death (in the sense of his mortal identity as the husband of Penelope) and life (in the sense of the restoration of that identity). The dynamic between them is mutually beneficial: Nausicaa gains confidence in her authority, and he achieves his return to Ithacan soil. Nagy suggests that any hero named in Homer could have been the recipient of cult. Perhaps we can imagine Nausicaa's arc, her story or one like it, being sung somewhere in the ancient Greek world by young girls transitioning into adulthood, with Nausicaa as the hero worth remembering. Here in our *Odyssey*, Athena brings Nausicaa and Odysseus together because each can benefit from the other, exemplifying how masculine and feminine authorities can work in harmonious balance and what it means for each to be a hero.

Andromache

The first time we meet Andromache, whose name means *fights with men*, in the *Iliad* is in a book six confrontation with her husband, Hector, on the walls of Troy, as a serving woman stands silently by holding their infant son. Hector's brother Helenus has sent Hector into the city to advise the women of Troy to offer Athena prayers and sacrifices. The bard has described Hecuba and the priestess Theano fulfilling Helenus' instructions but Athena denying their request to save the city. When the narrative then turns to the extended encounter between Hector and Andromache, it is with the knowledge of Athena's rejection, an omen that the city will fall.

> There, his richly dowered wife came at him, running
> Andromache, the daughter of great-hearted Eetion –
> Eetion who dwelled upon wooded Placus,
> In Thebes, under mount Placus, ruling over the people of Cilicia,
> His daughter had Hector, armed in bronze, as her husband.
> Then she met him face-to-face, and a serving woman went with her,
> Having their child upon her breast, as he was a tender-hearted baby,
> Son of Hector, beloved, resembling a star,
> Hector called him Scamander, but the others,
> Astyanax, lord of the city, for Hector alone protected Ilium.
> Now in silence he smiled seeing the child.
> Andromache made her stand near him, pouring tears.
> She grasped his hand, spoke a word, and named him,
> '*Daimoni*, your might will despoil you. You do not even pity
> Your infant child, and I too am without a share of it, soon the widow

Of you I will be, for soon the Achaeans will kill you,
All roused against you, it would be more profitable for me,
Missing you, to be lowered into the earth, for as yet no other
Comfort will there be when you pursue your destiny,
But grief, no father or mistress mother is there to me,
For truly, Achilles, born of Zeus, killed my father.
He sacked the well-populated city of the Cilicians,
Thebes of the high gates. He killed Eetion,
Though he did not strip him, having awe for him in his consciousness,
But he burned him with fire with his cunningly crafted armour.
And heaped around him the tomb of a hero, they planted elm trees around it,
Nymphs of the mountains, daughters of Aegis-bearing Zeus.
Seven brothers were in the great rooms with me.
They all went down into Hades in a single day,
For swift-footed Achilles, born of Zeus, killed them all,
Among the cows with a rolling gait and shining sheep.
My mother, who ruled over wooded Placus,
He led her away, then, along with her possessions,
But he released her again, having received immense compensation.
Artemis, shooter of arrows, shot her in her father's great rooms.
Hector, now you are my father and mistress mother,
And my brother, you are my blooming husband,
But come now, have pity and stand fast upon the citadel.
Do not make your son an orphan and your wife a widow.
Make the people stand beside the fig-tree, there where most of all
The city can be mounted, and the walls could be overrun,
For having come, their best men attempted this three times,
The two Ajaxes and highly renowned Idomeneus,
And the two sons of Atreus and the strong son of Tydeus.
Either someone told them, knowing well what the gods foretold,
Or their consciousness stirs them and leads them on.'

(Lines 394–438)

Consistent with the introduction of warrior heroes, a line of verse introduces Andromache by her name and her genealogy, 'daughter of great-hearted

Eetion', with a few lines devoted to identifying where her father lived, who he ruled over and who his daughter's husband is. As an introduction to a woman hero, this combination draws attention to marriage as a means of extending family networks, horizontally in time and vertically through time. In her speech, Andromache notes that Achilles, though he killed her father, had reverence for him and oversaw a hero's burial for him, symbolised by raising a *sema*, which I have rendered as *tomb of a hero*.[4] Eetion's heroic status seems further implied by the daughters of Zeus, the nymphs of the mountain, marking his tomb with elm trees. By emphasising her father's status as a hero, Andromache claims that status for herself, as the *Iliad*'s warrior heroes also do.

Andromache 'makes her stand' (*histemi*) opposite Hector, as Nausicaa makes her stand opposite Odysseus and warriors make their stands against each other in battle. Also in the scene is Astyanax, the product of Andromache and Hector's union. His presence is a reminder of all that is at stake for Hector: Astyanax is the descendant who would be charged with carrying on the story of his family, if he were in a city at peace and if his survival were guaranteed. The bard describes Hector as the lone protector of Troy, its bulwark, an association amplified by the setting of their encounter on the city's defensive walls. Andromache's speech suggests that this conflicts with his role as a father and husband, since it means facing danger that will leave his wife a widow and his son an orphan. As Andromache makes clear, she has no surviving family to protect her. Achilles did not kill her mother, who he returned, presumably to her father, in exchange for a large ransom, but he has killed her father and brothers who would have been in a position to do likewise for her.

The advice Andromache gives Hector, to make his stand from within the safety of the city's walls and to defend their most vulnerable entry points, echoes the advice one of his trusted Trojan comrades, Polydamas, gives him later. Hector confirms the soundness of the advice in his response to Andromache; he does not refute the wisdom of her strategy. But removing himself from battle would contradict his expectations for himself as the leading warrior of Troy. Though he anticipates the scope of the tragedy that will unfold, he cannot bring himself to stop its forward motion by protecting himself:

> Wife, all this concerns me too, but with exceeding dread,
> I would shame myself to the Trojan men and the Trojan women
>   of the trailing robes
> If aloof, I shrank from battle, as a bad man would,

> Nor does my consciousness command me thus, since I learned to be a good man
> Always and first to fight among the Trojans
> Winning great fame in song for my father and myself,
> For I well know this in my consciousness and my perceptions:
> The day will come when sacred Ilium will be destroyed
> Along with Priam and the people of Priam who are skilled with the spear,
> But the pain of the Trojans is not as much of a concern for me –
> Neither that of Hecuba nor lord Priam,
> Nor of my brothers or the many noble men
> Who would fall into the dust under hostile men –
> As is yours, when some bronze-clad Achaean
> Leads you, weeping, away from your day of freedom,
> And being in Argos, you would weave at another's loom,
> And you would bear water at Messeis or Hyperia,
> Very much against your will, a mighty necessity would press upon you,
> And seeing you pouring tears, some man would say,
> 'This is the wife of Hector, who was first in battle
> Among the horse-breaking Trojans whenever they fought around Troy.'
> When they will say that, it will be a fresh grief for you,
> The widow of such a man who could ward off the day of enslavement,
> But as for me, having died, a mound of earth would cover me over
> Before hearing your cries being dragged away.
>
> (Lines 441–461)

As noted earlier, the Greek word for *great fame in song* is *kleos*: a warrior becomes the subject of song because of his conduct in battle. To remain safely inside the city would then contradict both Hector's purpose and the honour he receives by fulfilling it. In this sense, it seems that Hector's choice is much like that of Achilles, his counterpart on the Achaean side: either to live a long, unremarkable[5] life or to die young but be eternal in song. Though Hector claims to be troubled by his wife's future enslavement and suffering, he is also aware that her lamentation will generate his fame. Hector himself does not make a direct correlation between lament and *kleos*, but the two are implicitly connected by his recognition that being 'first to fight' leads to both lament and *kleos*. The primary intentions of Hector and Andromache are thus incompatible. Her primary intention is for her husband to remain alive while his is to fulfil his function as a warrior hero, the function that leads him to achieve immortal fame. Andromache and Hector are trapped in an irresolvable paradox: his determination to fulfil his protective function as a warrior will lead to his death, which will lead to the fall of the city and the suffering of his wife, the outcomes his warrior skill are meant to prevent but which in this case will cause.

Following his speech, Hector reaches for his son, who is initially frightened by the apparatus of war in which Hector is cloaked, and utters a prayer for him:

> So speaking, shining Hector reached for his son,
> But the boy back toward his well-girdled nurse's breast
> He leaned, weeping, frightened at his dear father's appearance,
> Being alarmed by the bronze and the crest of his horsehair helmet
> And observing the helmet nodding dreadfully at the top.
> His dear father and mistress mother laughed.
> Straightaway, shining Hector took the helmet from his head,
> And he placed the beaming thing upon the ground.
> Then he kissed his dear son and swung him with his hands,
> And he spoke, praying to Zeus and the other gods,
> 'Zeus and you other gods, give this to be born,
> That this son of mine be distinguished among the Trojans, as I am,
> And in this way, to rule Troy mightily, with power and nobility,
> And may it be said of him that he was better than his father,
> Returning from battle, may he bear the blood-spattered spoils,
> Having killed a hostile man, may his mother rejoice in her perception of him.'
>
> (Lines 466–481)

As with the prayers of the Trojan women to Athena, Hector's prayer for Astyanax seems destined for rejection. If the fall of the city is imminent, as Hector seems aware, then there will be no Troy for Astyanax either to rule or to defend. The disconnect between Hector and Andromache's primary intentions echoes in the disconnect between Hector and his intentions for his son. If he were to remain inside the city, then the siege might extend indefinitely, and Astyanax could have a Troy to defend, but Hector's own choice to face Achilles rather than seek protection inside the walls renders his prayer forfeit, an outcome he seems resolutely determined not to confront. The baby's fear of the bronze and nodding crest of the helmet embodies the disconnect between Hector's role as a warrior and his role as a father. Astyanax consents to go to his father only after he has set aside his warrior paraphernalia, placing his helmet on the ground.

After speaking his prayer, Hector attempts to comfort his wife before returning to the battle:

> So having spoken, he put in the hands of his dear wife
> His own son, and she received him into her fragrant breast,
> Laughing through tears. Her husband felt pity observing her.
> He stroked her hand, spoke this word, and named her,
> '*Daimoni*, do not grieve excessively for me in your consciousness.
> For no man will hurl me into Hades beyond my allotted portion.
> Among men, I say no one can flee his portion,
> Once he has been born, neither the good ones nor the bad ones.
> But going into the house, take care of your own works,
> The loom and the distaff, and urge your handmaidens
> To go to their work, for battle is the concern of men,
> All of us who were bred in Ilium, mine most of all.'
> So having spoken, shining Hector took up his helmet
> Decorated with horsehair, and his dear wife stepped toward home,
> Repeatedly turning around, pouring thick tears.
> Quickly then, she arrived in the well-made house where dwelled
> Man-slaying Hector, and she found inside
> Serving women and roused lamentation in them all,
> And so they lamented for Hector in his home while he was still alive,
> For they did not claim that he would return from battle
> Fleeing the might and hands to come from Achilles.
>
> (Lines 482–502)

The comfort Hector attempts to provide Andromache is a recourse to fate: whatever his portion of life is cannot be altered or avoided. Since he cannot evade it, the proper course is to fulfil his purpose, the role that his skills and upbringing have scripted for him to be the best warrior and defender of Troy. If it leads to his death and Andromache's enslavement, then this too is to be understood as fated and accepted as such in the recognition that they will be participating in the cosmic plan. And they will be compensated in the eternal song that Andromache's grief will generate and into which her experiences are woven. Hector does not tell Andromache not to grieve but not to grieve 'excessively', beyond what is appropriate while he is alive. His instructions to her suggest that his purpose is to fight and hers to weave and to grieve, both in due measure.

Andromache's grieving has already begun in this exchange in book six: she and her community of women perform their laments though he 'was still alive'. Her expectation of and lamentation for his impending death, fuelled by his refusal to withdraw from battle, even when he is repeatedly warned to do so in later books, signifies the inevitability of it. Neither heeds Hector's apparent call for measure, a sense of proportion, in line 486. But she apparently does heed his parting words to return to her loom and distaff, which is where the narrative finds her in book twenty-two, when Hector has already been killed and lamented by Hecuba and Priam:

> So Hecuba spoke, weeping. She had not yet heard, the wife of Hector, for no trusted messenger had come
> To bear the message that her husband had stood fast outside the gates,
> But in an inner room of the high house, she was weaving at her loom
> A dark, gleaming, double-folded mantle, she was sprinkling into it patterns of dappled flowers.
> She was exhorting her beautiful-haired maidens throughout the house
> In order that they would set in motion
> A warm bath for Hector when he returned from battle.
> She was disconnected. She did not perceive that he was far away from baths.
> Owl-eyed Athena had subdued him at the hands of Achilles.
> She heard shrieking and wailing from the tower.
> Her limbs trembled, and her shuttle dropped to the earth.
>
> (Lines 437–447)

Elizabeth Wayland Barber's suggestion that the flowers Andromache is weaving may represent prayers, or perhaps a protective charm of some sort, is striking given that her hopes for Hector are not met, as Hector's hopes for his son will not be met. A garment meant to protect may instead become a funeral shroud for the warrior who was meant to defend the city from destruction but who has, in death, become a portent of its fall. The 'dark, gleaming, double-folded mantle' Andromache is weaving connects her to Helen, who weaves likewise in book three, and through this to the institution of epic. Helen is both the cause of the war, the generator of the story, and trapped inexorably in its tide. Andromache is a victim of the war and her grief a generator of its eternal memory, which in the historical ancient world was preserved not only in song but also dance and on cloth, pottery and monuments.

In this moment, however, Andromache's concern is not *kleos* but her husband's well-being. In the moment, she is 'disconnected' – the Greek word is *nepios* – from the news of her husband's death. In the larger sense, she is disconnected from the place of her husband's death in the cosmic fabric: it is part of a larger plan that heralds, per Hesiod, the end of the age of heroes. Her grief has eternal power because it is not only real and immediate but also because her experiences repeat again and again in the mortal world. They are simultaneously individual to Andromache in this moment and communal within and beyond Troy across time. In reverence for the eternal truth of this experience, which can take many guises, the bard describes in intricate and heart-rending detail the dread and terror that close around Andromache as she hears the 'shrieking and wailing' of the Trojans on the walls.

> She spoke again to her enslaved women with the beautiful hair, captured in war.
> 'Come here, you two, and follow me. I wish to see what works have been wrought.
> I heard the voice of my revered mother-in-law, and in my own self,
> The heart in my chest leapt up into my mouth, and my knees below
> Have stiffened. Some harm is near at hand for Priam's children.
> May my words be unheard, but very grimly
> I fear for my bold Hector. Achilles born of Zeus
> May have cut him off from the city, leaving him alone, and chased him across the plain,
> And has put an end to his grievous manliness,

> Which he bore, since he would never remain with the masses of men,
> But would run ahead, giving way to no one in his might.'
> So having spoken, she rushed through the rooms, equal to a maenad,
> Her heart shaking, and her handmaidens went with her.
> But when she came to the tower, and the men assembled,
> She made a stand upon the wall, gazing, and observed him
> Being dragged before the city. Him swift horses
> Were dragging towards the Achaeans' hollow ships, unburied,
> And gloomy night veiled her eyes.
> She fell backwards and breathed forth her life force.[6]
> She threw far from her head the glittering headdress that bound her,
> Her diadem and netting and plaited band,
> And the veil that golden Aphrodite gave her
> On the day when Hector of the glancing helmet led her
> From the house of Eetion, after he offered countless wedding gifts.
> Her husband's sisters and the wives of his brothers surrounded her.
> They held her, who was dazed to destruction.
>
> (Lines 458–483)

The presence, at the beginning of the scene, of enslaved women captured in war – the Greek word is *dmoee* – conveys the tragic cyclicality of what Andromache is living through in this moment. Her experience was presumably theirs first. Now it will be Andromache's, and in the future presumably someone else's since war has never been far from mortals. The pattern repeats, but the details and context vary. The epic embodies this dynamic interaction of repetition and variation in the system of its language, which threads the same phrases into different contexts.

Though she was disconnected when the narrative found her, the grief of the Trojans on the walls seems to have reconnected her; she anticipates what has happened to Hector, his inevitable destiny. After it is confirmed, the tearing off of her headdress symbolises the tearing down of protective walls that hold off chaos and disorder – in this case, Hector himself. Her community of women who will share her fate close ranks around her as she succumbs to her grief, which will also be theirs when their own fathers, husbands and brothers fall with the city. When Andromache recovers her senses, the lament she delivers focuses on the son for whom Hector delivered his fruitless prayer.

> But then, when she caught her breath, her consciousness
>   gathered into her perception.
> She spoke among the Trojan women in sudden bursts, lamenting.
> 'Hector, I am wretched. So we were born into one portion,
> We two, you in Troy, in Priam's house,
> But I in Thebes, under wooded Placus,
> In the house of Eetion, he nourished me when I was small,
> Ill-fated daughter of a doomed man, if only I had never been
>   born.
> Now you, to the house of Hades in the depths of the earth
> Are going, but you leave me in loathsome grief.
> A widow in the great rooms. As it is, your son is still an infant,
> Who you and I, most ill-fated, brought into the world. Neither
>   you to him
> Will bring anything profitable, Hector, since you are dead, nor
>   him to you.
> For even if he were to escape the Achaeans in war, bringer of
>   tears,
> Toil and sorrow always
> Will be his, for other men will take his father's land.
> The day a child is orphaned sets him apart from the friends of
>   his youth.
> He stands always with his head bowed down, his cheeks
>   pouring tears,
> In need, the child reaches for the comrades of his father,
> Tugging on the cloak of one man or the tunic of another.
> Having pity for him, one holds out a small cup.
> It wets his lips, but it does not wet his palate,
> Then a boy nurtured by both parents pushes him away from
>   the feast,
> Striking with his hands and attacks him with reproaches,
> "Be gone! Your father does not share the feast with us."
> The tearful child reaches for his widowed mother,
> Astyanax, who before was on his father's knees,
> He ate only bone barrow and the rich fat of sheep,
> But when he would cease playing as children do, and sleep
>   would take him,

He lay down on a bed in a nurse's arms,
Among soft bedding, full in his heart with good thoughts.
Now, his dear father having missed the mark, he will suffer many hardships,
Astyanax, as the Trojans called him, Leader of the city,
For you alone protected the gates and the great walls.
Now you lie beside the curved ships, far from your parents.
Quick-moving worms will consume what is left of you, once the dogs have sated themselves,
Naked, though your clothes lie in the great rooms,
Finely woven and lovely, having been crafted by women's hands,
But now, I will burn them all in a blazing fire.
It is of no use to you, since you will not be wrapped in them,
But they will carry the fame from the Trojan men and the Trojan women.'
So she spoke, weeping, and the women wailed with her.

(Lines 484–515)

Andromache's opening words speak to the married couple's interdependence. Though they are not of one mind, the blessing Odysseus spoke of to Nausicaa, their fate is of one essence. Hector's death signals the death of Andromache's freedom and as suggested in ancient myth narratives beyond the *Iliad* the death of Astyanax.[7] But while the hearer or listener is aware of Astyanax's death, Andromache does not yet know nor is she thinking ahead to the fall of the city. Her lament breathes into being an imagined future for Astyanax that explicitly contradicts Hector's prayer for him. Without his father to guide and protect him, Astyanax will not lead or defend Troy. Once loved and nurtured, he will be thrust into the margins and dependent on the whims of others.

The garments Andromache mentions at the end of her lament bring her presence in book twenty-two full circle. The garment she was weaving for Hector will not fulfil its purpose to clothe and protect him, but it might burn with his other garments in 'a blazing fire'. Fire, via Zeus and his thunderbolt, is associated with the immortalisation of a hero. Nagy notes that Elysium, one of several names for the idyllic place where heroes dwell in their afterlives, is connected to the verb *enelusion*, which refers to a place struck by lightning, which itself is connected to the power of Zeus.[8] The connection is exemplified in the myth narrative of Heracles as recounted by first-century BC historian Diodorus of Sicily. According to Diodorus, at the end of his life, Heracles was to be burned alive on a great pyre with his arms and armour. When the first flame was lit, lightning fell from heaven and set the pyre aloft. After it burned out, Heracles' companions could find no bones in the ash.

The reference to 'blazing fire' here may signal the cult hero who Hector will become while the ensuing lines simultaneously recognise that cult hero status in the future does not benefit the mortal man himself or his family in the moment. But it is the final line of Andromache's lament that most strikingly unites weaving, grieving and *kleos*: the garments woven by the women's hands and decorated with messages either to gods (via prayers) or mortals (via stories about heroes) will, in an act of grief and with the accompaniment of lament, be burned in a 'blazing fire' that carries the fame of Troy up to the wide sky, where it will become part of eternal memory.

After Priam brings Hector's body back to Troy, funeral rites are conducted for him, which will include burning his body on a flaming pyre, again evoking the immortalisation of Heracles and the institution of hero cult in historical Greece. But first, a series of two forms of lament is performed for Hector. Professional bards perform the funeral song – the Greek word is *threnos* – followed by his kinswomen who perform the laments – the Greek word *goos* – the first of which is performed by Andromache:

> After they had led Hector into his renowned house, next for him
> They set in place a carved bed and beside him were seated bards,
> Leaders of the funeral song, the mournful song.
> They sang the funeral song, and the women wailed in response.
> Shining-armed Andromache began the lament of him,
> Holding the head of man-slaying Hector with her hands.
> 'Husband, you were destroyed young from your life, and me a widow
> You now leave in the great rooms, our boy still an infant,
> Ill-fated, who you and I brought into the world. I don't suppose that he
> Will reach the prime of life, for before this, the city top to bottom
> Will be sacked, for truly, its own guardian himself has been destroyed.
> You protected it and kept safe its careful-minded wives and infant children,

Who presently will be born to the hollow ships,
And I with them. And you, my child, or I myself
Will follow. You will toil there in unseemly works,
Contending for a relentless master, or some Achaeans,
Taking you in their hands, will hurl you from the walls to baneful destruction,
Being angry that Hector killed his brother,
Or father, or also his son, since very many of the Achaeans
Took a bite of the vast land in the palm of Hector's hand,
For your father was not gentle in baneful war,
And that is why the people mourn him throughout the city.
You put accursed lamentation and grief into your parents,
Hector, but you leave me most of all in baneful pain,
For you did not stretch out your hands to me dying in your bed,
Nor did you speak to me some wise word, of which always
I would be reminded in the night and day, pouring tears.'
So she spoke, weeping, and the women wailed in response.

(Lines 719–746)

The presence of professional and personal mourners evokes the funeral of Achilles described in *Odyssey* book twenty-four, at which Thetis and her sisters sing the laments and the Muses the funeral song:

> The daughters of the old man of the sea made a stand on either side of Achilles,
> Lamenting piteously, they put all around him ambrosial garments
> All nine Muses in beautiful antiphonal voice
> Sang the funeral song. You observed there no one without tears
> Among the Argives, for so did the clear voice of the Muse move them.
>
> (Lines 58–62)

Odyssey book twenty-four is the only place in Homer's epics where the funeral of Achilles is described. Its placement in the final book of the *Odyssey*, on the heels of Penelope and Odysseus' successful *nostos*, brings the two epics full circle. It is a potent reminder of the unity of grief and *kleos*.

At Hector's funeral, women's grief is powerfully voiced by Andromache. Her lament echoes the concerns threaded through each of her previous speeches and expressed by Hector, and she now seems to be projecting ahead to her son's death, which she describes as the inevitable outcome of works of war. Hector 'was not gentle' in battle. His ferocity and might were the qualities that made him so valuable to the Trojans while alive and what make his son especially vulnerable after his death. As Andromache well understands, there will likely be no shortage of Achaeans with a personal grievance against Hector, whose friends and family members have fallen at his hands and who will now see an opportunity to extract compensation by destroying his helpless son. The cycle of vengeance fuels itself, which Andromache recognises, and her son will likely be one of its next victims.

Andromache is the first kinswoman to perform a lament, followed by Hecuba, and finally Helen. By the standards of historical lament, the order may be unexpected, since Helen is not his closest relative among the three women, and she is the cause of the war, which is the cause of Hector's death.[9] The responses to each woman's lament illuminate a meaning behind the organisation. The response to Andromache, 'the women wailed in response', evokes lament as a social institution. It evokes the grief of the community of women who held Andromache when she swooned on the walls of Troy and who share in Andromache's lament because they too have suffered or will suffer a similar grief. Hecuba's lament 'rousing unforgettable lamentation' evokes the sacred power of grief to eternalise the temporal. After Helen's lament, 'the boundless people burst forth their grief in response', suggestive of humanity as an infinite spiralling, endless and countless mass, all enfolded into this song at the moment it is sung in a sacred setting and context. Together, the women's laments suggest the cycle that generates epic song: powerful grief that stretches beyond the boundaries of the individual experiencing it, becoming enfolded into eternal memory and returned to the mortal world through the Muses. The beginning of this cycle lies with Andromache and her deeply personal grief at the destruction of her family unit in the temporal world. Both her family and her grief live eternally through epic, but the bard never allows us to forget that for Andromache, the woman, wife and mother in the moment, there is no compensation for her loss.

Penelope

Penelope is implied in the first word of the *Odyssey*: she is the wife to whom the 'husband, the versatile man with many plots and schemes', strives to return, accepting whatever suffering he will experience to achieve that return. As with Andromache and Hector, the fates of Penelope and

Odysseus are intertwined and mutually dependent. At Ithaca, Penelope's schemes shape the narrative, but it cannot be fulfilled without Odysseus. He strives to reclaim his mortal identity, but he cannot achieve this if Penelope chooses to remarry. Though initially separated by decades and distance, they share a single goal that requires the patience, trust and collaboration of each other.

Penelope makes her first appearance just over halfway into book one when she enters the public space where the bard Phemius is singing for her suitors, the topic of his song the disastrous return journeys of the Achaeans. Though there is no explicit mention of Odysseus, about whom no news has been heard, the song connects Penelope to her grief over his absence, as the song of Demodocus grieves Odysseus in book eight, and she asks the bard to sing a different song:

> The renowned bard was singing, and the men in silence
> Were seated, listening. He sang of the Achaeans' homecomings
> From Troy, which Pallas Athena ordained be ruinous.
> In the upper part of the house, she took heed of the god-inspired bard,
> The daughter of Icarius, circumspect Penelope,
> She came down the high stairway of her house
> Not alone, two trusted handmaidens followed her.
> When she, godlike among women, reached the suitors,
> She made a stand beside the post that held up the solidly made roof,
> Having a shimmering veil over her cheeks,
> A trusted handmaiden stood on either side of her.
> Shedding tears, she then addressed the bard of the gods,
> 'Phemius, you know many other songs for enchanting mortal men
> About the works of men and gods, who the bards made famous in song.
> Sing one of these, seated among the men as they in silence
> Drink wine, but cease from singing this song,
> Mournful to me, always, to the heart in my breast,
> This song wears it away, since unforgettable, insufferable grief came down on me,
> Being reminded that I forever yearn in my understanding
> For my husband, his fame broad throughout Hellas and in Argos.'

> But Telemachus, being prudent, spoke in response to her.
> 'Mother of mine, why do you begrudge the faithful bard
> To delight as his understanding moves him? Bards are not at this time
> The cause, but Zeus who is everywhere is responsible, for he apportions
> To men who toil, each one, according to his will.
> It is no wonder the bard sings about the Danaans' bad fate,
> For mortals bestow praise upon the song
> That is the newest one to meet their ears,
> So endure in your heart and consciousness to listen.
> For Odysseus was not the only one whose day of returning was destroyed
> By Troy, many others also were destroyed,
> But going into the house, take care of your own works,
> The loom and the distaff, and urge your handmaidens
> To go to their work, for public speech is the concern of men
> Alone, and mine most of all, for might in the house is mine.'
> And Penelope, being in a state of wonder, went back into the house.
> She put her child's prudent speech into her consciousness.
> Ascending into the upper part of the house together with her trusted handmaidens,
> She wept then for Odysseus, her beloved husband, until sleep,
> Honey-sweet upon her eyelids, put owl-eyed Athena.
>
> (Lines 325–364)

When Penelope enters the public space, which is associated with masculine authority and which the suitors have commandeered, she makes a stand (*histemi*) beside a pillar that holds up the roof, the same position Nausicaa adopts when she addresses her final speech to Odysseus in book eight. Drawing on the shared terminology of loom and mast and their connection to the verb *histemi*, Reyes Bertolin argues that markers of vertical space function as markers of authority.[10] The loom and the mast, when raised,[11] establish the separate spheres of masculine and feminine authority which, by virtue of being a single word in Greek, *histos*, are equivalent authorities. When 'making a stand' at the vertical pillar that holds up the house, Penelope is communicating to the suitors that she is the authority figure in the household.

Telemachus' response seems to subvert her claim to authority. First, he contradicts her request to the bard by highlighting that he is not the cause (the

Greek word is *aitia*) of either his song or the events that inspired it. Causation lies with Zeus. The bard is simply an instrument, here both of immortal inspiration and by the compulsion of the suitors. Telemachus then instructs her to return to her 'loom and distaff', as Hector advises Andromache to do in their *Iliad* book six exchange. In translation, Telemachus' speech can present, and has been interpreted, as bordering on the ridiculous since he is a young man, inexperienced and ineffectual at commanding control of the household, as evidenced by the suitors having overrun it. By contrast, Penelope has kept the household running for twenty-odd years[12] with her partner absent.

The bard's description of Telemachus, however, suggests that something more is happening in this scene than manifests in modern translation. Bertolin further suggests that the loom and mast apportion indoor spaces to women and outdoor spaces to men. If indoor and outdoor can also be correlated with private and public respectively, then Telemachus can be understood to be striving to assert himself as the masculine authority of the household who will complement Penelope as she practices her feminine authority. As noted, however, he has evidently not been in a position to establish himself as a compelling masculine authority thus far, making his speech seem unreliable.

But Telemachus has recently been consulting with Athena in her guise as Mentes. This name, as Nagy points out, is related to *menos*, meaning *strength* or *power*; *menos*, in turn, derives from the root *mne* – which means *mentally connect*.[13] We might then interpret Telemachus to be, with Athena-Mentes as the conduit, mentally connecting with the power or strength of his father. Athena has come to Ithaca to lead him into his adult role, and her influence flows through this scene. Penelope's reaction to Telemachus' speech seems to recognise the presence of an immortal. She is described 'being in a state of wonder', *thauma* in the Greek text, which indicates the presence of the immortal in the moment. Penelope absorbs her son's speech, which the bard describes as 'prudent' – the Greek is *pepnoumai*, literally *having breath* or *being alive*, which has been rendered *sensible, prudent* or *discreet* – and returns to her own rooms. What is 'prudent', 'sensible' or 'discreet' about Telemachus' speech? The next significant mention of Penelope suggests an answer.

In book two, Telemachus calls an assembly of elders, the first such assembly since Odysseus' departure for Troy, as the bard points out, a reminder that his absence has left Ithaca without its most potent leader. The elders worry that the city is in danger of outside attack, reminiscent of the fate that befell Troy and the cities around it, but Telemachus explains that the threat distressing him is coming from within his own house: the suitors who are consuming his supplies and pressuring his mother against her will to choose a husband from among them. Acknowledging that, given his young age and his father's absence, he is not strong enough to send them off alone, he asks for help. His concerns evoke Andromache's imagined fate for Astyanax in her second lament: a son without a father to lead and protect him is left vulnerable to the might of other men.

The elders are sympathetic, but the lead suitor, Antinous, retorts that Telemachus should not attribute the cause to them but his mother who has been deceiving them:

> She makes all have hope and makes promises to each man,
> Sending forth messages, but her understanding has other intentions.
> She pondered another trap with her perceptions,
> Setting it up on a great loom, to weave in the large room,
> A subtle and well-fitted thing, she spoke among us straightaway.
> (Lines 91–95)

The trap Antinous refers to is the shroud for Laertes, her father-in-law, which Penelope claimed she needed to weave before she could choose a new husband. Bertolin suggests that raising a loom in 'the large room', implied to be the public space where the suitors gather during the day, constitutes a proclamation of Penelope's independence: she sets up the marker of her feminine authority, the loom, in what is typically a masculine space, the public room. At night, when the suitors presumably departed to their own homes to sleep, Penelope would unravel her work, thus extending the project indefinitely. But in the fourth year of weaving and un-weaving her trap, Penelope is betrayed by enslaved women in the household, who inform the suitors of her deception. Setting up her authority, the loom, in a public space has left her vulnerable to discovery and compulsion. When the suitors catch her unravelling her work, they force her against her will to complete it, as she tells Odysseus in book nineteen (line 156).

Returning to the question of what makes Telemachus' book one instructions to his mother to return to her weaving 'prudent', an answer may be that he is reminding her where her authority and her cunning lie: with her loom and distaff, the instruments she used to set her trap in motion. Her shroud ruse functioned both metaphorically and literally: she trapped the suitors into stasis by claiming that she needed to weave the shroud. Now, she needs to spin a new trap, whether literally with her weaving or with some other application of her craft and cunning, and this time, Telemachus intends to unite her strategy with his might.

In his response to Telemachus at the book two assembly, Antinous believes that he and the suitors have Penelope cornered and confidently proclaims as much in the ensuing part of his speech:

> If she will as yet distress the sons of the Achaeans,
> The perceptions upon her consciousness, which Athena gave her –
> To be skilled in very beautiful works and noble perception,
> And shrewd counsel, of such a kind as we have not heard about up to this time, not even from the women of old,
> Who were the beautiful-haired Achaean women of former times,
> Tyro and Alcmene and well-crowned Mycenae.
> None of them is equal in understanding to Penelope –
> Then she does not observe properly this time,
> For in the meantime, they will devour your livelihood and property.
> As long as she holds this thought, which now at this very time
> Gods have placed in her chest, great fame in song she
> Will make, but for you, yearning for your lost livelihood.
> We will neither go to our own homes nor anywhere else
> Until she herself is to marry whichever of the Achaeans she chooses.
>
> (Lines 115–126)

Antinous acknowledges that Penelope is preeminent among women in skill, perception and council, outshining even the best of the Achaean women of her time or the past, and that Athena herself is the source of Penelope's gifts. But he then claims that her schemes will benefit her alone, earning her 'great fame in song', *kleos* in the Greek, but costing her son his livelihood. In making this claim, Antinous reveals a failure to understand how *kleos* functions. It is not individual. A song of fame emerges from the dynamic among everyone connected to the heroes, immortals and mortals. The *Iliad* is a monument to this: the godlike wrath of Achilles does not affect only him or even his chief antagonists, Agamemnon and Hector. Each of these men are connected to other mortals and immortals who will be drawn into their conflicts. Achilles' wrath ripples out across the cosmos, affecting relationships on Olympus via Thetis' request that leads to strife between

Hera and Zeus and among the gods who favour heroes on opposite sides. It visits destruction on the Achaeans via Achilles' refusal to re-join the battle. Beyond Troy, it will cause boundless grief for the families of the heroes who are killed because of his absence. Within Troy, it destroys the Trojans who he kills in the moment and who will see their civilisation collapse. It destroys even Achilles' own dearest companion, Patroclus, and ultimately Achilles himself. No one escapes either harm or benefit, depending on the context. Each life is a single thread, but its meaning derives from the pattern into which it is woven in the fabric both of the cosmos and of the epic song, which memorialises all, victors and victims.

Further, Antinous' speech exposes that he is disconnected from understanding Penelope's *kleos* in particular. It derives from her ability to deploy her skill, perception and strategy to restore her family into a functional whole. As such, it is not she alone who receives Athena's gifts and favour but each member of her family. Athena works through all three to achieve the reintegration of their unit, which then has implications for the people of Ithaca in the present and time to come. Each of the suitors has a family who mourns his death, and the deaths of so many leading young men, who may have had future sons of their own, may leave the city vulnerable. It also presumably restores Odysseus to power within the community and ensures a leadership position for Telemachus in the future. By holding Odysseus' place, Penelope not only strives to restore her husband to herself but also father to son, current and future leaders of Ithaca whose descendants will carry the family's story forward. In this way, the *kleos* of one is defined by the *kleos* of all, in time and for all time.

The prudence or discretion of Telemachus' speech to his mother in book one, then, is that he recognises her feminine authority as essential to his success. Unlike Antinous, Telemachus recognises that they will succeed or fail together. Rather than underestimating her importance to his success, sending her to her loom and distaff may be a signal that he recognises the need to complement her feminine authority with his masculine authority. She must spin the schemes not in full view of their antagonists but concealed from them, and he must be ready to project strength in his speeches and have the physical might to uphold his words. The suitors' response to his speech in book one manifests that he is not yet ready, but Athena's interventions are laying the groundwork. Penelope's sense of wonder reflects that she perceives the presence of a god-breathed plan and understands that she must weave a new cunning, a new scheme, to hold off the suitors, and that she does.

This new scheme is set in motion in book eighteen, after Odysseus has returned to Ithaca disguised as a beggar, and its source, as ever, is Athena:

> Then the goddess, owl-eyed Athena, placed upon her perceptions
> For circumspect Penelope, the daughter of Icarius
> To appear before the suitors, so that she might most inflame
> The consciousness of the suitors and become honoured
> Even more than she was before with regard to her spouse and son.
>
> (Lines 158–161)

Immediately following, Penelope announces to her housekeeper Eurynome her intention to present herself to the suitors and counsel her son. Eurynome advises Penelope to beautify herself before going, but Penelope dismisses the notion on the grounds that Odysseus' departure from Ithaca destroyed her beauty. She instructs Eurynome to fetch two trusted handmaidens as escorts into the public space, and after Eurynome departs, Athena sets in motion the next step of her plan:

> There Athena, the owl-eyed goddess, had another intention.
> She poured honey-sweet sleep around the daughter of Icarius.
> Reclining, she lay down to sleep, all her joints loosening
> Themselves along the sofa, meanwhile the goddess of Zeus
> Gave Penelope ambrosial gifts in order that the Achaeans would wonder at her.
> First, she washed her beautiful face with the beauty
> Of ambrosia, of such a kind as well-crowned Cytherea[14]
> Rubs on her body when she joins the passionate dance of the Graces,
> And she set in place for her to appear taller and fuller,
> More luminous than freshly sawed ivory.
>
> (Lines 187–186)

The ambrosia Athena anoints Penelope with is suggestive of the desirability associated with Aphrodite (Cytherea). It also evokes Hera cloaking herself in ambrosia before her seduction of Zeus in *Iliad* book fourteen. The immortal gift Athena bestows to Penelope is portrayed as potent and cosmic, amplifying the significance of the moment. It also draws attention to the interdependence of the immortals' domains. As with authority in the mortal world, authority in the immortal one is diffuse and complimentary, each necessary to the plans and intentions of the other. This is also evidenced in the creation of Pandora, who receives gifts from a host of gods in *Works and Days*.

When Penelope wakes up, she descends to the public room with her trusted handmaidens to fulfil her intentions. She first confronts Telemachus, scolding him for allowing the suitors to mistreat the beggar (Odysseus) and suggesting that his 'perceptions are neither in accord with fate nor showing understanding' (line 220). Telemachus assures his mother that he recognises the suitors' harmful thinking and lack of understanding and notes that the beggar has demonstrated full command of himself. As with their public exchange in book one, their exchange in this moment operates on two levels, the overt and the concealed. On the surface, they appear to be discussing the beggar's mistreatment by the suitors in the context of sacred hospitality rituals, Penelope expressing her concerns and Telemachus reassuring her that he recognises the suitors for what they are. Below the surface, another potential conversation is taking place. How it is interpreted depends, to some extent, on whether one believes Penelope has already recognised Odysseus, a question we will return to shortly.

Immediately after Penelope's exchange with Telemachus, the suitors remark on her beauty, prompting Penelope to reiterate a version of her earlier claim to Eurynome:

> Eurymachus, truly, the excellence seen in my form and stature,
> The deathless ones destroyed it when they went to Ilium,
> The Argives, and with them went my own spouse, my Odysseus
> If returning, he were to care for my life,
> In this way, my fame in song would be greater and more beautiful,
> But now I grieve, for so many are the harms a *daimon* has set
>   in motion against me.
>
> (Lines 251–256)

She then recalls Odysseus' parting words to her in which he acknowledged that he might be killed at Troy and advised her to take care of their household and his parents, even more while he is away than she has been already. When their son has 'grown a beard', signifying entering adulthood, she may then remarry and leave their home behind (line 269). Conceding that the hateful time has arrived, Penelope claims that everything Odysseus predicted has come to pass. He has died far away; their son has become an adult, and she must now choose a husband. But she grieves that it must be from among these subpar suitors:

> 'But another grim pain has come upon my heart and consciousness,
> This behaviour was not correct for suitors in past times to make

> Towards the noble daughter of a wealthy father.
> Those who wished to woo her contended with one another,
> These same men led in oxen and stout sheep,
> To be a feast for those dear to the bride, and they gave shining gifts.'
> So she spoke, and much enduring, godlike Odysseus rejoiced,
> Because she was drawing out gifts from them and enchanting their consciousness
> With honey-sweet words, but her way of understanding had other desires.
>
> (Lines 274–283)

The end of her speech reveals that, though the bard has not focalised him, the disguised Odysseus has been in the background all along. Now, he is delighted to see Penelope extracting gifts from and enchanting the suitors. Readers or hearers might recall the story Odysseus told the Phaeacians about Circe: she enchanted his companions and robbed them (though temporarily) of their humanity. Penelope is not here enchanting with potions but with her 'honey-sweet words' and the power of ambrosia, immortalising armour with which Athena anointed her, and this will lead the suitors to irreversible death. The bard reports that her beauty weakens their bodies and dulls their minds while her words invite them to compete for her by offering splendid gifts. Claiming to accept that she must remarry provokes the suitors to believe they have worn her down and won the game, but as Odysseus observes, Penelope has other intentions.

The precise nature of those intentions is never explicitly stated and has generated spirited debate. Antinous complains in the book two assembly that Penelope's behaviour has been duplicitous, that she conceals her true intentions, and Odysseus observes likewise here. For Antinous, it is a harm but for Odysseus a benefit. Returning now to the question of when Penelope recognises Odysseus, Homer does not, perhaps cannot, provide a ready answer because to do so would contradict Penelope's characterisation. She is *periphron*, her epithet, which translates literally to *thinking all around* and is rendered here, as elsewhere, *circumspect*. Penelope's forethought, cunning and endurance enable her to conceal her intentions, within the narrative from the men around her who strive to win her and from us, the hearers or readers of her story. Like the suitors, readers or hearers are left to wonder what she knows and when she knows it, and this is part of what makes her powerful. Her actions and intentions cannot be anticipated unless someone else knows and exposes them.

When Penelope first announces her intention to descend to the public room, she informs Eurynome that she wishes both to present herself to the suitors and to advise Telemachus. This 'advice' she offers presents as a rebuke of his behaviour and understanding. On the surface, it can sound like a mother nagging her adolescent son. But if Penelope knows, or at least suspects, that Odysseus has returned or will do imminently, and has been moved by Athena to press the suitors towards a crisis, her conversation with Telemachus may have a pointed purpose to test her son. Is he prepared to stand by his father? Is Odysseus, if he has returned, prepared to fight the suitors? What are Athena's intentions for the family? Penelope does not presume to know for certain and has the forethought to plan for numerous potential eventualities.

Shortly after the suitors present their gifts, Penelope requests to speak with the 'beggar'. Eurynome brings a chair for him, and Penelope opens the conversation by asking the three familiar questions put to visitors: Who are you? Where are you from? Who are your people? In response, Odysseus praises her, comparing her to a good king:

> Woman, no one among mortals upon the boundless earth with
>   you
> Could quarrel, for truly, your fame in song reaches the wide sky,
> As that of a blameless king, one who fears the gods,
> Ruling among many blameless men,
> He upholds righteousness, and the ink-dark earth bears
> Wheat and barley, trees heavy with fruit,
> Sheep give birth steadily, and the sea supplies fish,
> From his good guidance, the people under him thrive.
>   (Book 19, lines 107–114)

His speech is notable for its praise of Penelope as a king[15] and for his reference to her *kleos* having already reached 'the wide sky'. But he declines to answer her questions, claiming that remembering them fills him with grief, and it would be improper to lament in her home. Since laments are traditionally sung by women, Odysseus is here associating himself with a traditionally feminine responsibility as a complement to the traditionally masculine responsibilities he attributes to Penelope through his simile. Doing so calls attention to his and Penelope's shared experiences. Both have endured grief and been coerced by more powerful forces, Penelope by her more than one hundred suitors and Odysseus by the goddess Calypso. But rather than thriving in his absence, Ithaca has come under attack by the suitors. It is losing its resources and vitality, as Penelope herself earlier suggested when she described her beauty being 'destroyed' by Odysseus' departure for Troy: she functions as a metonym for Ithaca itself.

Odysseus' simile recalls an earlier one used by the bard in book four when he compares Penelope to a cornered lion. Lion similes are also applied to warrior heroes in the *Iliad*, particularly to highlight their ferocity and might, but the simile is used more sparingly in the *Odyssey*. In the book four instance, the bard applies it to Penelope to highlight her vulnerability:

> As much as a lion ponders when among a crowd of men,
> In fear as they circle around him to lead him into a trap,
> So was Penelope pondering as honey-sweet sleep came upon her.
> (Lines 791–793)

Penelope is a cornered lion surrounded by men attempting to lead her into a trap, but the lion too has power. Returning to her book nineteen conversation with Odysseus, Penelope's response to him merges grief and *kleos*: she both laments her circumstances and 'sings her fame', which she connects somewhat pointedly to her excellence in traditional feminine authorities, weaving and strategy:

> Then circumspect Penelope responded to Odysseus,
> 'Guest-friend, truly the excellence seen in my form and stature.
> The deathless ones destroyed it when they went to Ilium,
> The Argives, and with them went my own spouse, my Odysseus.
> If returning, he were to care for my life,
> In this way, my fame in song would be greater and more beautiful,
> But now I grieve, for many are the harms a *daimon* has set in motion against me,
> For many of the greatest men who rule over the islands
> Dulichium and Samos and wooded Zakynthos,
> Who sustain themselves around far-seen Ithaca herself,
> They woo me against my will, consuming my household.
> Therefore, I take heed neither of guest-friends nor of suppliants
> Nor even of messengers, who are skilled workmen of the people.
> No, I melt away, my dear heart longing for Odysseus.
> While the suitors urge for a wedding feast, I spin traps.
> My first, which a *daimon* breathed into my consciousness, was a large cloth,

Setting it up on a great loom, to weave in the large room,
A subtle and well-fitted thing, I spoke among them straightaway,
"Young men, my suitors, godlike Odysseus has been killed.
Eager though you are for my wedding, be steadfast, wait for the cloth
To come to fulfilment, so my weaving is not destroyed in vain.
It is a burial shroud for Laertes, the hero, for when
Destructive fate takes him down, laying him out in death.
Let me not be resented by the women of Achaea
For allowing a man of great status to lie without a cloth."
So I claimed, and their proud hearts and understanding were persuaded.
There, by day, on a great loom, I wove,
But by night, placing myself beside the fire torch, I unravelled,
So I escaped unnoticed for three years, and I won over the Achaeans,
But when the fourth arrived, and the season drew near,
The moons having waned around many days, it reached fulfilment
At that time, because of enslaved women, having no cares, like dogs.
Having come upon me, the suitors caught me and threatened me with their words.
Thus, though against my will, I brought it to fulfilment, by force.
Now, it is possible neither to escape marriage nor a certain other
Scheme do I find, as of yet. My parents urge me
To marry, and as the suitors devour, my child grieves.
He perceives them, for already, he is such a kind of man
To care for a house, to whom Zeus grants glory,
But now, tell me your race, from what place are you?
For you do not come from a tree, neither from a rock, as was spoken long ago.'

(Lines 123–163)

As suggested in the final three women's laments in the *Iliad*, lament and *kleos* are intertwined in Penelope's speech, one flowing into the other: Penelope's grief at Odysseus' absence and the invasion of the suitors led her to devise the ruse that has led to her song of fame. Across the *Odyssey*, she grieves and laments her troubles, and these too are woven into the song of Odysseus' return. Now, she claims to be unable to escape remarriage and to have no new scheme, but in actuality, a new one has already been set in motion. Athena placed the idea in Penelope, and she prompted the suitors to compete for her by observing the proper rituals.[16] Penelope again mentions her beauty having been destroyed when Odysseus went to Troy, using similar language as when she mentioned it first to Eurynome and again to the suitors. The language she uses to describe her ruse mirrors Antinous' narrative of it in book two. If Penelope suspects or believes that she is speaking with Odysseus, or someone who will carry the message to him, her speech is especially striking for what it indirectly communicates: she has spun schemes to hold off the suitors, and their son is already the kind of man who can defend a household. But the time has come when Odysseus will need to show his power if the family's reunion is to be fulfilled.

If he is not yet ready to take on the suitors, however, it could be dangerous for Penelope to reveal either him or her knowledge of him. Odysseus himself makes this point after his conversation with Penelope when she asks Eurycleia to wash his feet, noting that he 'is the same age as your leader' (line 317). In the course of fulfilling the request, Eurycleia recognises a scar on Odysseus' leg, cries out his name and attempts to catch Penelope's gaze to reveal that her husband has returned. But the joint effect of Athena's intention and Odysseus' might forestall her:

> So Eurycleia said, and she looked at Penelope with her eyes,
> Wanting to point out her beloved husband being in the house,
> But Penelope was able neither to look nor to notice,
> For Athena turned her perceptions, but Odysseus,
> Reaching with his right hand and seizing Eurycleia by the throat,
> Dragged her toward him and spoke out,
> 'Foster-mother, why do you want me to be destroyed, you who nursed me yourself
> Upon your breast? Now having suffered many pains,
> I have come to my fatherland in the twentieth year,
> But now, since you recognise me, and a god has put it in your consciousness,
> Stay silent, so that no one else in the great rooms realises,
> For if you do not, I make it known, and it will surely come to fulfilment,
> If a god by me overpowers the illustrious suitors,
> Not even you being my nurse will ward me off when the other
> Enslaved women captured in war I kill in my great rooms.'
> (Lines 476–490)

Athena 'turning [Penelope's] perceptions' has been interpreted to mean that the goddess distracted Penelope so that she would not notice Odysseus and Eurycleia's conversation. Interpreting it in this way can seem to render Penelope a bystander in Odysseus' story rather than a hero who herself has the support and guidance of Athena to determine the proper moment to reveal that she knows Odysseus has returned. To do so in the public space among the suitors would be wildly dangerous, as they might overpower him and destroy not only Odysseus but also Penelope and Telemachus. Both Penelope and Odysseus have secured Athena's favour because of their forethought and cunning, because they would not be so foolish, so disconnected from how things work, that they would fail to evaluate the implications of their actions. Odysseus did not make the mistake of Agamemnon, striding back to his home expecting to be welcomed warmly; he slunk back in humble disguise. Likewise, Penelope has not, like Clytemnestra, become distracted by the attentions of her suitors. While he is testing her, she too may be testing him, as Athena is testing them both.

After Eurycleia professes her loyalty and completes her task, Odysseus and Penelope resume their conversation, and Penelope asks the 'beggar' to interpret her dream in which an eagle descends to destroy the geese in her house. He replies that the dream clearly indicates her husband will return and destroy the suitors. In response, Penelope immediately announces her intention to hold a contest among her suitors: whoever can string the bow of Odysseus and shoot an arrow through twelve axes will be the next man she marries. Again, if we believe that Penelope recognises him or believes that he bears a true omen of Odysseus' return, then her announcement of the contest invites her husband to reveal his might in the context of the proper ritual: he must win her in marriage again by defeating her other suitors.

That night, Odysseus tosses and turns, urging his heart to endure but unable to find rest until Athena appears to him and affirms that he has her support. She declares that they two alone[17] could defeat an army, then causes sleep to wash over him. Immediately after he falls asleep, the focus flows into the perspective of Penelope, who is likewise awake and grieving:

> When sleep took hold of Odysseus, dissolving the cares in his consciousness,
> Relaxing his limbs, his knowing and trusted wife woke up,
> Seated on her marriage bed, she lamented,
> But when her weeping was satiated, in accordance with her consciousness,
> She, godlike among women, prayed to Artemis, first before all,

'Artemis, revered goddess, daughter of Zeus, if only already for me
You would seize an arrow, shooting it into my chest, casting out my consciousness,
Straightaway, now, either a violent storm, snatching me up,
Would take me away, bearing me along a gloomy path,
Or would throw me in the stream of encircling Ocean,
As when a violent storm carried away the daughters of Pandareus.
The gods destroyed their parents, and they survived them,
Orphaned in the great rooms, godlike Aphrodite cared for them
With cheese and sweet honey and pleasant wine.
Hera gave them, above all women,
Beauty and understanding, and holy Artemis lofty stature.
Athena taught them to perform glorious works.
When divine Artemis ascended to high Olympus,
Begging to bring to fulfilment fruitful marriage for the girls –
To Zeus, who delights in thunder, for he well knows all
Fate, all that is fated and un-fated for mortal people –
Storm winds snatched up the maidens and carried them off,
And gave them to the furies of abomination to take care of them,
So I wish those who have homes on Olympus would destroy me,
Or that Artemis of the beautiful locks would shoot me, in order that Odysseus,
Seeing him, I too would arrive under the hated earth.
I would not delight the perceptions of any lesser man.
But enduring holds off evil, when someone
Weeps by day, grieving deeply at heart,
Sleep takes hold in the night, for it causes him to forget everything,
The good and the bad, since it wraps itself around the eyelids,
And yet, a *daimon* put in motion against me bad dreams,
For this night, someone resembling Odysseus was sleeping beside me,
Such as he was when he went away with the army, yet my heart
Rejoiced, since I did not claim it to be a dream, but the day was already here.'
So she said, and straightaway, golden-throned Dawn arrived.

(Lines 56–91)

The first two lines of this section create a sense of fusion: Odysseus' limbs loosen just as his trusted wife awakes, as if her vigilance is a reaction to his rest. Her immediate reaction is to lament and pray, and the goddess she directs her prayer to is Artemis, a goddess associated with the bow and the protection of innocents. Recounting the myth of the daughters of Pandareus as a simile, Penelope wishes for a swift death that would reunite her with Odysseus rather than 'delight the perceptions of any lesser man'. Assuming again that Penelope knows Odysseus has returned and has set up the contest to provide him the opportunity to defeat the suitors and reclaim his place as her husband, her prayer can be understood as an expression of anxiety about the events to come on this day.[18] If Odysseus is not able to defeat the suitors, if they strike him down with his or any other bow, then Penelope would rather be struck down with him than marry one of the suitors who are inferior to him.

Concluding her prayer, Penelope reflects that a *daimon* must have given her bad dreams since she felt Odysseus to be beside her. A specific explanation for the grief she experienced upon waking and realising he was not there may lie in the epithet used to announce Dawn. Penelope's prayer is followed 'straightaway' by the arrival of 'golden-throned Dawn'. Two epithets used to describe Dawn in Homer are 'rosy-fingered' and 'golden-throned', which Kerry Hartwick notes are metrically equivalent in the Greek.[19] Considerations of metre, then, would not determine which epithet is used in this instance; either would fit. Hartwick proposes that the different epithets are focalising devices for receivers of the story that enable them to keep track of and anticipate events, and 'golden-throned' heralds significant days. Its use at the end of this passage may portend a cosmic occurrence, signified by Dawn's 'golden throne': the contest of the bow will be held on this day, which is also a feast day for Apollo, who, like his twin sister, is associated with the bow. And it is the day when Odysseus will defeat the suitors in the contest for Penelope.

As the day unfolds, Athena provokes the suitors to increasingly outrageous behaviour, intending to fuel Odysseus' anger and eager ferocity to attack when the time comes. Omens warn the suitors repeatedly, though they disregard the signs, and embolden Odysseus in his assurance of the immortals' approval and favour. He prepares to launch his attack, and in book twenty-one, prompted by Athena, Penelope fetches the bow of Odysseus:

> But when Penelope, godlike among women, arrived at the inner room,
> She stepped upon the oaken threshold, which a craftsman

Had smoothed knowingly and straightened with a carpenter's line
And fastened a door post and added a shining door.
Straightaway, she nimbly loosened the leather strap of the door handle,
Thrust the key in, and drove up the bolt of the door,
Aiming straight, it roared loudly, as a bull does,
Feeding in a meadow, so clanged the beautiful doors,
Being struck by the key, they spread open quickly before her.
She stepped upon a high platform. There, large chests
Had been made to stand. Inside these, garments smelling of incense had been placed.
Reaching out, she took the bow from a peg
And its case, a shimmering object that covered it,
Seating herself down there, on the spot, setting it upon her dear knees,
She wept exceedingly, shrilly, and took out the bow of the master of the house.
After she had satisfied herself with much weeping and wailing,
She walked to the large room to go among the illustrious suitors,
Holding the back-stretched bow in her hands and the quiver
Holding arrows, many groan-causing arrows were in it.
The handmaidens with her carried a case. There, iron
Much of it was put, and bronze, prizes of the master of the house.
When Penelope, godlike among women, arrived at the suitors,
She made her stand beside a pillar of the solidly made roof,
Having a shimmering veil over her cheeks.
A trusted handmaiden stood on each side of her.
Straightaway, she spoke among the suitors and delivered these words:
'Hear me, bold suitors, who this house
Attack, eating and drinking continually, always,
The house of a man who has been away for a long time. Nor any other
Pretext are you able to make with your words
But setting in motion to marry me and make me your wife,
But come forward, suitors, since this prize now appears,
For I will set out the great bow of godlike Odysseus,

> And whoever can stretch the bow most easily with the palm of his hands
> And shoot an arrow through all twelve axes,
> I will follow him at once, abandoning this house
> Of my wedded husband, exceedingly beautiful, quite full of life,
> That I suppose I shall ever call him to mind just as in a dream.'
> (Lines 42–79)

The bard's attention to the storeroom's construction and contents – iron and bronze, weapons and incense-scented garments – frames it as a shared space in which the works of men's and women's hands are placed alongside each other. It signifies that for a community to thrive requires both, working harmoniously together, as Odysseus and Penelope have been doing, and sharing unity of mind and feeling, as Odysseus and Penelope do. The events of the day will determine whether the family is restored or irrevocably torn apart. Penelope's heightened emotion as she retrieves Odysseus' bow focalises the tension and uncertainty that she is experiencing in the moment. As her prayer to Artemis earlier suggested, the contest is a risk that could lead either to restoration or destruction. Penelope is mindful of Athena's presence, but the full scope of the gods' intentions cannot be known by mortals. In the *Iliad*, Hector enjoyed the favour of Zeus and the support of Apollo, but that support served a larger end of which Hector was tragically unaware, and which would lead to the fall of his city, the death of his only son and the enslavement of his wife.

Appearing before the suitors carrying the bow, Penelope upbraids them for their sacrilegious behaviour before announcing the terms of the contest and her intention to marry whoever can prove himself Odysseus' equal by stringing his bow and shooting the axes. Her prefatory remarks make clear that she does not believe any one of them to be Odysseus' equal, and her closing ones attest to the strength of her attachment to him: even if forced to follow another man into marriage, she will always be thinking of the house of Odysseus, which could be said to function metonymically to represent Odysseus himself, as Penelope earlier functioned metonymically to represent Ithaca. This sense is amplified by the final two lines. Translated line by line, it is 'wedded husband' that is put with 'quite full of life', which Odysseus is, though the suitors do not know it. The final line of her speech is especially telling, since Penelope woke up that day having believed that Odysseus was beside her. In mind and feeling, it could be said that he was.

Eumaeus, the masculine counterpart of Eurycleia, is instructed to set up the axes, and he weeps after doing so, earning a sharp rebuke from

Antinous. When Eumaeus departs with another loyal household member, Odysseus follows them out and questions them: would they fight alongside their leader if he were to return? When Eumaeus affirms that he would with a prayer to the gods, Odysseus reveals his scar, the same token of identification that revealed him to Eurycleia, and the men set to planning their attack.

Back in the great room, none of the suitors manages to string the bow, which Antinous attributes to the feast day of Apollo. He suggests suspending the contest for the night and making an offering to the god of the bow the following day, after which they can try again. The suitors approve of his plan, but Odysseus returns and demands an opportunity to test the power of his limbs with the bow. Outraged at the suggestion, they threaten to destroy him, prompting Penelope to intervene. Surely the beggar does not expect to win her as a wife, she claims, adding that it is wrong for them to mistreat a guest of their host, Telemachus. If she knows that the beggar is Odysseus, her words add weight to the suitors' missteps, since they are mistreating their host himself, a violation of the sacred law of hospitality, the same violation that set the Trojan war in motion and led to the destruction of Troy and the Trojans.

One of the prominent suitors, Eurymachus, notes that it would be embarrassing for them if the beggar succeeds where they failed. He worries that they would become the objects of rumour, which prompts a scornful reply from Penelope and a familiar exchange between her and Telemachus:

> Again circumspect Penelope addressed him:
> 'Eurymachus, in what way is it a good report throughout the land
> To be consuming the household of a man, dishonouring
> The best of men? With whom do you reckon over this disgrace?
> This guest-friend is exceedingly great and well built.
> He vows that he is the son of a father from a noble race of men.
> Now, give him the bow with the polished shaft in order that I can see,
> For in this way, I will declare, it will be brought to fulfilment.
> If he can stretch the bow and if Apollo will grant his prayer,
> I will put clothes upon him, a cloak and a chiton, beautiful garments.
> I will give him a sharp javelin, a protection from dogs and men.
> And a two-edged sword. I will give him sandals under his feet.
> I will send him whichever way his heart and consciousness command him.'

> But Telemachus, being prudent, spoke in response to her,
> 'Mother of mine, regarding the bow, no one of the Achaeans besides me,
> Has more power over who I wish to give it and also to deny it,
> Neither as many as are lords throughout rocky Ithaca,
> Nor as many islands toward horse-nourishing Elis,
> Of them, none will constrain me against my will, unless I should will it to be so,
> Once and for all, for anyone to give the guest-friend this bow to bear,
> But going into the house, take care of your own works,
> The loom and the distaff, and urge your handmaidens
> To go to their work, for the bow is the concern of men
> Alone, and mine most of all, for might in the house is mine.'
> And Penelope, being in a state of wonder, went back into the house.
> She put her child's prudent speech into her consciousness.
> Ascending to the upper part of the house together with her handmaidens,
> She wept then for Odysseus, her beloved husband, until sleep,
> Honey-sweet upon her eyelids, put owl-eyed Athena.
>
> (Lines 330–358)

Structurally and in the repetition of language in the Greek, the above exchange recalls the scene between Penelope and Telemachus in book one: she makes a bold public speech, in the first instance to request Phemius sing a different song, here to present a catalogue of the gifts she will provide the beggar if he succeeds in stringing the bow and driving an arrow through the axes. Telemachus responds to assert his authority in the household and advise her to return to her loom and distaff, again inspiring wonder and consent from Penelope, who returns to her rooms and weeps for her husband until sleep washes over her, via Athena.

The speeches of Telemachus and Penelope in the passage above incorporate identical lines from the book one exchange. Penelope addresses a man in the public room, Phemius in book one and Eurymachus here, and Telemachus, 'being prudent', speaks 'in response to her'. He opens his speech with the same address, 'mother of mine', and the final four lines of his speech are identical to the ones in their book one exchange, with one exception. In book one, he declared that 'public speech is the concern of men'; here, it is 'the bow is the concern of men'. Together, his book one and twenty-one speeches highlight the two qualities associated with masculine authority, the same qualities necessary for his full transition into adulthood: public speech and might. Penelope's reaction in the final five lines above is rendered identically to those in book one. In both cases, Penelope recognises, via 'being in a state of wonder', the presence of an immortal hand and returns to her rooms to weep and sleep, in this instance to wait for news of the outcome of the contest. The variation within the repetition suggests that the maturation of Telemachus has reached fulfillment, and he is now prepared to be his father's son. He does not only look like his father's son, as Helen expressed in their book four meeting, but can act like him too by standing beside him as he fights the suitors to reclaim his wife and home.

The subtext in the book one exchange was that Penelope needed to focus on spinning a new scheme while Telemachus needed to make a compelling show of might. Here, assuming again that Penelope is aware the beggar is Odysseus, Telemachus appears to be signalling his mother that the slaughter is at hand. Once Odysseus strings the bow, he will not relinquish it willingly. In the event the gods have set this crisis in motion to bring about the destruction of Odysseus and Telemachus, unbeknownst to them, as they did to bring about the destruction of Hector in the *Iliad*, it would be prudent for Penelope to absent herself. She can only feign ignorance of the plan if she is not present when the slaughter begins, at which time it is unlikely she would be able to conceal where her loyalties lie.

Throughout the slaughter and its aftermath, Penelope remains concealed in her rooms behind locked doors. When Eurycleia delivers the news of Odysseus and Telemachus' success, Penelope is disbelieving. She insists that, if the suitors have been killed, it was by the hand of an immortal who was outraged by their bad acts, but Odysseus has lost his homecoming and his life in some distant place. Eurycleia reveals that she recognised Odysseus by his scar when she washed his feet and attempted to get Penelope's attention, but she failed to notice. Penelope brushes this off, replying,

> Dear foster-mother, it is difficult for you the everlasting gods'
> Plans to discern, even though you have great wisdom.
>
> (Lines 81–82)

Penelope's 'circumspect' nature can make her reaction seem puzzling and seems to support the theory that she truly does not know the beggar is Odysseus. She has been given the news she professed to long for: Odysseus has returned and vanquished the suitors. But rather than being jubilant, she is restrained and suspicious. Her own words to Eurycleia suggest the reason for her behaviour, which will become explicit in her final exchange with Odysseus later in book twenty-three: no mortal, no matter how wise, can discern the plans of the gods. To believe that he or she does is an invitation to their own destruction, a pattern that plays out repeatedly in the *Iliad*, most starkly with both Achilles and Hector. Achilles believes he knows his options because his mother shared a prophecy with him, but refusing to return to battle leads to the death of Patroclus, which leaves him no option *but* to return to battle to avenge him. Hector stands fast to face Achilles believing his brother is beside him only to realise at the last moment that Athena has deceived him. Penelope has been patient and enduring for twenty years, and she will not succumb to recklessness now, when the outcome she has worked for is so close at hand.

Nevertheless, she consents to descend to the public room to witness the suitors lying dead and to meet the man who killed them:

> So speaking, she stepped down from the upper room, many things her heart
> Was turning over, whether she should question her dear husband from far apart,
> Or whether, drawing near, she should kiss his head and receive his two hands.
>
> (Line 85–87)

There, she finds Odysseus leaning against a pillar, but from a seated position beside the hearth, evoking Hestia, goddess of hearth and home, whose name alternately can mean *fireside*, *household* or *family*, and conferring the status of a sacred occasion to the family's reunion. Odysseus' seated position by the pillar and hearth with Penelope seated beside him depicts the husband and wife who are united in mind and feeling as equivalent authorities. Penelope sits in silence for a long while, as 'astonishment reached her heart' (line 93). At some moments, he resembles the man she remembers, but his disguise, 'his rough clothes', render him unfamiliar (line 95). The tension is finally broken by Telemachus, who bursts out,

> Mother of mine, no mother, having a harsh consciousness,
> Why in this way do you turn away from my father, not even with him
> Sitting, do you neither inquire nor investigate with a word?
> No other woman in this way having undergone suffering in her consciousness

> Could stand apart from her husband, who having suffered so
>   many harmful things,
> Has returned in the twentieth year to the land of his father,
> Your heart is always more solid than a stone.
>
> (Lines 97–103)

In his speech, Telemachus has essentially given voice to the *kleos* of Penelope, to what has enabled her to achieve the family's reunion and for what she will be remembered. She has been immovable as a stone, enduring her suffering rather than allow herself either to waver or be deceived. To Telemachus, it appears excessive, but the excesses of heroes can be what earns their *kleos*. Achilles' excessive grief that morphs into excessive rage and destruction are what he is remembered for. Andromache too is remembered for her excessive grief, a grief so powerful that it becomes immortal, and Hector for his extreme dedication to fulfilling his purpose as the bulwark of the Trojans, even though he knows that it may lead to his death. Odysseus and Penelope both are remembered for their capacity to endure excessive suffering in the hope of fulfilling their return to each other.

Telemachus' speech prompts Penelope to introduce what will become the subject of her final test of Odysseus:

> Now circumspect Penelope spoke to him,
> 'Child of mine, the consciousness in my chest is astonished.
> I am capable neither to speak to him nor to ask him a word,
> Nor to look him directly in the face. If truly
> He is Odysseus, and he is come home, he and I very surely
> Will perceive one another in the preferred way, for there is to us
> A token, which we two know, having hidden it from others.'
>
> (Lines 104–110)

The reference to a token is a familiar conceit in ancient myth narratives: a hero is separated from his or her family and reunion is achieved by some mark, memory or object(s) that identifies him or her. The token that revealed Odysseus to Eurycleia and Eumaeus was his scar, which they were well aware of, having cared for him from a young age. Athena reveals Odysseus to Telemachus by amplifying his appearance. To the suitors, Odysseus reveals himself by stringing his bow, though as with so many other signs, they miss the meaning until he uses the bow to send arrows into their chests. The token that will confirm Odysseus' identity must be something only they two know, and it works both ways. If

Penelope uses it to test Odysseus, then he knows that she cannot have revealed it to anyone else. If she had, then knowledge of it could reach the ears of any man planning to deceive her, and it would no longer be an effective test of Odysseus. Thus, by the end of Penelope's speech, her loyalty to him is confirmed:

> So she spoke, and godlike Odysseus, much enduring, smiled,
> Then he quickly spoke to Telemachus words with wings,
> 'Telemachus, allow your mother now in the great room
> To make a proof of me, she will perceive quickly and in an excellent way.
> Now, because I am dirty, and I wear rough garments on my skin,
> For this reason, she holds me in no honour and up to this time does not claim me for who I am.
> We must ponder how to bring events to the best outcome, for killing any one man among the people,
> Even one who does not have many helpers left behind to avenge him,
> The killer flees, abandoning his kin and native earth.'
>
> (Lines 111–122)

Odysseus concludes his speech by drawing Telemachus' attention away from the private matter between husband and wife and towards the problem that faces them as leaders of Ithaca. They have not slaughtered one man but more than one hundred, and these men have families who will demand compensation or retribution for the deaths of their sons. Telemachus submits to his father's direction, declaring his willingness to follow wherever his father directs him to go. The members of the household dress in their best and dance robustly as the bard sings to the accompaniment of his lyre. The illusion – and reality – is of a wedding feast, but not the one that passers-by might imagine. Hearing the music and dance, they will expect that Penelope has chosen a husband from among her suitors. She has, but that husband is Odysseus. In this way, the deaths of the suitors will at least temporarily remain concealed.

While Odysseus' ruse is being carried out by the household, Eurycleia bathes and anoints him with oil and dresses him in fine clothes, and Athena completes the task by pouring grace and beauty over him and amplifying his stature and the thickness of his hair. In this guise, he presents himself to his wife:

> Stepping from the bath in his form identical to the immortals
> He seated himself again on a chair and made his stand,
> Facing his wife, and towards her he spoke these words,
> '*Daimoni*, in you among all women
> Has been given a hard heart by those who dwell on Olympus.
> No other woman in this way suffering in her consciousness
> Could keep away from her husband, who having suffered so many harmful things,
> Returned after twenty years to the land of his father,
> But come, foster-mother, spread a bed for him, in order that
> I may lie down, for truly, the heart in her perceptions is made of iron.'
>
> (Lines 165–174)

The speech Odysseus addresses to Penelope echoes that of Telemachus earlier, with both repetition (lines 170–171) and variation: this is her husband, not her son, addressing these words to her. He knows what their token is, which they two have hidden from others. He invites Penelope to test him by asking Eurycleia to 'spread a bed for him', and she complies:

> In turn, circumspect Penelope responded,
> '*Daimoni*, I am neither exalting myself nor disregarding you,
> Nor am I very astonished, but I know very well what kind of man you were,
> When you went from Ithaca in the long-oared ships.
> But come, Eurycleia, spread a well-stuffed bed
> Outside the well-built inner room, the one he himself crafted,
> Setting out the well-stuffed bed there, throw down bedding,
> Fleece and cloaks and shining blankets.'
>
> (Lines 175–182)

Penelope does not dispute his claim that 'the heart in her perceptions is made of iron'. She clarifies that she sees them as equal: she is neither elevating herself nor attempting to diminish him. He calls her *daimoni*, an acknowledgement of the immortal power present in her, and she responds in kind. In contrast to the wills of Andromache and Hector, which are fixed on opposing ends, the wills of Odysseus and Penelope are united in mind and feeling, united in a common end. He has invited her to test him, and she sets that test in motion, echoing his request of Eurycleia to set out a bed for him, adding the crucial detail that she should set out the bed that 'he himself crafted'.

> So she spoke, testing her spouse, but Odysseus
> Sorely vexed, addressed his careful-minded wife,
> 'Oh woman, truly this word you spoke is exceedingly heart-grieving to my consciousness.'
>
> (183–186)

After his outburst, Odysseus reveals that the bed cannot be moved because it is built into a tree, then launches into a detailed twenty-line description of how he built the bed (notably, one line for each year he was absent). Their marriage bed being built into a living tree provides a complementary opposite to trees in the *Iliad*: they are mentioned repeatedly in similes that compare heroes who have fallen in battle to trees that are felled to be repurposed for ship timber or chariot wheels. For Odysseus and Penelope, the heroes who live to be reunited, the living bed seems a striking symbol of the nature of their *kleos*: they are remembered for enduring their separation and recovering their 'mortal identities' as husband and wife.

Was Odysseus truly surprised and angered by his wife's instructions to lay out the bed he himself crafted, or is he satisfying the test, proving to Penelope that he is the man who built the bed whose secret only they two know? As with so many other questions, this one can be and has been debated or dissected from endless angles. However one answers these questions, his speech concludes with Penelope finally succumbing to the impulse she had when she first heard of the suitor's slaughter:

> So he spoke, and her knees and her dear heart loosened,
> Recognising the steadfast signs that Odysseus indicated to her,
> She then ran straight to him, pouring tears.
> She threw both her hands around Odysseus' neck and kissed his head and addressed him,
> 'Do not be angry with me, Odysseus, since beyond all others,
> You have understanding among men, the gods sent misery,
> They begrudged us two remaining beside each other
> To delight in our youth and to reach the threshold of old age.
> But now, do not be angry with me or resentful
> That I did not, when I first saw you, treat you with affection,
> For the consciousness in my dear chest always
> Shivered that the words of some mortal man would beguile me,

> For having come, they deliberated many harmful advantages.
> Not even Helen of Argos, born of Zeus,
> Would have mingled in love in the bed of a man from another people,
> If she had known that the sons of the Achaeans, devoted to Ares,
> Intended to lead her back home to her land and her people.
> Truly, a god stirred up unseemly acts for her to do.
> Before then, she did not store up in her consciousness delusion,
> Baneful, from which grief reached us from the start,
> But now, since you have already recounted the token
> Of our bed, which no other mortal man has seen,
> But only you and I and one serving woman alone –
> The daughter of Actor, who my father gave me when I came here,
> Who guarded the doors of our well-built inner room,
> You have persuaded my consciousness, even with it being exceedingly unyielding.'
>
> (Lines 205–230)

Penelope's heart 'loosens', no longer an unyielding stone. By explaining the construction of the bed, Odysseus has 'indicated' the sign that he is truly her husband, that their union is approved by the gods, and she can let down her guard, allow her heart to soften and trust the man sitting before her. The story of the Trojan war comes full circle with Penelope referencing Helen, whose removal from her home and husband resulted in the removal of Odysseus from his. Both were led by a god, Helen away from her home by Aphrodite, Odysseus back to his home by Athena. Telemachus was correct that no other woman could have stayed away from the man claiming to be her husband after twenty years, and it is this very quality that preserved her and enabled Odysseus to achieve his return home from Troy, his *nostos*.

When Penelope concludes her speech to Odysseus, it 'stirred from inside him a greater longing to lament', and he weeps (line 231). The wording is poignantly reminiscent of Priam's supplication to Achilles in *Iliad* book twenty-four: He asks the warrior who has killed his son, and whose body the father seeks to recover, to remember his own father, who will one day be mourning his son's death as Priam is mourning Hector's. His speech 'stirs from inside [Achilles] a longing to lament his father' (line 507). The repetition of these formulaic phrases in two vastly different contexts connects the *kleos* of these four heroes. By seeing themselves in each other, Priam and Achilles experience reintegration, for Achilles with the father of his beloved companion's killer, for Priam with the killer of his son. It is a heart-rending recognition of their mutual connection, their shared experience, and in this moment, they transcend the man-made boundaries of 'friend' and 'enemy'. The ending of the *Odyssey* bestows the joyful reunion that the Trojan heroes and Achilles are denied. Odysseus and Penelope's unity of mind and feeling is expressed in a simile in which 'home' and 'Penelope' fuse:

> He wept, holding his heart-gladdening, trusted, knowing spouse,
> As welcome as when land becomes visible to swimmers,
> Who Poseidon their well-wrought ships into the sea
> Shatters, weighing them down with strong winds and waves,
> A small number escape the grisly sea to reach land,
> Swimming, much brine congeals around their skin,
> Gladly they step on land, having escaped harm.
> Just so, her spouse was welcomed by Penelope, beholding him.
> At this time, she could not quite release his neck from around her two luminous arms.
>
> (Line 232–240)

Odysseus has one more revelation to share with Penelope, a prophecy from Tiresias that Odysseus will again be drawn far from home. He does not want to reveal it in this moment when they are finally celebrating their hard-fought reunion, but Penelope insists,

> Tell me about this trial, since I suppose hereafter
> I will hear it talked about. It would not be inferior to learn it straightaway.
>
> (Lines 261–262)

> Then Odysseus of many devices spoke in reply,
> '*Daimoni*, why do you again urge me exceedingly, encouraging me
> To tell it? But I will speak, and I will conceal nothing.'
>
> (Lines 263–265)

Addressing her as *daimoni* at this moment when she is compelling him to reveal his full story fulfils yet another circle: the genesis of 'songs of fame'.

They begin in stories of grief, loss and reunion that are passed by word of mouth, words with wings that spread across the ages. Odysseus submits to Penelope's request, reporting the prophecy. She shares all that she endured at home while he was away, and he tells her the story of his wanderings, the elaborated version he recited for the Phaeacians now presented as a condensed summary reported by Homer.

If Odysseus and Penelope had lived a long, happy life together, never being torn apart by war, then they would not be remembered for their endurance, cunning and dedication to each other. Their grief has become the source of their *kleos*, but on this occasion, their joyful reunion after twenty years of war and wandering is woven into their 'song of fame'.

Afterword

THE WORLD IN HOMER

THE HOMERIC EPICS tell stories about the heroes who historical listeners would presumably recognise as immortal forces they worship, but the narratives themselves – about conflict and brutality, sacrifice and grief, devotion and reunion – are so timelessly human that we can find meaning in them even without recourse to their own cultural contexts. This is the paradox and the gift of Homer: 'he' is at once among the most familiar figures to us through his texts and the most obscure as a historical person. Whether describing a mother's love, a warrior's anger or an adolescent's need to prove him- or herself, Homer's insights into human dynamics remain as startlingly relevant as his world can feel remote. Yet we can say little with certainty about where he was from or where and how his songs came to be written down.

Not only modern readers but ancient ones too wanted an 'author' to connect with, as we want to know who this Homer was who could convey the experiences of warriors and mothers, enslaved swineherds and barley grinders, young people on the cusp of adulthood and esteemed elders with such acute sensitivity and insight. Since as early as the third century BC, scholars and readers have sought answers to the question of who Homer was and been denied definitive answers. Since that time, the *Iliad* and *Odyssey* have been experienced in some way uninterrupted. At all times since they first appeared, somewhere in the world, in some way, humans have been engaging with Homer's epics. Memorising and reciting them in Greek, reading them in translation, composing poetry, dramas, films, operas and symphonies in conversation with them, creating visual images inspired by them, writing novels and anthologies that retell them, producing scholarship that analyses them.

What we can take away from this abundance of literature, music, art, and scholarship around Homer is that there are as many ways to engage with, retell and interpret the epics as there are readers of them. And sometimes, not even direct readers but anyone who has encountered Homer's ideas, plots and figures may engage with them in some way. When we talk about Homer, we are talking not only about the texts of his epics that have survived into our time but also about the readers of those texts who have influenced our perception of them. Our experience of Homer is necessarily filtered through countless others' experiences of Homer. Thus, to approach Homer and the men and women whose voices his epics carry, to hear them through the noise and static of millennia of reception, we may begin by asking why these songs were deemed so important that they travelled so far and wide. We may wonder, too, why they were written down at all. Exploring potential answers to these questions takes us back to the beginning, to the period when he first enters the historical record in the sixth century BC.

Roman rhetorician Quintilian described Homer as 'the river from which all literature flows', and Homer's epics have inspired millennia of artistic and scholarly production. But while they became the beginning of a literary tradition, they also heralded the end of an oral one. If a person called Homer, who orally composed epics that were something like our *Iliad* and *Odyssey*, existed, we have no way of recovering who this person was. The noun *homeros* can mean *hostage*, *captive* or *pledge for maintaining unity*. The latter reflects the function that the epics assumed in the classical period as sacred texts that explained the Greeks' cosmology, rituals and common culture. Used as a proper noun, the name *Homeros*, Latinised as Homer, was attached to eight epics about the Trojan war and its aftermath from the sixth century BC onwards. Together these epics told the story of the war, from its origins through its aftermath. By the end of the classical period in the mid-fourth century, however, only the epics that were transmitted via a textual tradition and that have survived into our time as the *Iliad* and *Odyssey* were believed to have been composed by Homer, and they were, likely not coincidentally, believed to be the best of them.

As noted above, the earliest references to Homer in connection with narratives about the Trojan war appear in written sources from sixth-century Athens. As Graziosi notes in *Inventing Homer*, her study of the early reception of Homer, these ancient sources do not refer to texts or poems but to songs, which reportedly travelled orally from this figure referred to as Homer, to those closely associated with him, to civic leaders who brought the songs back to their respective cities. Recitations of these songs were incorporated into sacred festivals to honour the gods and heroes of cities, most famously the Great Panathenaea in Athens.

Ancient sources seemed to relish telling stories about Homer – where he was from, what he was like, how he spent his time. Graziosi notes that these stories tend to be inconsistent and conflicting, but two recurring features are descriptions of him as impoverished and blind. The latter is a quality linked with prophets, seers and (in the *Odyssey*) bards, which speaks to the idea that gifts from the gods come with a price. In this case, immortal gifts of vision into the eternal require the sacrifice of vision of the ephemeral.

Graziosi further notes that no extant sources connect the figure of Homer, as a poet, composer or song-maker, to a written text. Nor do any describe him writing his songs down or even possessing a text of his songs. Unlike his rough contemporary Hesiod, who with Homer provides the earliest sources for Greek mythological narratives and who tells stories about himself in his poems, the Homeric epics do not refer to who composed them, and they make only two passing references to something resembling writing. Instead, they refer, via the description of bards, to a creative process of composing songs orally in the act of performing them. We encounter two of these in the *Odyssey:* Phemius in Odysseus' home of Ithaca, and Demodocus in the Phaeacian court that Odysseus visits on his way home. The latter is described in terms that evoke Homer himself. He is blind, and the gods have given him 'the whole song' from which he can 'bring solace in whichever direction his consciousness moves him to sing' (book eight, lines 44-45).

Dating Homer and the origins of his epics

As with the question of Homer's identity, when the epics were composed remains concealed behind a veil of uncertainty. Greek written inscriptions begin to appear in the mid-eighth century BC. Based on the belief that it takes at least a generation or more to learn how to use a new technology, in this case written language, it has been theorised that the Greek alphabet was probably adapted in the early eighth century, some arguing as early as 800. Prior to the development of this Greek alphabet, there is no surviving evidence of Greek speakers using written language to record myth narratives, though earlier writing systems had existed.

One theory has suggested that the alphabet was adapted to record the epics. Another has argued that a bard called Homer may have impressed someone who had learned the already extant alphabetic system and who then decided to apply it to record the bard's songs. Yet another has proposed that a bard called Homer existed long before writing, and his epics were passed down orally until someone wrote them down, perhaps no earlier than the sixth century BC. Theories abound, each leaving a trail of intriguing questions but no definitive answers.

Complicating the question of Homer's identity and dating, the language of the epics cannot be pinned down to one time or place. They incorporate a range of dialects from different parts of the ancient Greek-speaking world as well as references within the surviving texts that situate them in a range of historical periods. Some language and references seem to have come down from the Bronze Age historical period (approximately 3300–1200 BC) or even earlier while others may be as late as the end of the eighth century BC. Nor can it be assumed, from the language, references and themes, that the basic stories of the *Iliad* and *Odyssey* are Greek in origin.

The Near Eastern epic of *Gilgamesh*, whose earliest extant tablets date to the third millennium BC, may offer insight into pre-Greek myths and legends. Unlike Homer's epics, whose earliest texts have been treated as transcripts or scripts for oral performance, surviving versions of *Gilgamesh* are believed to be scribal compositions rather than remains of oral performances. While Homer's epics grow increasingly less multiform after they are written down, *Gilgamesh* retains its multiformity even as it is passed down in written language. Alongside these differences exists a significant commonality: both *Gilgamesh* and the Homeric epics are believed to have had a role in ritual worship of gods and demigods, and the gods and demigods whose stories these epics narrate were also worshipped in sacred rituals during the time their stories were circulating.

In addition to sharing ritual significance, versions of *Gilgamesh* feature themes, characters and narratives that echo in Homer's epics. A few notable examples include anxiety about leadership, the importance of supplicating immortal forces and the need for mortals to reconcile with their mortality. Further, Homer's Phaeacians and *Gilgamesh*'s Uta-napishti both live outside of time. Homer's Odysseus and Gilgamesh both descend to the land of the dead. The companions of Homer's Odysseus die after consuming the cattle of the Sun god; *Gilgamesh*'s Enkidu dies after he and Gilgamesh kill the bull of heaven. In Homer's *Iliad*, Aphrodite complains to her mother Dione, whose name is a feminised version of Zeus, the sky god, who is Dia in Greek; in the Standard Babylonian version of *Gilgamesh,* Ishtar complains to her mother Antu, whose name is a feminised version of Anu, the sky god. In both Homer and *Gilgamesh*, gods' immortality renders them unable to relate to human consequences. The similarities are striking enough to suggest that Homer may descend from a cultural continuum with roots in the Near East.

As noted above, our Homer is texts that we refer to as 'poetry', a sub-genre of literature. But the uncertainty around who composed them, when they were composed and where they were composed alerts us that these texts differ fundamentally from literature that we are accustomed to encountering. Though we categorise them as literary texts, the earliest known references to Homer's epics are not to poems but to songs. Though they are composed in what we think of as a literary metre, their content predates written language. Though they are attached to an 'author', no reliable extant evidence exists about this person. Though they are composed in Greek, an antecedent of them, *Gilgamesh*, emerged from the Near East. Though they tell stories about gods and heroes, these gods and heroes were not treated as fictions but as immortal forces that were worshipped in historical time. These incongruities invite us to investigate, then, what these texts that we have received into the modern period are doing, how what they are doing diverges from our modern concepts of literature, and what the implications are for approaching and understanding these texts and the women within them.

On a thematic level, the *Iliad* and *Odyssey* are cosmological narratives: they tell stories about the relationships between immortal forces and mortal bodies. The *Iliad* is concerned with events during the Trojan war, the *Odyssey* with its aftermath. In both, the immortals are intimately involved with mortal outcomes. The events in the *Iliad* are described as fulfilling 'the plan of Zeus', and the gods descend into battle on behalf of their favourites, even directly fighting each other. In the *Odyssey*, Athena guides Penelope, Telemachus and Odysseus to ensure the latter's successful return home.

As Graziosi and Johannes Haubold explore in *The Resonance of Epic*, when Homer's epics are set against contemporaneous cosmological texts, notably Hesiod's *Theogony* and *Works and Days*, they seem to carry the listener through a transition: from a time when mortals and immortals were in direct and consistent communication in the *Iliad* to a time when immortals communicate less directly and consistently with mortals in the *Odyssey*. Hesiod's texts narrate this transition in macro terms. *Theogony* presents a genealogy of the gods, from the creation of the cosmos to the ascension of Zeus and the Olympians, concluding with a catalogue of their notable god and demigod children. In *Works and Days*, Hesiod explains why mortals must toil and suffer (because it is the will of Zeus) and provides practical advice for living a just and prosperous life. Framing his narrative in *Works and Days* are two myths that we have considered briefly since both bear on the Homeric epics: the five ages of mortals and the creation of Pandora.

The first three ages of mortals created by the immortals are all named for metals. First is the gold age, who live free of suffering. When this age ends, the mortals are honoured as *daimones*, superhuman forces, who watch over and bring wealth to mortals. The second and third ages, silver and bronze respectively, each successively devolve. The silver race fails to honour the immortals sufficiently, angering Zeus, and the excessively violent bronze age destroys itself. The fourth is the age of heroes, the predecessor of the 'current' age, the age of iron, to which Hesiod belongs. The wars at Troy for the sake of Helen and at Thebes bring the age of heroes to an end. But Zeus resettles the *olbioi heroes*, blissful heroes, to a *makaron nesoisie*, island of the blessed, where they live without cares. After Prometheus gives mortal men fire against Zeus' wishes, the god punishes men by giving them Pandora, in whom pleasure and pain are interwoven.

It is tempting to map the events of Homeric epics onto the cosmology of Hesiod: Hesiod's Trojan war is the one in which Homer's Achilles and Odysseus fight. Helen, like Pandora, is a figure who brings both pleasure and pain. Like the mortals of Hesiod's time, Odysseus must accept and endure his suffering. However, Graziosi and Haubold's word 'resonance' encourages a more flexible association. The worlds of Homer and Hesiod can be understood to have emerged from the same cultural consciousness that believed heroes belonged to an earlier generation of mortals who were descended directly from and in close communication with the gods. After fulfilling their mortal lives, these heroes of myth became immortal forces who were worshipped in ritual during the historical time of Homer and Hesiod. As Nagy has expressed, through the narratives of Achilles and Odysseus, the Homeric epics communicated to Greek speakers what is most essential to remember about the heroes they worshipped in seasonally recurring ritual festivals. The myths and the rituals framed each other.

Oral storytelling

It is commonplace to say of Homer that he worked within 'a tradition of oral storytelling', but the implications of this can be harder to conceptualise for modern readers within a literate culture. When we speak of literature, we are referring to compositions constructed in written language. These may – as with Vergil's *Aeneid* or Shakespeare's *Julius Caesar* or John Keats' 'Ode on a Grecian Urn' or James Joyce's *Ulysses* – interact with pre-existing myths, legends and history, but these literary texts are expected to function as self-contained wholes. Each element is expected to serve the coherence and unity of that whole. Originality with respect to syntax, diction and themes is lauded.

These expectations are subverted when we are confronted with the orally composed epics of Homer. In them, we encounter frequent repetition of phrases, scenes and story patterns. Characters may drop in for one scene and never be heard from again, without seeming to move the narrative in what we would deem, by the standards of literature, an essential way. Descriptive phrases attached to the names of immortals and heroes are repeated again and again, sometimes seeming to contradict events of the moment. Even large blocks of text may reappear across the epics. A variety of verse forms, notably lament, lyric and epigram, appear stitched into the larger epics. Details within the narratives do not always correspond: books one and eighteen of the *Iliad*, for example, provide different explanations for Hephaestus' physical disability. The epics are composed in dactylic hexameter but attempts to scan them in Greek as one would a modern English poem can quickly turn frustrating.

Translators, popular writers and scholars have, in the past, dismissed these qualities as unsophisticated and simplistic, markers of a less developed system. This criticism has especially been levelled at 'formulas' – the repeated phrases, scenes and story patterns, which are the epics' building blocks – with some English translators opting to scrub them out entirely. By striving to reconstruct the thought world of ancient listeners and composers, the works of scholars such as Milman Parry, Albert Lord, John Notopoulos, John Miles Foley, Gregory Nagy and Casey Due, among others, have illuminated the unity and coherence of the oral storytelling tradition out of which the Homeric epics are composed. Homer, then, is not 'inferior' or 'unsophisticated' literature because it is not 'literature'.

One way for modern readers to conceptualise how formulas work in Homer is by thinking of Lego. The blocks are 'formulaic': they come in a set number of sizes and colours, yet depending on how they are put together, they can create structures of astonishing complexity, sophistication and originality. Viewing such structures, we can see the formula, but we can also see the ingenuity enabled by the adaptability of the building system.

Instrumental in opening new avenues to understanding Homer as orally composed was the research of Milman Parry in the early part of the twentieth century, which revealed that Homeric diction was built on a system of formulas that predate literacy in Greek. Formulas are used to build what are commonly referred to as 'type scenes' (for example, scenes of feasting, dressing, receiving guests, making sacrifices), and type scenes are used to build songs. Here, the word 'song' highlights that Homeric compositions did not come to life on a length of papyrus but emerged in performances. The implications of this are significant. They raise questions about singularity, which we are accustomed to expecting in the study of literature: we want to know which is the 'true' text – the true Shakespeare, the true Mary Wollstonecraft Shelley. If Homer's epics were transmitted orally, and texts of them were not, as Graziosi notes, important enough to merit mention, and the earliest recorded versions were scripts or transcripts, what did it mean for a song to be recognised as the work of 'Homer'?

Anyone who has performed in or attended performances of the same 'script' may notice that no two performances are exactly the same. The audience participates in the creation of meaning and the shaping of a particular version of the 'script', whether a bard singing with a lyre in homes as we see depicted within Homer or a rhapsode reciting the epics at a festival in archaic and classical Greece. Nagy notes that audiences in Homer can request particular versions of the song, as in the *Odyssey* when Odysseus asks Demodocus to sing about the Trojan horse or ask the singer to stop and sing a different song, as Penelope does to Phemius. Studies of other song cultures bear out some of these theories as well. Hearers within an oral traditional system know the stories being performed, and they hold special meaning for these hearers. The meaning of the story emerges in the interaction between the performer and the receivers.

After Parry's premature death in 1935, his associate Albert Lord carried on his research, and he proposed two concepts coexisting in Homeric song: the essence of the story that remains stable (for example, that the Trojan war occurred and that Odysseus returned home to Ithaca after it) and the variability associated with performances, each of which was itself a discrete work of art. As Lord and Parry discovered in their study of twentieth-century Serbo-Croatian bards, while the researchers noted variations across performances, the bards themselves asserted that they performed the 'same' song each time.

Yet it remains that what we have received in the modern world is a set of texts, through manuscripts, papyrus fragments, references and summaries. What happened across these thousands of years is complex, difficult to untangle and the topic of ongoing debate. As Graziosi has expressed eloquently of the *Iliad*, it is 'a text that is not a text'. A central question that continues to be debated, then, is not only whether there was an 'original' Homeric text but also, if there was, whether we could ever access it. Perhaps it is more accurate to think not of an 'original' text that could ever be recovered but of the first time a Homeric performance was recorded in written language. Perhaps, too, this first time is not necessarily more 'Homeric' than performances that were recorded subsequently. The word Nagy favours for referring to the multiplicity of Homeric *Iliad*s is 'multiformity': the idea that there is not one Homeric *Iliad* but potentially many that archaic and classical Greek audiences would have recognised as

'Homeric' epics. The repetition and variation draw attention to both what is distinct and what is part of the recurring cycle of human experiences and events, which are evoked in ritual.

John Miles Foley suggests that rather than conceptualising Homer as an 'author' in the literate sense, perhaps he can be better understood as a personification of bardic tradition.[1] A fragment of a marble relief dating to the third century BC known as the *Apotheosis of Homer* can offer a way of conceptualising Homer in this way. The relief features four levels. On the bottom level, Chronos (Time) and Oikoumene (the Inhabited World) crown a seated Homer, who holds a sceptre and a scroll. Personified figures of the *Iliad* and *Odyssey* sit at his feet. On the right-hand side, various figures lead a sacrificial bull to an altar set in front of the bard. Hands and torches are raised in worship. The second and third levels may depict the slopes of Mount Helicon, populated by the nine Muses and Apollo playing his lyre. At the top, Zeus and Mnemosyne (Memory), the parents of the Muses, look at one another. Returning to one potential meaning of Homer's name, *a pledge for the maintenance of unity* invites us to think of Homer as the hero of oral storytelling and oral storytelling as a system that fused past, present and future together through seasonally recurring, communal re-enactments performed under the watchful eyes of the immortals.

Homer in the world

Recent years have seen a flood of novels that retell ancient myths centring women's perspectives. Circe, Clytemnestra, Atalanta, Elektra and Ariadne have all featured, to name just a few. A shared stated intention among these novels is a desire to recover the voices of ancient mythical women. Two questions this intention invites are: what does it mean to have a voice in the myths of the ancient world, and to what extent are we as modern readers equipped to hear these voices? To explore these questions, it is helpful to examine the categories around which we organise our world and to set them alongside those that organised the ancient Greek world from which Greek mythology and Homer emerged.

We began to examine these categories in the previous section, suggesting that the Homer of archaic and classical Greece could perhaps better be thought of as a tradition rather than an individual and as dynamic songs that unfold across time in performance rather than as static texts fixed in time at the moment they are written down. Across this book we have attempted to attune our minds such that we can hear Homer's women. In the process, we have begun to perceive that the categories we use to organise our modern world are not interchangeable with those that the ancients used.

Myth, legend, history

When we encounter ancient myths in modern novels, we do so as readers of fiction. Generally speaking (though not always), modern readers do not approach ancient myths as sacred stories about the immortals and heroes they worship in the present. As noted in the previous section, archaic and classical Greeks would have engaged with these myths in communal settings, often also in the context of sacred rituals to propitiate immortal forces who they hoped would apply their power for the city's advantage. Implied in this approach is that we read myths through the lens of categories that did not yet exist for the earliest ancient people who told, heard and saw myth narratives.

One significant difference is that we tend to treat myth, legend and history as discrete categories in ways that seemingly did not exist when the epics were written down, whether in the eighth or the sixth centuries BC. This began to change across the classical period, and we can debate the extent to which, even today, these categories can be seen as distinct. Nevertheless, it is important to note that we have different ways of understanding these phenomena that the ancients did not. As permeable as boundaries may be, we create categories to organise our world, and these categories reveal what is important to us. For us, then, it seems important to differentiate myths (cosmological stories that explain the origins of the world and the place of immortals and mortals within it), from legends (stories that may have had a grain of truth and that became grander and more embellished over time), from history (past happenings that can be documented).

The Homeric poems incorporated – and generated about themselves – myths, legends and history without seeming to need to differentiate among them. The epics tell us about immortals and heroes. They feature names that can be associated with documentable historical places and people, as, for example, the words Achaeans and Ilium have corollaries in the Near East during the Bronze Age historical period. The epics tell stories about a war and a homecoming hero, both potentially historical realities, even if we cannot definitively tie them to the specific figures and events

Homer sang about. These conflations invite us to be mindful, when we are trying to hear Homer's women, of modern terms, concepts, and modes of thought that we may import into our reading of Homer.

The Bronze Age: history and myth

The historical Bronze Age was characterised by urban, literate societies that were administratively distinct but linked via trade and trade routes, which enabled cultural exchanges among civilisations on three continents in the Mediterranean basin. Evidence of these cultural exchanges live on in the resonances across stories that have come down to us from the ancient world – notably the *Iliad*, *Odyssey*, Babylonian epic *Gilgamesh* and creation myth *Enuma Elish*, the Hebrew Bible and Hesiod. The Bronze Age collapsed dramatically around 1200 BC, likely a consequence of a series of stressors – climate change, drought and famine, migration, invasion, civil strife. After the collapse, the Greek world seems to have lost its writing system until alphabetic writing appears in the eighth century.

A question that inevitably arises when we talk about Homer and Trojan war mythology is: was there really a Trojan war that corresponds with the Bronze Age collapse? As with the figure of Homer, the answer to this question is not straightforward. That there were wars is almost certain, and archaeological finds support the possibility of a war in the region referenced in the epics during the historical Bronze Age. Whether it was the war Homer sang about, we cannot know definitively. For the Greeks, the Trojan war was truth not necessarily because it was factually accurate but because it communicated true experiences that people lived through which eternally recurred: peace was fragile because conflict was inevitable, and war brought on destruction for all involved.

The stories, or parts of the stories, we refer to collectively as 'Greek mythology' may have been carried forward for hundreds, perhaps even thousands, of years, from the Bronze Age and earlier, but they are set in a mythical (in the modern sense) past, at a time when immortals and heroes were perhaps too close for comfort. As suggested by Hesiod's *Works and Days*, and as is evident in the *Iliad* and Odyssey, heroes were excessive, potentially both protective and destructive figures. Their conflicts spilled over into the immortal realm, causing strife to break out among the gods and goddesses who fought one another on behalf of their favourites. For there to be stability and balance, the age of heroes had to come to an end. This mythical past has, at times, been conflated with the Bronze Age historical period. The confusion may in part arise because of Hesiod's 'bronze age of heroes' and the presence of Bronze Age historical elements within the epics. The confusion can also arise due to our own desire to map the myths onto the past, but the certainty and clarity we seek was not necessarily of concern to the ancients who passed on the stories of their immortals and heroes.

Reception of mythology

As we have seen, not only Homer but also Greek mythology more broadly is not a collection of texts but a collection of stories that concern mortal bodies and immortal forces and that had special meaning for the people who told them. Parts of these stories may have existed for hundreds or potentially thousands of years, predating the Greeks themselves. Homer and Hesiod are the oldest textual sources for these stories in the Greek language and thus have been described as providing Greek speakers a template for understanding the immortal forces they honoured in ritual. Since the first texts about them appeared, stories about these gods and heroes continued to be narrated in verse and prose and performed in public across the pagan Greek and Roman worlds until approximately the fourth century AD.

Across this roughly one-thousand-year period, the Greek world moved from largely oral – meaning that texts were created for a particular context and were experienced in some kind of performance – to literate. In *Homer's Text and Language*, Nagy argues that the shift from orality to literacy in the Greek world was a gradual process that occurred across the archaic, classical and Hellenistic periods. According to Nagy, this shift corresponds to the Homeric epics becoming less fluid and more fixed, which reaches its peak during the second century BC, when the texts assumed the status of scripture and Homer the status of a figure of divine authority.

During this literate period, verse and prose continued to be performed and recited, but texts were also travelling great distances, being collected in libraries and studied by scholars. In addition, these texts could be read by people who not only were not present at a particular performance but also could be receiving that text in a very different social and political context. It is at this point that we can begin to speak of 'poetry' produced by 'writers', meaning individuals who composed within a literate culture, attached their names to their work and understood that it could travel beyond its context and be experienced as texts rather than performances.

Another important shift occurred during this period that influenced the evolution and reception of Greek mythology up to our own time, which is the conquest of the Greek world by the Roman Republic during the second and first centuries BC. In 27 BC, a few years after Roman leader Octavian's defeat of Cleopatra, the Greek-speaking queen of the Ptolemaic empire centred in Alexandria, and Roman general Antony, the Roman Republic became the Roman Empire, and Octavian became its first emperor, Augustus Caesar. The emerging empire needed a foundation myth that would legitimise it, and Roman poet Vergil provided that myth with the *Aeneid*, his epic that simultaneously pays homage to Homer and seeks to supplant it as a foundational text.

Composed during the transitional period between Republic and Empire, the *Aeneid* narrates Aeneas' flight from the ravaged, burning city of Troy with his father (past) and son (future), his wanderings across the Mediterranean in search of a new home and his discovery that the Trojans' ancestral homeland was Rome all along. There, Aeneas fulfils the imperative thrust upon him to found a new empire, which will in turn avenge the sack of Troy by conquering the Greek world. That 'Greeks' did not exist in Homer – they were called Achaeans, Danaans and Argives – is cleverly elided, as is that the Achaeans and Trojans are not represented as inherently 'friends' and 'enemies'.[2] In Homer, destructive conflicts arise because of personal grievances: the Achaeans come to Troy because Paris violated Zeus' sacred law of hospitality when he left Sparta with his host's wife, Helen. In crafting his epic for the empire, Vergil self-consciously blurs the boundaries between myth and history, as we would think of those terms in our time, framing the emperors of his time as descendants of Aeneas. In doing so, he infuses the establishment of the Roman Empire with a sense of cosmic intention and the emperors, who would be deified, with immortal favour.

Arguably the most influential Roman poet to our understanding of 'Greek' mythology is Ovid, who, like Vergil, composed during the reign of Augustus but a generation later. Characteristic of Empire poetry, Ovid likewise intertwines myth and history. His *Metamorphoses* is a cosmological poem that purports to cover the totality of history, from the origin of the cosmos to the historical present of Ovid's time. It is a veritable encyclopaedia of Greek myths told, self-consciously by Ovid, through a Roman lens. The poem appropriates Greek myths to explore the relationship between power and vulnerability, not as in the Greek world in performances at sacred festivals to honour gods and heroes but in court contexts to demonstrate imperial power and all its implications. The poem's title, *Metamorphoses*, is a transliteration in Latin of the Greek word meaning *transformation*; in the first line, Ovid shifts to the Latin word, *mutatas*, brilliantly and economically embodying one of the poem's themes from the first line. A pattern across the poem is the suffering that falls heavily on those who challenge powerful forces, as Ovid himself perhaps understood or would come to understand, given he would spend the final decade of his life in exile.

When we read modern myth anthologies and novel retellings, we are often reading a blend of different versions of myths pulled from both Greek and Latin texts which were composed and experienced in vastly different social and religious contexts. Characterisations and events portrayed in Greek reception of Greek mythology – via Homer, Pindar, Hesiod and the classical Athenian tragedians Aeschylus, Sophocles and Euripides, among others – may be mixed with characterisations and events portrayed in Roman reception of Greek mythology, such as by Augustan poets Vergil in the *Aeneid* and Ovid in the *Metamorphoses*, among others. Both are brilliant Roman epics that have had a lasting influence on Trojan war mythology and more broadly on what we call 'Greek' mythology, but they are Roman interpretations of Greek mythology that were composed for their own social and political contexts. Generally, in archaic and classical Greek narratives, composers of verse are engaging with the storytelling tradition at large. They are composing narratives for performance at sacred festivals. In the Hellenistic and Roman empires, poets engage not only with a tradition of telling stories about immortals and heroes but also with specific texts and the composers associated with them. While poetry continued to be publicly presented, it was not necessarily in a festival context, and it could travel as a text beyond the boundaries of its performance.

Not only myth anthologies and retellings but any discussion of Greek mythology, including this one, is necessarily partial and requires curation, and any time there is a curation process, there is a purpose. Some versions and episodes are highlighted, others omitted, to develop a particular interpretation on the part of the composer. This is not so different from how classical and archaic composers constructed their narratives, which is why myth narratives from these periods can be so variable. Thus, when we speak in broad terms about 'Greek' mythology, we are often referring to a vast range of contradictory and complementary approaches and depictions. This is especially important to bear in mind when we speak about mythical women because both Greek and Roman versions can vary considerably in how they depict these women, and in both cases, while the material lives of women in composers' own time may influence how they depict them, we cannot map one onto the other with precision.

Homer's women are not necessarily Sappho's, Aeschylus', Euripides' or Apollonius of Rhodes', nor are they Vergil's or Ovid's. Each composer or poet tells the familiar stories for his and her own purposes, as do modern novelists, poets and playwrights. Each may be 'true' to her or his time and experiences, and all benefit from being approached within the context of their creations. By understanding how the myths are approached and why they are approached that way, whether from the perspectives of composers or receivers of them, we enable ourselves to be drawn into the dialogue that Homer invites, both within 'his' epics and around them: to explore what it means to be human, to grapple with events bigger than we can control and to wrestle back agency by creating even from the most devastating and heart-breaking experiences something beautiful, meaningful and lasting.

Appendix 1

WORD GUIDE

IN THE PREFACE, I touched on my general thought process and approach to translation and what I hoped to make visible by including my own renderings of selected passages from the *Iliad* and *Odyssey*. This section is intended to draw attention to words and concepts that are especially challenging to translate into Greek, how I've chosen to render them and the inspiration and lasting questions behind my choices.

A challenge of rendering Homer is that his epics feature several dialects associated with different times and places in the ancient world, including inherited phrases whose meaning was debated even in antiquity. This is also what makes Homer so thrilling to read in Greek and tempting to translate. Each word, many of which have been subjected to extensive study and debate, holds many possible meanings. The choices we make among these meanings are, as noted above, driven by various and at times competing necessities that have had consequences especially on how women in the epics are understood. My intention here is to bring as much transparency as possible to the challenges associated with rendering Homer's Greek into any modern language and to invite dialogue over the choices.

Two inspirations that have strongly influenced me are not derived from research but are purely lived experiences. Those are growing up as a native speaker of modern Greek and travelling to Greece annually for extended periods of time. Living the Greek language and culture has inevitably shaped my reception of Homer, as Homer's insights into human dynamics, approaches to immortal forces and vocabulary have shaped Greek language and culture from the seventh century BC onwards. Whether or not Greeks have always had access to the texts of Homer, aspects of his language suffuse the Greek language, even as it has evolved and been reshaped, and in the lived experience of Greek speakers.

We can see this in the repeated presence of the exclamatory statement *o po po*,[1] which is still in use. It lives on in the bits of what we might call folk wisdom[2] and humorous asides.[3] Culturally, the importance we find in Homer of dialogue and debate, of recognising personal grievance as the source of conflict rather than the inherent 'goodness' or 'badness' of a people or culture at large, of differentiating the laws of men from the laws of the immortals and the central place of family and hospitality have all been carried forward by Greek-speaking communities across time, whatever political forces have governed their lives in other respects. This is not to say that these values are unique to or shared by all Greek speakers but that the Greek language itself carries resonances of Homer.[4]

Having grown up in this language has inevitably sensitised me to these aspects of Homer in ways that cannot entirely be quantified. But one way that it makes its way into my translations is especially with my preference for concreteness over abstraction (more on this below in the context of specific words). A second is in my sensitivity to the dual presence of everyday and sacred meanings coexisting within the same word. Another final significant influence is that it has sensitised me to how much is lost in translation any time we move from one language to another. Having spent my lifetime moving between these two languages, Greek and English, I have experienced every day how impossible it is to be literal, how much has to be sacrificed from one language to another and how easy it is to misunderstand something because it seems familiar.[5]

Breath of life (*Iliad*), mortal identity (*Odyssey*) – *psyche*

The Greek word *psyche* troubled me in my intention to render words consistently for readers in translation. I worked from Nagy's description of the *psyche* as the animating breath of the hero in life and the 'conveyer' of the hero's identity after the mortal body's death. The challenge for me was to keep it consistent across the *Iliad* and *Odyssey*, which I ultimately decided against.

In the *Iliad*, *breath of life* felt like the appropriate choice because the epic is concerned with mortality, with the hero facing his death and releasing his mortal body.[6] In the *Odyssey*, however, Odysseus is not striving to reconcile himself with his *psyche* leaving his body. Rather, he is striving to recover his *psyche*: 'He experienced at sea many sorrows upon his consciousness / Striving to recover his *psyche* and the *nostos* of his companions' (book one, lines 4–5). In this case, to render *psyche* as *breath of life* would not quite make sense, since Odysseus is, in the narrative sense, still alive. Drawing inspiration from Nagy's description of the *psyche* as the conveyer of the hero's identity, I felt *mortal identity* would be most apt: Odysseus is striving not only to return home but to regain his mortal identity as the husband of Penelope.

Cause – *aitia*

As with so many Greek words, *aitia*, from which derives the word 'aetiology', holds many meanings. As a noun, it can refer to a charge or accusation, an occasion or opportunity, a cause or a source. Its verb form can mean *to charge, accuse, censure,* or *blame*. I chose to render it *cause* to restrain, as much as possible, from judgement. In his first speech in *Odyssey* book one, Zeus says, 'Alas! See how at this time mortals *aitionmai* the gods' (line 32). We could assume from this that Zeus is complaining that mortals 'blame' the gods, and this is how it has typically been translated. I preferred to render this line, and others like it, 'Alas! See how at this time mortals assign causation to the gods', because I hoped to highlight the dynamic between immortal and mortal wills that seems to preoccupy the ancient Greeks. Who is the first mover? Is it the immortals or the mortals themselves? Is Fate the sole source of outcomes? What role do human strengths and frailties play in how the immortals work through them? These do not have clear and definitive answers in Homer, but they are fascinating to explore through and with his creations.

Circumspect – *periphron*

The most literal translation of *periphron* is *thinking all around*, and it is the epithet applied to Penelope and Eurycleia in the *Odyssey*. After much thought and experimentation, I came to believe that *circumspect*, a popular choice in existing translations, captures the many qualities that make up Penelope's character and that enable her to achieve her *nostos* with Odysseus. She is discreet, vigilant, guarded and watchful. She has foresight, patience and the capacity to approach a problem from a variety of perspectives.

Colour words

What I referred to earlier as the 'concreteness' of the Greek language most influenced me in how I rendered Homer's colours. In every instance that

I can think of, what we call colour words have, in Homer, some observable presence in the material world, whether it is an object itself (e.g. steel, ink, honey, blood) or a quality that emerges from an observed phenomenon (e.g. the play of light and surface).[7] For this reason, I opted to tether what we might think of in more abstract terms – white, black, light, dark – to a corollary in the natural world.

As anyone who has travelled to Greece may have noticed, the sun is exceedingly strong and nearly ever-present, and this impacts how we experience colours. The light it casts on the Aegean heightens its natural gradations of colour: it can appear at times clear on top and dense and dark on the bottom, much as the mixture of water and wine may have appeared to the ancients, hence perhaps Homer's *wine-coloured* or *wine-dark* sea. Dawn's throne is *golden*, suggesting both the metal and the brilliance of light reflecting off it. Her fingers, though, are *rosy*, a reference to roses (perennial in temperate climates). The *dark, gleaming* wool Arete spins and cloth Andromache and Helen weave is *porphyrein* in Greek, used also to describe reflected light off of blood and troubled waters.

What we often see rendered as *white* and *dark* provided an engaging challenge, but here again, each usage could potentially connect to the observable world. When *dark* is described as *melas*, I rendered it *ink-dark*. When it is described as *kyaneos*, I rendered it *steel-dark*, and when it is describing clouds associated with Zeus, *kelainefis*, I rendered it *blood-dark*. Similarly, nothing is necessarily 'white' in Homer, as we might imagine the colour. The word often translated as *white* is *leuko*, but this word can refer to the play of light and surface or to a density of colour (or lack thereof). This can be seen in a line describing Penelope in book eighteen: 'More luminous (*leuko*) than freshly sawed ivory' (line 186). We might immediately be inclined to associate ivory with the colour white, but freshly sawed ivory might also be especially susceptible to a flash of light. Ino is similarly described as *Leukothea*, which has been translated as *the White Goddess*, but if her transformation into an immortal occurred the moment she entered the sea, as a version of her myth attests, and if Zeus were believed to have immortalised her as he is described immortalising Heracles, with a thunderbolt, could *leuko* speak again to the play of light and surface?

Consciousness – *thumos*

The word *thumos* presents a challenge conceptually, and I cannot say that my choice to render it *consciousness* feels exactly right. According to Nagy, the *thumos* is the 'realm of consciousness', the life force of the hero, incorporating both emotive and rational capacities, as with *perceptions/phrenes* below. Ruth Padel describes the *thumos* as an animating force that drives desires and actions.[8] Translations have typically rendered it *heart, spirit, mind, feeling* or *thinking*. As is also true of *perceptions/phrenes*, it was important to me to translate the word consistently so that readers who do not have Greek would be able to recognise that the same word was being used in different contexts. Thus, to translate it as either/or depending on context was not satisfying for my purpose. In one sense, this is impractical since the word may not mean the same thing each time it is mentioned. In another sense, it allows me to forestall making the judgement about which meaning is being invoked and leave it for the reader to ponder. The compromise I chose was *consciousness*, which I settled on for two reasons: (1) to differentiate it from *phrenes* and (2) to capture the idea of the life force, the fully conscious self.

The one exception to my 'repeat what is repeated' rule with regard to *thumos* is when it is paired with *megas* in the epithet that describes heroes: *great-hearted*. It was simply too unwieldy and slightly ridiculous to render it consciousness, so I deferred to the wisdom and choice of past translators.

Daimoni

As noted earlier, Nagy describes a *daimon* as a 'superhuman force' that intervenes in mortal affairs. To render *daimon* as 'superhuman force' felt both clunky and incomplete, since it is a particular application of superhuman force. I chose to leave this word untranslated, not only because I discuss the meaning of it at length in the introduction but also because some words ultimately resist our attempts to translate. I appreciate this acknowledgement when I am reading texts translated from languages I do not have knowledge of, and so it seemed appropriate to invoke the practice with a word that appears sparingly but significantly.

Disconnected – *nepios*

Typically, *nepios* is translated as *fool*, which strikes me as a fine rendering of the context in which it is used. I chose *disconnected* in part to avoid introducing a judgement of the context. My choice was also inspired by a highly illuminating study of the word conducted by Susan Edmunds in *Homeric Nepios*. Edmunds makes a compelling argument that the word is used of adults who have become, in some way, disconnected from the cosmic fabric. The word can be used of children but is not a synonym of 'child'. What makes adults *nepios* seems to be that they have not read and interpreted the signals correctly or have failed to remember what is important. The companions of Odysseus, for example, fail to heed the warning not to eat the sacred cattle of Helios. Similarly, the suitors of Penelope repeatedly ignore the signs that their behaviour has exceeded the bounds of proper conduct. In *Iliad* book fifteen, Hera notes of herself and the other immortals, 'We were *nepios* when we desired to be apart from Zeus in our intentions' (line 104), and Andromache, in *Iliad* book twenty-two, is *nepios* when she weaves a garment for Hector because, unbeknownst to her, he has already died.

Divine wrath – *menis*

In his study on the concern for anger control in classical antiquity, *Restraining Rage*, William Harris notes that Greek has many words for 'anger-like' emotions. *Menis* is associated especially with the gods and with lasting anger that, once set in motion, is difficult to dispel. *Menis* is famously the first word of the *Iliad* which describes the particular kind of anger that Achilles experiences and which persists until the final book. I chose to render it *divine wrath* because I wanted to emphasise that part of Achilles' arc in the epic is to accept his mortality, to accept that he must die, despite having an immortal mother, and that divine wrath in a mortal body is not sustainable, either for the mortal directly or for his community.

Fame in song – *kleos*

As noted earlier, *kleos*, like *kudos*, can be and has been rendered *fame* or *glory*. Because I am interested in drawing out the nuances of meanings in specific words and enabling the reader of Homer in translation to see them in context, it was important to me to differentiate between the kinds of glory each of these words implies and to be consistent in how I rendered them. This is especially important because *kudos* and *kleos* do not seem to be exactly interchangeable forms of 'fame' or 'glory' in Homer. *Kudos* seems to refer to fame and glory conferred in the moment while *kleos* seems connected especially to the fame conferred by having one's name sung about and heard eternally in epic. It is the fame of being woven into the song that reaches the 'wide sky', the fame that becomes eternal. This seemed most noticeable when Hecuba speaks of the *kleos* of Priam but describes Hector as the *kudos* of the Trojans.

Fate – *moira*

The Fates in Greek are the *Moirai*, in their personified form three sisters who spin the thread of human life, apportion that person's life and decide when it will end. *Moira* can also refer to one's allotted portion of a sacrificial feast. When it is treated as a personified immortal, I render it *Fate*. For example, when Hecuba entreats Priam not to risk his life attempting to recover Hector's body since the immortals have decided he should die 'far away from his parents' (line 211), she says, 'mighty Fate for him / Spun this thread when he was born' (lines 209–210). When *moira* is treated as one's portion of life, I render it *portion*, as when Hecuba laments Hector in book twenty-two, 'now, death and your portion have reached you' (line 436). Though it can seem discordant in translation, *portion* enabled me to meet two of my criteria: to use concrete language that corresponds to observable phenomena and to use words that convey the sacred meanings woven through the epics.

Many plots and schemes – *polytropos*

Polytropos is the famous (or infamous, depending on one's point of view) epithet of Odysseus. Appropriately, point of view can shape how it has been rendered. My personal favourite might be Robert Fagles' *man of twists and turns*, which captures Odysseus' ability to adapt to his environment, shift the perspective of the stories he tells and slip out of the traps laid for him, even if he does require the assistance of immortals to do so. I thought about using a literal rendering along the lines of *many ways*, but it felt flat and too abstract. I chose *many plots and schemes* because it alludes not only to the many storylines Odysseus weaves himself into, both in the tale of his wanderings recited to the Phaeacians and his 'lying tales' told in Ithaca, but also to his ability to execute a trap and see it through.

Names for divine forces

In the preface, I discuss the distinction Nagy draws between *daimon* (superhuman force interceding in mortal concerns, also discussed above) and *theos* (a god). In addition to these, there is *athanati*, which is literally *without death* and which I render *the deathless ones*. The gods collectively are also referred to in the text as *the Olympians* or *those who dwell on Olympus*. The epithet *dia* invokes the name Zeus within it, and I render it *of Zeus* when it refers to an immortal and *godlike* when it refers to a hero, since *o theos* is usually implied to mean Zeus.

Owl-eyed – *glaukopis*

This is the famous epithet for Athena. While *glaux* does mean *owl* in ancient Greek, I cannot recall encountering it in Homer, though Athena does turn into birds of prey in both the *Iliad* and *Odyssey*. The word *glaucos* is used to refer to a quality of light, hence the popular options *grey-eyed* or *gleaming-eyed*. The two options I vacillate between (to this day) are *gleaming-eyed* and *owl-eyed*. Ultimately, I decided on the latter because I liked the conversation, debate and questions it invites. Where does the word come from? When and where does Athena come to be associated with the owl? Given Athena's propensity for revealing her presence by transforming into a bird of prey, it seemed fitting to signify that in her epithet.

Perceptions – *phrenes*

As with *thumos*, *phrenes* (the singular is *phren*) is a difficult and much debated word that is exceedingly challenging to express in translation. *Phrenes* can be connected to intellectual, emotive and intuitive capacities. In Homer, the word typically appears in its plural form, which is why I use *perceptions* and not *perception*. According to Padel, *phrenes* can be 'containers' that hold emotions, a piloting force that drives the *thumos* and responsive in both the thinking and feeling sense. As Nagy notes, context can dictate how it is rendered, either as *thinking* and *mind* or *feeling* and *heart*. My choice to render it *perceptions* is not entirely satisfying to me, but it was a way to differentiate it from *thumos* while also both tethering it to thinking and feeling capacities and leaving the meaning somewhat open to discussion and debate.

Portion or allotted portion – *moira*

See 'Fate' above.

Prize – *kudos*

See *kleos* above.

Authoritative story, public speech – *mythos*

As the word *heros* is transliterated as *hero*, the word *mythos* is where we derive our word *myth*. Generally (but not always) for us, a myth tends to mean a story about gods and heroes told in the past by people who believed in them (in some form) but who are not presently figures of worship. In Greek, a *mythos* could be a story, speech or word. In *The Ancient Greek Hero in 24 Hours*, Nagy devotes considerable attention to the shades of meaning contained in this word. What struck me especially is his discussion of *mythos* as an 'authoritative' speech or words spoken for the record. In the passage from *Ion* in my epigraph, I rendered it *authoritative story* to convey that it would be a story familiar to its audience, whether it was heard recited at a festival, sung at home or seen depicted visually in a city. In Telemachus' (in)famous response to his mother in book one, I rendered it *public speech* since this evidently seems to be the skill he is contrasting with Penelope.

Slaves captured in war – *dmoee*

As with anger, ancient Greek uses several words to express different forms of enslavement. One used in the *Odyssey* seems especially significant when we view Homer's epics together as depicting two facets of human experience, war and peace, and that is *dmoee*. The word can be used to refer to an enslaved person in general. It also is used to refer specifically to people who became enslaved by being captured during or after a war. Given that the *Odyssey* depicts post-war life, the repeated use of *dmoee* feels pointed, a way to weave a memory of the Trojan women's fate into an epic that does not depict them but also that does not allow us to forget them. Because I neither wish to generalise human suffering nor believe Homer does so, I rendered the word *dmoee* as *slaves captured in war*.

Way of understanding, mind, intention – *noos*

Noos designates the rational, as opposed to emotive, capacity associated with what we might think of as the mind, thinking and understanding. In the passages from Hesiod and Homer I have included, it is seen paired with Zeus and Athena to indicate their plans. In the passages I have included, it is also paired with mortals to suggest that they understand what is happening and what needs to happen. Here again, I had to make compromises with my goal to render words consistently, primarily to benefit coherence and flow in English, and to differentiate between mortals and immortals. When *noos* is used with an immortal, I have rendered it *intention*. When it is paired with a mortal, I have rendered it *understanding* or *mind*, depending on which seemed to fit most fluently with the rest of the line.

Appendix 2

GODS AND HEROES OF THE *ILIAD* AND *ODYSSEY*

Gods and Goddesses

Zeus
A son of Cronus and husband of Hera, Zeus is the leader of the Olympian gods and goddesses. His domains are the sky, lighting and thunder. Through omens, he is associated with eagles. Via the *Iliad*, he is also known for granting Thetis' request that her son Achilles be honoured, which leads to the deaths of Patroclus and Hector, which in turn prefigure Achilles' own death and the fall of Troy.

Hera
A daughter of Cronus, Hera is the wife of Zeus and goddess of marriage. She is also associated with seasonality and timing. In the *Iliad*, she supports the Achaeans and often sends forth Athena to put her intentions into effect.

Athena
Athena is the daughter of Zeus (and the goddess Metis). Her domains are strategic warfare, crafts and schemes. In the *Iliad*, she supports the Achaeans in the Trojan war, intervening in the thoughts, plans and actions of heroes, sometimes by her own volition and other times at the prompting of Hera and Zeus. In the *Odyssey*, she ensures the fulfilment of Odysseus' homecoming by working through Telemachus, Penelope, Odysseus and Phaeacian Nausicaa.

Hephaestus
Hephaestus is the son of Hera and Zeus. He is the god of fire and the forge and is associated with craft. The *Iliad* provides two complementary and contrasting narratives about the origins of his disability, in both versions as a result of being thrown from Olympus. He credits Thetis for nursing him back to health and crafts armour for her son, Achilles.

Poseidon

A son of Cronus, Poseidon is the brother of Zeus and god of the sea and earthquakes. His support lies with the Achaeans in the Trojan war. In the *Iliad*, he is known for having built Troy's famed walls with Apollo and for his antagonism with Zeus. In the *Odyssey*, Poseidon is angry with Odysseus for having blinded his son, Polyphemus, and works against his return but ultimately concedes to it, since the other gods support it.

Aphrodite

In Homer, Aphrodite is the daughter of Zeus and Dione (a feminine form of the Greek word for Zeus, *Dia*). The goddess of desire, seduction and beauty, Aphrodite brought Paris and Helen together, leading to the outbreak of the Trojan war. In the *Iliad*, she advocates for the Trojans and is the protector of Trojan princes Paris and Aeneas. The latter is her mortal son by Trojan prince Anchises.

Apollo and Artemis

Apollo and Artemis are the twin son and daughter of Zeus and Leda. Both are associated with the bow. Apollo is also a god of prophecy, poetry, music, plague and healing, and Artemis is a goddess of the hunt and protector of innocents. Both fight on the side of the Trojans in the war. Apollo is instrumental in the narrative. He sends the plague that leads to the quarrel of Agamemnon and Achilles, delivers the stunning blow to Patroclus that precedes Hector's deathblow and ensures that the immortals do not forget Hector after he is killed.

Ares

Ares is the son of Zeus and Hera and is a god of brutal war and bloodlust. He is associated with gruesome battle. Warrior heroes are said to suffer *by the hands of Ares* in Homer.

Xanthus (Scamandros)

Xanthus is a river god known for fighting Achilles in *Iliad* book twenty-one and being defeated by the fire of Hephaestus at Hera's prompting.

Iris

In the *Iliad*, Iris is known as a messenger of the gods. Notably, in book three, she leads Helen to the walls of Troy to observe the duel between her past and current husbands, Menelaos and Paris respectively, and she summons Thetis to Olympus for the final assembly in book twenty-four.

Themis
Themis is the goddess of good order and associated with cosmic balance and proper conduct. She appears at few but significant moments in the *Iliad*, implying in those moments that events are about to be set right. Notably, she is the first person Hera greets in book fifteen when she returns to Olympus intending to uphold Zeus' instructions.

Hermes
Hermes is the son of Zeus and Maia and a god of travellers, thieves and cunning. In the *Odyssey*, he is best known for providing Odysseus with the antidote to Circe's charms and potions and for leading the shades of the slaughtered suitors into Hades in book twenty-four.

Calypso
A daughter of Titan god Atlas, Calypso is a nymph who lives on Ogygia. In the *Odyssey*, she holds Odysseus captive for seven years, wanting to make him her husband. She releases him reluctantly and resentfully only after being ordered to by Zeus.

Circe
Circe is the daughter of Helios who lives on the island of Aeaea. In the *Odyssey*, she is known for her charms and potions that transform men into pigs and for providing Odysseus with the advice he needs to return home.

Ino
In the *Odyssey*, Ino is a sea nymph who enables Odysseus' safe arrival on the island of the Phaeacians. Poseidon spots him sailing away from Calypso's Island and angrily summons storm wins to harass him. Pitying him, Ino gifts him her immortal veil. Beyond the *Odyssey*, Ino is one of four daughters of Cadmus, all of whom endure suffering and wandering as a result of their relationships with immortals. When Ino throws herself into the sea to end her suffering, Zeus pities her and transforms her into a sea nymph.

Captive women

Helen
Known for her beauty and weaving, Helen of Sparta is the daughter of Zeus and Nemesis, a goddess of revenge. Her first husband is Spartan leader Menelaos, with whom she has a daughter, Hermione. Helen is best known

as the cause of the Trojan war after Aphrodite brought her and Trojan prince Paris together, leading to her removal from Sparta. After the war, she returns there with Menelaos.

Thetis
Thetis is the daughter of the sea god Nereus, who was forcibly married to mortal king Peleus, and mother of Trojan war hero Achilles. In the *Iliad*, she is credited with saving Zeus after rebellious immortals bound him and taking care of Hephaestus when he was gravely injured. Both gods reciprocate her care of them, Zeus by granting her request to honour Achilles, which sets the events of the *Iliad* in motion, and Hephaestus by crafting new armour for Achilles.

Chryseis
Chryseis is a priestess of Apollo and daughter of priest of Apollo, Chryses. After the Achaeans capture her, she is given to Agamemnon as a war prize. When her father appeals for her return with a generous ransom, Agamemnon rudely sends him away. Chryses appeals to Apollo to send a plague that will destroy the Achaeans, ultimately forcing Agamemnon to return her.

Briseis
In the *Iliad*, Briseis is best known as the war prize who Achilles and Agamemnon quarrel over. When the Achaeans sacked her city, Achilles killed her brothers and husband, and Briseis was captured and given to him. After Agamemnon was forced to return Chryseis, he took Briseis from Achilles, leading to the quarrel that prompts him to petition his mother, which launches a central conflict of the *Iliad*.

Eurycleia
Described in the *Odyssey* as the daughter of Ops, Eurycleia is an enslaved member of Odysseus' household who is loyal to his memory and his wife and son at Ithaca. She was purchased by Odysseus' father, Laertes, who 'honoured her in the great room equivalent to his wife' (*Odyssey* 1.432). She served as the foster-mother of Odysseus and Telemachus.

The Achaean heroes

Agamemnon
Agamemnon is the king of Mycenae, son of Atreus, older brother of Menelaos, husband of Clytemnestra and father of Orestes. In the *Iliad*, he is

the commander of the combined Achaean forces at Troy and characterised by his thirst for fame and spoils and his at times ineffective leadership skills. His failed return to Mycenae, where he was killed by his wife's lover upon arriving, provides a foil for Odysseus' successful return in the *Odyssey*.

Achilles
The mortal son of the sea nymph Thetis and Peleus, the mortal leader of Pythia, Achilles is characterised by his martial prowess, godlike wrath and grief. His name means *grief of the people*, suggesting that he can be understood both as the cause of grief and the occasion for grief. His mother reveals a prophecy about him that he can choose either to return home to Pythia to live a long but unremarkable life or die at Troy but achieve immortality in song. This choice ceases to exist after the death of Patroclus, since Achilles' desire for vengeance drives him back into battle and, beyond the *Iliad*, his death at Troy.

Patroclus
In the *Iliad*, Patroclus is the dearest companion of Achilles. Characterised by both his skill as a warrior and gentleness as a friend, Patroclus rebukes Achilles for refusing to help his Achaean comrades and enters battle himself dressed in Achilles' armour, where he is killed by Apollo at the hands of Hector. Achilles' desire to avenge Patroclus overcomes his feelings of resentment against Agamemnon, driving the narrative to its fulfilment.

Menelaos
A son of Atreus and younger brother of Agamemnon, Menelaos is the commander of the Spartan forces and the first husband of Helen. In the *Iliad*, Menelaos is characterised by his concern for his fellow Achaeans who he is aware are suffering and dying on his account. Back in Sparta with Helen in the *Odyssey*, Menelaos welcomes Telemachus hospitably, sharing the story of his return, which (like Agamemnon's) acts as a complement and foil to Odysseus'.

Odysseus
Odysseus is the son of Laertes and Anticleia, leader at Ithaca, husband of Penelope and father of Telemachus. At Troy, he is the leader of the forces from Ithaca and valued for his strategy: he conceived of the Trojan horse ruse that enabled the Achaeans to defeat Troy. In the *Odyssey*, he is characterised by his willingness to endure suffering in order to return to

his family and for the strategies and stories he deploys to achieve his ends. Like Penelope, Odysseus receives the gifts of Athena, which enable him to fulfil his return.

Penelope
Penelope is the wife of Odysseus and mother of Telemachus. Like her husband, she is characterised by her endurance, cunning and strategy and by Athena's patronage of her. Her weaving enables her to control the narrative of the *Odyssey*. By claiming that she cannot remarry until she has woven a funeral shroud for her father-in-law, she holds off her suitors. As Odysseus tests the loyalty of the Ithacans, Penelope tests his identity, maintaining control of his return to and the fulfilment of their reunion.

Ajax, son of Telamon
Ajax Telamon is the commander of the forces from Salamis. His defining qualities are his exceptional size and strength. He is considered the second-best Achaean warrior after Achilles. His best-known feats include his eagerness to engage in single combat with Hector, which closes with a draw, and his vigorous defence of the Achaean ships when the Trojans, led by Hector, threaten to burn them to the ground.

Diomedes
The son of Tydeus, Diomedes is commander of the forces from Argos. He is portrayed as one of the younger leaders and characterised by his brash courage and skill at public speaking. After Achilles withdraws from battle, Diomedes receives the support of Athena, enabling him to fight even against immortals, Aphrodite and Ares. In one of his memorable scenes, Diomedes refuses to fight Glaucus, the Trojan ally, on the grounds that they are guest-friends through their grandfathers.

Nestor
Commander of the forces from Pylos, Nestor is an elder warrior who is joined by his son Antilochus. He is known for having participated in quests with the previous generations of heroes and for his wisdom, sage advice and long stories.

Tlepolemus
The grandson of Zeus and son of Heracles, Tlepolemus is commander of Rhodes' forces at Troy. He memorably faces a son of Zeus, Trojan ally Sarpedon, in single combat and is killed by him.

The Trojan Heroes and their Allies

Priam
Priam is a leader of men at Troy, father of Hector and Paris (among other children) and husband of Hecuba. In one of his best-known scenes in *Iliad* book three, Priam greets Helen warmly and invites her to provide a catalogue of the Achaean heroes. His most memorable scene involves his reconciliation with Achilles in book twenty-four, when Priam insists on travelling into the Achaean camp to recover his son's body from his killer.

Hecuba
Hecuba is a leader of women at Troy and the mother of Hector and Paris. Hecuba is portrayed overseeing sacred rituals. She directs an appeal to Athena for Troy's protection, which the goddess rejects. Hecuba also instructs Priam to seek an omen from Zeus before departing for the Achaean camp, which he obeys. Hecuba performs three laments for Hector and is one of the final voices heard in the *Iliad*.

Hector
A son of Hecuba and Priam, husband of Andromache and father of Astyanax, Hector is the city's preeminent defender and a favourite of Apollo. Hector's choices echo those of Achilles: he can choose to remain inside the city, endeavouring to protect it from within, or face Achilles in battle and likely lose. Hector chooses the latter and becomes the subject of songs of lament by the Trojan women and Helen, suggesting the origin of epic fame.

Andromache
Andromache is the wife of Trojan leader Hector and the mother of their son, Astyanax. She is perhaps best known for her poignant exchange with her husband on the walls of Troy, when she entreats him to defend the city from inside the protective walls. Her name means *fights with men*, evoked in the resistance she displays to Hector's desire to face Achilles in combat. The laments she delivers for him before and after his death can be understood as the foundations or origins of epic.

Paris (Alexander)
Prince of Troy, son of Hecuba and Priam, brother of Hector, second husband of Helen, Paris is known as a favourite of Aphrodite, for breaking the law of hospitality by removing Helen from Sparta while visiting there and for his good looks and at times reluctance for battle.

Aeneas
Aeneas is the mortal son of Aphrodite and Trojan prince Anchises. In the *Iliad*, Aeneas is described as fated to survive the fall of Troy and carry on the Trojan line. Both Aphrodite and Apollo step in to ensure his survival early in the epic. During Achilles' deadly rampage after Patroclus' death, Poseidon, though he supports the Achaeans, intervenes to protect Aeneas out of deference to Fate.

Glaucus
Glaucus is a captain of Lycia, a Trojan ally. His two most memorable scenes are with Diomedes and Sarpedon. In the former, Glaucus reveals that he is the grandson of Bellerophon, promoting Diomedes to throw down his weapons and declare them guest-friends. With Sarpedon, Glaucus discusses the responsibility of leaders and nature of heroism.

Sarpedon
A captain of Lycia, Sarpedon is a beloved son of Zeus who the god repeatedly wants to save, against the dictates of Fate. Both Hera and Athena warn him of the consequences of doing so, and Zeus concedes to their council. He allows Sarpedon to die but weeps tears of blood onto the battlefield and orders his body returned to his people for burial. In *Iliad* book twelve, Sarpedon tells Glaucus that leaders receive the richest rewards because they take the greatest risks. If they did not have to die, he would not enter battle willingly, but since death is their fate, they should strive to participate in remarkable deeds.

Appendix 3

THE NARRATIVES OF THE *ILIAD* AND *ODYSSEY*

THE *ILIAD* IS set in the tenth year of the Trojan war between the Trojans and the Achaeans (they are also alternately referred to as Argives and Danaans in Greek texts, and in some Latinised translations as 'Greeks'). Following the invocation of the goddess, the bard recounts the war's inciting incident: a quarrel between the commander of the combined Achaean forces, Agamemnon, and the Achaeans' best warrior, Achilles.

In the wake of a successful raid of a neighbouring community, Agamemnon claimed as his war prize Chryseis, a priestess of Apollo and daughter of a priest of Apollo. When her father, Chryses, comes to the Achaeans with a substantial ransom to recover his daughter, they are prepared to grant his request, but Agamemnon refuses to return her and crudely dismisses him. As Chryses departs in anger and dismay, he prays to Apollo, who in response unleashes a plague that decimates the Achaean ranks. Hera prompts Achilles to call for an assembly of the Achaean leaders, and he confronts Agamemnon, who is insulted. Though he resentfully agrees to return Chryseis, he demands compensation for releasing his prize and appropriates Achilles' war prize, Briseis, as that compensation.

Achilles in turn is aggrieved and refuses to fight for Agamemnon any longer. He asks his mother, the sea goddess Thetis, who Achilles recalls describing how she preserved Zeus against rebellious Olympian gods. He asks her to supplicate Zeus on his behalf, asking him to restore her son's honour, and she complies. Zeus is troubled by her request, aware that it will cause strife with Hera, his wife who is a staunch defender of the Achaeans, but he cannot refuse the request. At a tense assembly on Olympus, Hera confronts him, and the two wrangle, with Hera eventually backing down after he threatens her with violence. Hephaestus chides the two for quarrelling, noting that immortals should not allow their peace to be disrupted by mortals.

Zeus sends a deceptive dream to fill Agamemnon with false confidence by convincing him that the Achaeans are finally on the brink of victory. He calls an assembly to test the men by informing them that he has received an omen indicating the Achaeans will not succeed in sacking Troy, but his plan backfires. Chaos ensues as the men rush for their ships to return home until Hera sends Athena to restore order. Odysseus commandeers Agamemnon's sceptre and races through the ranks of men ordering them not to retreat. At a subsequent assembly, Odysseus and Nestor effectively rouse the men, declaring it would be disgraceful to return home defeated. Agamemnon regrets his quarrel with Achilles, aware that Troy will not be defeated as long as there is strife between them. After the Achaeans feast, they prepare for battle, and the bard calls on the Muses to reveal their names and places of origin through him. Zeus sends Iris to warn the Trojans of the Achaeans' movements, and the bard names the Trojan leaders and their allies.

Paris impulsively decides to fight Menelaos but thinks better of it when he catches sight of the warrior. After Hector berates him, Paris offers to fight a duel against Menelaos, with both sides agreeing to abide by the results. Menelaos is eager to preserve his comrades from further suffering on his behalf. Iris is sent to bring Helen, who she finds weaving the story of the war onto a mantle, to the walls of Troy, where Priam and the elders will observe the contest. Though the elders revere her beauty as the work of an immortal, they recognise her danger and wish she would be returned. Priam, however, welcomes her warmly and asks her to catalogue for him the Achaean leaders. On the field, as Menelaos is on the verge of defeating Paris, Aphrodite envelops Paris in a mist and carries him to the safety of his bedchamber, then summons Helen to his side. Helen resists angrily until Aphrodite threatens her with destruction.

At an assembly among the gods, Zeus provokes the anger of Hera and Athena by suggesting the gods contrive how to make peace between the two sides. Hera will not accept the idea that her labours on the Achaeans' behalf will come to nothing, and Zeus agrees to obey her, sending Athena to provoke a Trojan into breaking the truce. When the fighting resumes, Agamemnon attempts to rouse the Achaeans by challenging the men's fighting spirit, which is met with some resentment. The armies clash, and the bard catalogues the duels fought, including the names of the victors and the vanquished and brief epitaphs for the fallen.

Athena gives her patronage to Diomedes, empowering him to fight even Aphrodite and Ares at various points. He has his moment of excellence, cutting down Trojans, until he tries to kill Aeneas, who is fated to survive. Three times Apollo warns him to back down, and the third time, Diomedes obeys, avoiding his own destruction. Athena and Hera work on behalf of the Achaeans until Zeus orders the immortals to retreat from the field, allowing the Trojans to gain the advantage. Diomedes and Glaucus are on the brink of duelling when they realise that they are bound by the law of guest-friendship; instead of fighting, they exchange armour, though the bard notes that Glaucus must have been addled when he did so since his own armour was much more valuable.

Helenus instructs Hector to return to the city and exhort his mother to lead the Trojan women in prayers and sacrifices to Athena. Hecuba follows his instructions, offering among others a garment woven by skilled women captured in war, but Athena rejects the prayer. Andromache confronts her husband, begging him to consider the fate of his wife and son if he is killed in battle and urging him to defend the city from inside the walls. Hector sympathises with her but cannot justify his role as the best warrior of the Trojans by seeking safety over battle. He instructs her to return to her loom and distaff since battle is the concern of men and his most of all.

As deaths pile up on both sides, Athena and Apollo agree to contrive a rest for the weary warriors. They prompt Hector to challenge the best of the Achaeans to a duel. With Achilles refusing to fight, Ajax is the best on the field. During the duel, Apollo ensures Hector's protection until a draw is called via an omen from Zeus. After, the Trojans support returning Helen to the Achaeans, but Paris refuses. The Achaeans build a protective wall around their ships without offering sacrifices to the gods, offending Poseidon. Zeus promises him that the wall will be destroyed. When the fighting resumes, Zeus insists that the gods remain on the side lines as he watches the two armies battle, and the Achaeans suffer losses. Hera berates Poseidon for allowing the Achaeans to die, but he refuses to oppose Zeus, whose power exceeds theirs. Urged on by Hera, Athena prepares to re-enter the battle, but Iris warns her of Zeus' wrath. She backs down, echoing Hephaestus' earlier assertion that immortals should not fight over mortals.

Agamemnon realises that disrespecting Achilles was a mistake and sends an embassy to appeal to him with gifts, but Achilles rejects the offer. Agamemnon did to him what Paris did to Menelaos, and he will not fight under his authority. He recalls a prophecy that his mother shared with him: he can choose either to return home to live a long but unremarkable life or to remain and die at Troy but be honoured. No gifts or prizes are worth his life, which cannot be recovered once lost. His father-figure at Troy, Phoenix, attempts to persuade him by retelling the myth of Meleager, who similarly refused to fight until the last moment and lost the esteem of his peers, but Achilles is unmoved. He will only fight if his own ships are threatened.

Odysseus brings the news back to Agamemnon and later carries out a night raid with Diomedes, whose impulse for recklessness is checked by Athena.

The two sides clash again, and the Achaean leaders are injured. Observing the Achaeans struggling, Achilles sends Patroclus for news, and he is filled with compassion for his Achaean comrades. Nestor suggests that he enter the battle in Achilles' armour, in the hopes that the Trojans will be frightened into backing off. Patroclus carries the news back to Achilles as the battle moves ever closer to the Achaeans' ships. Believing he holds the favour of Zeus, Hector becomes increasingly bold, ignoring a bird omen that Polydamas interprets to mean that the Trojans will not succeed in destroying the Achaeans' ships. Zeus inspires his son Sarpedon to drive forward, and he reminds his comrade Glaucus that they fight on the front line because they receive the greatest honours. Since they cannot avoid their fate, they must throw themselves into battle. Hector succeeds in tearing down the Achaeans' wall.

Confident that none of the gods will defy him, Zeus turns his attention away from battle, but Poseidon takes the opportunity to encourage the Achaean leaders. Zeus drives the Trojans forward but is mindful that he does not want the Achaeans defeated. The bard continues to catalogue the duels. When the Achaeans rally, Polydamas succeeds in convincing Hector to retreat and regroup. Noticing Poseidon rousing the Achaeans, Hera resolves to distract Zeus by seducing him and enlists Sleep to help her by promising to grant him one of the Graces for his wife. Her ruse is successful, but Zeus is enraged when he awakes and sees Poseidon fuelling the Achaeans. Hera insists that she supports his intentions and carries his orders back to Olympus.

When Ares learns that his son on the Trojan side has been killed, he prepares to re-join the battle, but Athena stops him since his act of defiance could cost them all. Poseidon is insulted, affirming that he shares the same status as Zeus based on their shared genealogy, but agrees to abide by Zeus' will as long as he does not attempt to circumvent fate: Troy must be allowed to fall. Determined to fulfil his promise to Thetis, Zeus resolves to allow the Trojans to set fire to the Achaean ships, after which the Achaeans will be allowed victory. When the Achaean ships are threatened, Patroclus hopes to convince Achilles to save them and rebukes his hard heart when he refuses. As the fire spreads, and the Achaeans' spirits flag, Achilles agrees to allow Patroclus to wear his armour into battle, emphasising that he is to return as soon as the ships are safe. The ruse works, and the Trojans flee in terror. In the heat of battle, however, Patroclus is fuelled with a fighting spirit and surges forward.

When Patroclus duels with Sarpedon, Zeus wants to save his son and is warned not to by Athena, since it would cause other gods to want to save their children as well. He agrees to allow Sarpedon to die but sends Sleep and Death to recover the body and transport it to Sarpedon's home in Lycia to receive funeral rites. Patroclus drives towards Troy's walls and is warned three times by Apollo to back down but refuses. Apollo stuns him in the back, and then Hector delivers the deathblow. The Achaeans fight desperately to preserve his body, but Hector captures Achilles' armour. When the Achaeans bring Patroclus' body back to Achilles, he is distraught. Thetis hears him from the depths of the sea and rushes to his side. She orders him to remain out of battle until she can secure him new armour from Hephaestus. Hera sends Iris to instruct Achilles to appear before the emboldened Trojans to frighten them into retreat. Athena cloaks him with her shield and places a burning cloud over his head. He releases three piercing cries, terrifying the Trojans. Later, he leads laments for Patroclus. Athena anoints him with ambrosia to preserve his strength while he refuses to eat or drink, and Thetis anoints Patroclus with ambrosia to prevent his corpse from decomposing.

Hephaestus gladly fulfils Thetis' request, crediting her with caring for him after he was thrown off Olympus. The following day at dawn, Thetis presents the armour to Achilles. He calls an assembly to announce his return to battle. Agamemnon admits he was deluded when he allowed their conflict to escalate, noting that even Zeus was once vulnerable to delusion when he boasted about the impending birth of his son Heracles, and Hera foiled his plans for his son. When Achilles rides into battle, Zeus grants the immortals permission to join the fight on whichever side they choose. Achilles ruthlessly cuts down the Trojans, who the bard catalogues. His rampage offends the river Scamander, who orders him not to glut him with corpses. Achilles refuses, and the river attempts to drown him. Hera sends Hephaestus to overpower Scamander with fire until Hera finally orders him to back down, reiterating that immortals should not fight over mortals. Ares attempts to attack Athena, but she knocks him out with a boulder. When Aphrodite attempts to aid him, Athena punches her in the chest.

Concerned for Hector, Apollo returns to Troy. The Trojan warriors have fled into the city, but Hector has stayed behind, determined to face Achilles. His parents plead with him from the walls to come into the city, but he refuses. Athena deceives him into believing his brother is beside him. At the last moment, he realises the deception and chooses to die courageously, throwing himself at Achilles, who strikes him down then ties him by the heels to his chariot and drags his body around the city. Priam and Hecuba lament him, and their grief is echoed by the people. Andromache hears the wailing from inside her room, where she is weaving a mantle. Rushing to the walls in fear, she sees Hector and faints. When she revives, she performs a lament for him.

Returning to his camp, Achilles leads a lament for Patroclus and continues to refuse food or drink. Patroclus visits him in a dream and accuses him of neglect for not performing his burial rites. At dawn the following day, Achilles conducts the funeral rites then holds funeral games in his honour. Overseeing the games, Achilles manages the conflicts that erupt among the Achaean competitors, including a quarrel between Ajax and Odysseus after Athena propels Odysseus to victory over him, and skilfully negotiates the distribution of prizes. After, he continues to attempt to desecrate Hector's corpse, but the gods continue to preserve it.

At the final assembly of Olympus in the *Iliad*, Apollo confronts the other gods for allowing the pious Hector to be dishonoured. Zeus agrees that Achilles must return the body but will not allow it to be removed by stealth. Thetis herself must order her son to return Hector's body to Priam. Zeus summons her to Olympus, and she obeys. After informing her of the debate among the immortals, he asks her to carry his order to her son, and she again consents. Zeus sends Iris to instruct Priam to recover his son's body. Hecuba is initially against the idea and urges Priam to request an omen. When it returns favourable, he sets off with a ransom, safely guided by Hermes.

When Priam appears at the feet of Achilles, he and his Myrmidons are overcome with wonder. Priam kisses Achilles' hands and begs for the body of his son, asking Achilles to think of his own father. Priam's gesture and words move Achilles to tears. After the two men weep together, Achilles insists that they share a meal, and following the meal, they admire one another with a sense of wonder. Priam returns with Hector's body, and funeral rites are carried out, at which time Andromache, Hecuba and Helen each perform a lament. The *Iliad* ends with the funeral rites for Hector.

The *Odyssey* opens with the bard invoking the Muse to sing about a husband attempting to return home from Troy and the trials he encountered trying to recover his life and the homecoming of his companions, whose recklessness resulted in their destruction. The narrative then moves to an assembly of the gods at which Poseidon is absent. Zeus discusses Aegisthus, who was warned not to court Agamemnon's wife but did so anyway. He killed Agamemnon when he returned from Troy and was subsequently killed by Orestes, Agamemnon's son. Affirming that Aegisthus' impiety warranted his death, Athena asks her father why he allows a pious man like Odysseus to remain the captive of Calypso. Zeus claims the cause is Poseidon, who is angry at Odysseus for blinding his son, but agrees to order his release, and Athena goes to Ithaca to embolden his son, Telemachus.

In the guise of his father's guest-friend Mentes, Athena visits Telemachus, who explains that his home has been overrun by suitors who court his mother against her will. She advises him to call an assembly to censure the suitors and seek help from the elders and to travel to Pylos and Sparta to consult with his father's comrades from Troy. Before departing, she fills Telemachus with courage and intention. Later, in the hall where the suitors have gathered to feast on the household's provisions, a bard entertains them with a song about the disastrous homecomings of the Achaeans. Hearing the song from her upper room, Penelope descends to the hall to ask Phemius to sing a different song since this one fills her with grief and longing for her husband. Telemachus advises his mother not to interfere with the bard and to return to her loom and distaff, since public speech is the responsibility of men, his most of all since might in the house belongs to him. She receives his words with a sense of wonder and returns to her rooms to weep and sleep.

The following day, Telemachus calls the assembly. The city elders feel sympathy for him, but the lead suitor Alcinous responds roughly that he should look to his mother, not the suitors, as the cause of his problems. Her behaviour with the suitors is deceptive. She encourages some but has plotted against all. For four years she claimed to be weaving a funeral shroud for Laertes, after which she would choose a husband, but her enslaved women revealed that Penelope was secretly unravelling her work. Antinous advises Telemachus that his mother will achieve fame in song while he loses his livelihood and asserts that as long as Penelope remains in Ithaca the suitors will not depart until she chooses a husband from among them. After the assembly, Telemachus resolves to travel to Pylos and Sparta. Athena aids him in the guise of Mentor, an adviser of his father's. Before setting off, he instructs Eurycleia, the enslaved woman who nursed him, to keep the news from Penelope until she asks for him.

Telemachus and Athena-Mentor arrive in Pylos on a feast day to Poseidon and are welcomed warmly by Nestor, who recounts the Achaeans' troubled departure from Troy. Many of the Achaeans behaved impiously in the wake of the city's fall and were punished. He recounts a quarrel between Agamemnon and Menelaos that led them to set off separately. Menelaos was blown off course to Egypt, and Agamemnon returned home and was killed by Aegisthus, who had persuaded the good-hearted Clytemnestra to betray her husband. Nestor encourages Telemachus to visit Menelaos and hear his story, sending his own son, Pisistratus, as Telemachus' escort.

In Sparta, Menelaos is preparing for the weddings of his children. Recalling his time at Troy, he describes Odysseus as the comrade dearest to him for his cunning. Both he and Helen, now back at Sparta with him, recount stories about Odysseus. First Helen describes helping Odysseus when he snuck into Troy on a spy mission. Menelaos responds by sharing how Odysseus kept the Achaeans who were hidden in the Trojan horse safe when Helen tried to lure them out by mimicking their wives' voices. Menelaos shares his story of wandering and becoming trapped on an island but achieving his escape through the advice of a sea nymph. Menelaos predicts that Odysseus will return, kill the suitors and reclaim his place.

Menelaos wants Telemachus to stay for a long visit, but Telemachus insists that he should not stay away too long. In Ithaca the suitors are furious when they learn Telemachus travelled for news of his father and plot to ambush and kill him upon his return. A herald loyal to Penelope, Medon, reveals the plot to her, and she is distraught when she discovers that Telemachus has left the island. Eurycleia assures her that he is protected by an immortal.

At a second assembly of the gods, Athena notes that Odysseus has still not been released while his wife's suitors plot the murder of his son. Zeus sends Hermes to Calypso, ordering her to release Odysseus, while Athena returns to Ithaca to ensure Telemachus evades the suitors' plot. On Ogygia, Calypso resents being forced to release Odysseus, noting the gods envy goddesses falling in love with mortals. She rescued and cared for Odysseus and wants to keep him for her husband. But she acknowledges that he longs to return to his Penelope, though it means giving up immortality and enduring suffering. When she informs Odysseus that he may leave if he wishes to, he is suspicious, worried the goddess is planning him some harm, but she swears an oath that her offer is sincere. He builds a raft, fitting it with a mast and sail, and departs but has to fight for his survival after Poseidon sends a storm to harass him. The sea nymph Ino sees him struggling for his life and gifts him her immortal veil to carry him safely to the shores of the Phaeacian land, where he is fated to find his return. Initially suspicious of the goddess's intentions, Odysseus refrains from using the veil but ultimately is forced to when his own strength is insufficient.

Athena guides him safely to shore, where he collapses in exhaustion. While he sleeps, Athena visits Nausicaa, the young daughter of Alcinous, in a dream to scold her for not taking responsibility for essential household tasks. Upon waking, Nausicaa secures a cart from her father and with an escort of handmaidens brings the washing to the river on whose banks Odysseus sleeps. Awakened by the girls' shouts, he emerges from the bushes naked and caked in brine, terrifying all but Nausicaa, who stands her ground and confronts him. Supplicating her with flattering words comparing her to the goddess Artemis, Odysseus secures a hospitable response from her. She gifts him clothes to wear and advises him how to supplicate her mother, Arete, who will ultimately decide whether he can achieve his return home. On his way, he prays to Athena and later encounters her in the guise of a young girl. She echoes the advice of Nausicaa and ensures he reaches Alcinous' home safely. There, Odysseus declares himself a suppliant and is welcomed accordingly.

Arete questions him about his identity and his clothing, and he admits to his earlier encounter with their daughter. Odysseus reveals that after the comrades he travelled from Troy with were killed, the gods brought him to Calypso, who held him captive for eight years against his will. After she released him, Poseidon harassed him until he finally landed on the shores of the Phaeacians, where Nausicaa kindly provided him a garment in which to clothe himself. She did not guide him personally because it could be viewed as improper. Arete orders a bed for him, and the household sleeps.

The following day, preparations are made for Odysseus' departure. A feast is held, and a bard sings of the quarrel between Achilles and Odysseus at the start of the war, prompting Odysseus to weep. Athletic games are held, at which Odysseus initially declines to participate out of respect for his host, but he is drawn into the discus throw after another participant insults him. After his shot lands far beyond the others', Odysseus recounts his success at Troy, noting that he is not at full strength following his trials at sea. Alcinous calls for another song from Demodocus, and he sings of Hephaestus trapping his adulterous wife Aphrodite with her lover Ares in an inescapable net, only agreeing to release them at Poseidon's urging. The song is followed by a dance, after which Alcinous orders gifts be brought to send home with Odysseus.

After Arete advises Odysseus to secure his bag of gifts with a strong knot, Nausicaa shares a goodbye with Odysseus, asking him to remember her since she saved his life. Odysseus promises to pray to her as to a goddess. Later, he requests from Demodocus the song of the Trojan horse, but when the song provokes him to weep, Alcinous asks him who he is and why the song has caused him to grieve. Odysseus introduces himself with his name, patronymic and place of origin and begins his story.

Zeus sent him many troubles when he departed from Troy. His ships were blown off course, landing on the island of the Cicones, where they sacked the city but did not depart quickly enough and ended up losing more men in a subsequent battle. A typhoon then blew the survivors to the land of the Lotus-Eaters, who did not harm them but who gave them the fruit of forgetting. Those who ate it no longer cared if they returned home and had to be brought back to the ships by force. After escaping the Lotus-Eaters, they next landed on the island of the Cyclops, where Odysseus insisted, against his men's wishes, on seeking ties of guest-friendship with Polyphemus, a Cyclops son of Poseidon. But the Cyclops are too powerful to care about Zeus' laws, and rather than extend hospitality, Polyphemus devoured two of his men for dinner and two more the following morning. Odysseus devised a plot to blind Polyphemus and escape his cave by tying himself and his men under the Cyclops' rams when he let them out to graze. But Odysseus could not resist revealing himself as he and his men sailed away, and Polyphemus prayed to his father to avenge him.

At their next stop, they encountered Aeolus, caretaker of the winds, and he welcomed them hospitably, gifting them a bag of winds that would carry them back to Troy. Odysseus concealed the nature of the gift in the bag, and while he was sleeping, his comrades became suspicious and released the winds too soon. Just as they could see smoke from the fires of Ithaca rising into the sky, the winds blew them back to Aeolus, who refused to help them a second time since a god must be against them. Leaving Aeolus behind, they landed on the island of the giant Laestrygonians, who destroyed all of his ships and men save Odysseus' own. From there they escaped to Aeaea, the island of Circe. Only one of the first men sent out to scout the island returned, revealing that Circe had turned the others into swine. Odysseus set off in his armour to confront her, encountering Hermes along the way. The god prepared him for the meeting by providing him with a herb to counteract Circe's drugs and enchantments and advising him how to interact with her.

She was shocked when Odysseus failed to transform and made to attack her, but she adopted the position of a suppliant and invited him to bed. Forewarned by Hermes, he made her promise not to harm him. Later, he convinced her to transform his men back to their human forms, and she complied. They remained with Circe for a year until Odysseus' men prompted him to set off for Ithaca again. Circe advised them how to secure their return: they must first visit Tiresias in the underworld and secure a prophecy from him. Following Circe's instructions, Odysseus had his meeting with Tiresias and consulted also with his mother. Breaking off his story, Odyssey is eager to set off for Ithaca. Arete orders more gifts, and Alcinous compliments Odysseus' story as being like that of a bard and asks him to continue.

Odysseus recounts his conversations with Agamemnon and Achilles. Agamemnon warned Odysseus by sharing his own return story, though he acknowledged that Penelope could be trusted. Achilles declared that he would rather be enslaved to a mortal than be the best among the shades of Hades.

Odysseus spoke to many spirits, but one refused to engage with him, Ajax, who held a grudge against Odysseus because Athena allowed him to win Achilles' armour at his funeral games. After leaving Hades, Odysseus and his men returned to Aeaea, where Circe provided advice that complemented Tiresias' prophecy. With their guidance to lead him, Odysseus was able to hear part of the Sirens' song by having his men tie him to the mast of the ship as they passed them. He faced the six-headed Scylla and lost six of his men rather than face Charybdis and lose them all. Odysseus wanted to sail past the island where Helios' sacred cattle dwell, but the men insisted on stopping. Odysseus warned them that they must not eat the cattle. But while he slept, hunger overcame his men, and they decided to eat the cattle. As they left the island, Zeus destroyed their ship out of respect for Helios, and only Odysseus survived and was carried to Ogygia.

With Odysseus having completed his story, the Phaeacians transport him back to Ithaca while he sleeps on the deck of the boat. Upon its return, out of respect for Poseidon, who did not attempt to subvert Odysseus returning to Ithaca in it, the ship is turned to stone.

Now that Odysseus has returned to Ithaca, Athena reveals herself, and the two plot how he will defeat the suitors. Odysseus initially mistrusts her, which pleases Athena, but she assures him of his success. He asks her to weave him a plan, and she disguises him as a beggar. He visits Eumaeus, his swineherd, and is pleased with the man's proper observance of hospitality and the care he takes with his former leader's livestock. The two share stories, Eumaeus explaining how he came to be enslaved and Odysseus claiming to be a man from Crete who was also exploited. When he assures Eumaeus that Odysseus will return, Eumaeus warns him that Penelope and Telemachus do not trust the news travellers bring.

At Sparta, Athena hastens Telemachus home. Before his departure, Menelaos and Helen each present gifts, the latter a woven garment for Telemachus' future wife instructing him to leave it with his mother until his future marriage. Athena guides him safely past the suitors' trap and engineers his reunion with Odysseus. After Athena reveals Odysseus to his son, she instructs him to go in his beggar disguise to the hall where the suitors are gathered. Led by Antinous, the suitors consider whether to find another way to kill Telemachus, but one of the suitors suggests attempting to determine the intentions of the gods before acting against him. Later, Penelope appears before the suitors to upbraid them for their disrespectful treatment, reminding Antinous how Odysseus once protected his father.

Telemachus recounts to his mother the news he heard from Menelaos, but a seer overhears and prophesies that Odysseus has already returned to

Ithaca and will kill the suitors. Later, when Odysseus appears in the hall, he claims to have once been a wealthy man who always shared with those in need and asks Antinous to share his portion with him, but he responds violently. The other suitors object, reminding him that gods sometimes visit the mortal world in disguise to test them. Later, the suitors arrange for Odysseus to fight another beggar, assuming that he will be defeated, but instead, he knocks the other man senseless.

Athena places in Penelope a desire to appear before the suitors and beautifies her before she descends to the public hall. After speaking with Telemachus about the treatment of the beggar, she announces her intention to remarry but scolds them for courting her improperly, without proper gifts, secretly pleasing Odysseus, who is watching the proceedings in disguise and understands that Penelope has other intentions. Athena fuels the suitors to further insult and abuse Odysseus to stoke his outrage for the slaughter to come. One of the enslaved women loyal to the suitors, Melantho, abuses Odysseus, filling him with violent rage.

Penelope asks to speak with the beggar, and the two exchange stories. She describes her grief at losing her husband to the Trojan war effort and her scheme to hold off the suitors, while he tells another version of his man-from-Crete story in which he claims to have met Odysseus. Penelope asks him to describe what Odysseus was wearing, and he recounts the clothes and ornaments Penelope dressed him in before his departure. Eurycleia is asked to wash his feet and recognises Odysseus by a scar on his leg. She attempts to get Penelope's attention, but it is elsewhere, with Athena's assistance. Odysseus warns Eurycleia on threat of death not to reveal him, and she assures him of her loyalty. Later, Penelope asks for Odysseus' advice regarding a dream she had, and he predicts her husband will return and kill her suitors. She announces her intention to hold a contest among them with Odysseus' bow and to marry the man who can string it and drive an arrow through twelve axes.

The following morning, a feast day for Apollo, Odysseus and Penelope both feel agitated and anxious. The suitors and enslaved members of the household loyal to them continue to abuse Odysseus. When they do so in front of Telemachus, he threatens them with violence, shocking them. The contest with the bow is held, but none of the suitors can string it. When Odysseus asks for a turn, the suitors are outraged. Penelope intervenes to insist the beggar have a turn, but Telemachus again sends her to her loom and distaff, affirming that the bow is the concern of men, his most of all since might in the house belongs to him. After Penelope leaves, Odysseus lifts the bow, and the suitors immediately threaten him, but Telemachus orders them to stop. Amused by his now forceful behaviour, they do not resist when Eumaeus gives Odysseus the bow but are shocked when he strings it and sends it through the twelve axes. He gives Telemachus the sign, and the slaughter begins, the first victim being Antinous.

Odysseus and Telemachus, with Athena's support, kill all the suitors but spare Medon, the loyal herald, and Phemius, the bard, who sang under compulsion. Odysseus questions Eurycleia regarding which of the women in the house are loyal to Odysseus. Twelve identified as disloyal are hanged, by Telemachus' order, to make their deaths more painful. After the hall is purified, Eurycleia is instructed to fetch Penelope and the loyal women. Penelope initially expresses disbelief at the news but agrees to meet with Odysseus. They sit together by the hearth in silence, until Telemachus bursts out a criticism of his mother. Odysseus restrains him, assuring him that he and Penelope have their own token of mutual recognition and instructing him to remember that they must consider how to negotiate the release of the suitors' slaughter. While Telemachus instructs the household to perform music and dance to give passers-by the impression that a wedding is taking place, Penelope and Odysseus test each other. He asks for a bed since his wife does not recognise him, and Penelope affirms the request, asking Eurycleia to bring the bed Odysseus himself crafted. Odysseus bursts out in anger that the bed cannot be moved and explains how he carved it into a living tree in their bedroom. With Odysseus having now revealed the token, she embraces him, and the two exchange stories of their time apart.

Hermes leads the suitors' shades to the underworld, where they tell their story to Achilles and Agamemnon, who discuss Achilles' funeral and Agamemnon's unfortunate murder upon his return to Mycenae. In Ithaca, Odysseus reunites with his father Laertes in one of their orchards, and the three generations – Laertes, Odysseus and Telemachus – face the grieving and angry families of the slaughtered suitors. When violence erupts among them, Athena fuels Laertes to a moment of martial success but ultimately calls for an end to the fighting, with the consent of Zeus. Odysseus feels moved to continue the violence, but Athena restrains him. He obeys the goddess, exchanging oaths for peace with the suitors' families.

NOTES

Preface

1. The works of Gregory Nagy are especially illuminating of this dynamic.

Introduction

1. See 'The Mast and the Loom: Signifiers of Separation and Authority'.
2. See 'Remarks on the Interpretation of Some Ambiguous Textile Terms'.
3. See Evy Johanne Haland, 'Athena's Peplos: Weaving as a Core Female Activity in Ancient and Modern Greece'.
4. See Marie-Louise Nosch, 'The Loom and the Ship in Ancient Greece. Shared knowledge, shared terminology, cross-crafts, or cognitive maritime-textile archaeology?' In *Texts and Textiles in the Ancient World*, edited by Henriette Harich-Schwarzbauer.
5. See Elizabeth Wayland Barber, *Women's Work: The First 20,000 Years, Women, Cloth, and Society in Early Times*.
6. *Daimoni* is the vocative case, used for direct address.
7. See Gregory Nagy, *The Ancient Greek Hero in 24 Hours*.
8. See F. A. Wilford, 'DAIMON in Homer', for three contexts in which a *daimon* is invoked in Homer: when a hero oversteps mortal limits by confronting a god, when an external event that affects the hero is credited to a *daimon*, and when an internal thought, idea or feeling within a hero is credited to a *daimon*.
9. See Gregory Nagy's *The Ancient Greek Hero in 24 Hours* for an exploration of this term, its meaning and its significance.
10. See Gregory Nagy's *The Best of the Achaeans* for a discussion of the relationship between the Muse and the bard.
11. An illuminating discussion of this is also in Nagy's *The Best of the Achaeans*.
12. Note how often these stories involve someone's suffering: Penelope and Odysseus here exchange the stories of the trials they each endured while apart. The story Menelaos tells Telemachus in *Odyssey* book

three also concerns his trials attempting to return to Sparta after the Trojan war. Nestor repeatedly tells stories about overcoming trials in both the *Iliad* and *Odyssey*, and the story repeatedly referenced about Agamemnon in the *Odyssey* concerns his death at the hands of his wife's lover and the vengeance his son extracted on his behalf.

Part 1 – Queens

1. This is Hephaestus, one of whose epithets is 'Ambidexter'.
2. Note that in Homer the source of Hephaestus' disability is an accident – either Zeus (in book one) or Hera (in book eighteen) throwing him from Olympus, not a stated deficiency in Hera's capacity to produce him.
3. Helen 'escapes the notice' of the Trojan women who might criticise her.
4. Penelope unraveling the funeral shroud for Laertes 'escapes the notice' of the suitors for three years.
5. See P. Considine, 'Some Homeric Terms for Anger'.
6. See Gregory Nagy, *The Ancient Greek Hero in 24 Hours*.
7. See Elizabeth Wayland Barber's *Women's Work: The First 20,000 Years, Women, Cloth, and Society in Early Times* for a fascinating discussion of what this belt might have looked like and signified.
8. See 'Seeing Hera in the *Iliad*'.
9. Note that in book twenty-three, the shade of Patroclus visits Achilles to reproach him for neglecting to conduct the rites that will shepherd Patroclus on his journey. Various ancient sources attest to the importance of appeasing the dead with proper funeral rites and the fear of incurring the wrath of the dead by neglecting to do so.
10. This refers to Artemis.

Part 2 – Captives

1. See *Helen: The Evolution from Divine to Heroic in Greek Epic Tradition* by Linda Lee Clader for a more in-depth study of these facets of Helen.
2. Meaning Laertes.
3. Meaning he does not want to sleep in a storeroom.
4. See Margaret Alexiou, *The Ritual Lament in Greek Tradition*.
5. See Casey Due, *Variations on a Homeric Lament by Briseis*.
6. See Laura Slatkin, *The Power of Thetis and Selected Essays*.
7. See L. Clader, *Helen: The Evolution from Divine to Heroic*.
8. Alexander is Paris.

9. Note the resonance with Hecuba's laments for Hector, in which she says that Hector was killed by Athena at the hands of Achilles as well as the description of Patroclus' death: Apollo stuns him, and Hector delivers the death blow.
10. See Gregory Nagy, *The Best of the Achaeans*.
11. See 'Helen and the Last Song for Hector'.
12. See, for example, Theocritus, *Idyll 18: The Marriage Song for Helen*.

Part 3 – Goddesses

1. In *The Best of the Achaeans*, for example, Nagy explores the sacred meaning of the word for *feast, dais* in Greek, which signifies not only a meal but specifically eating the meat of a sacrificial animal.
2. This is Apollo.
3. See *Weaving Truth: Essays on Language and the Female in Greek Thought*.
4. 'His son' is Heracles.
5. 'That one' refers to Aegisthus.
6. 'He wants to die' might suggest not only that he wants to die rather than remain captive but also that he wants to return to the flow of time and mortal life, though that will mean eventually dying.
7. 'They' are Odysseus and Diomedes, with whom he carries out the raid.
8. 'The grandson of Aeacus' is Achilles.
9. See Barber's *Women's Work*.
10. Thus, the *Odyssey* begins not in the middle of the story but where it needs to begin to develop the theme: See '"Reading" Homer Through Oral Tradition'.
11. In *The Ancient Greek Hero in 24 Hours*, Nagy defines the mystical meaning of *nostos* as *return to life and light*, which influenced my decision to render it as such.

Part 4 – Heroes

1. I include this notion of Hades as a transitional place from Nagy's formulation.
2. The Greek word is *homophrosyne*, the quality that describes Penelope and Odysseus' connection and which enables them to achieve their reunion; they share one goal and one way of thinking, which not even time and distance can sever.
3. See *Wonder and the Marvellous from Homer to the Hellenistic World*.
4. Nagy discusses the meaning of *sema* as *the tomb of a hero* in *The Ancient Greek Hero in 24 Hours*

5. Unremarkable in a rather literal sense here, a life that would not be remarked upon, spoken of, sung about.
6. She has breathed out *psyche* in Greek, which has been interpreted to mean she has fainted.
7. See, for example, Euripides' *Trojan Women*.
8. See *The Ancient Greek Hero in 24 Hours*.
9. See Maria C. Pantelia's 'Helen and the Last Song for Hector' for more on the organisation of the laments for Hector and Margaret Alexiou's *Women's Lament in Greek Tradition* for more on the historical institution of lament.
10. See 'The Mast and the Loom: Signifiers of Separation and Authority'.
11. The warp-weighted looms depicted in vase images from the classical period are vertical and thus can be said to be 'raised' or 'made to stand', reflected in the connection between *histos* (loom) and *histemi* (make to stand).
12. Numbers in the ancient Greek texts do not necessarily mean the same as they do in modern times. 'Twenty years' may have meant 'a long period of time' rather than twenty literal years. Smaller numbers that tend to repeat, notably three, seven and twelve, may be connected to the number of days allotted for sacred events.
13. In *The Ancient Greek Hero in 24 Hours*.
14. Meaning Aphrodite, for whom 'Cytheria' is an epithet.
15. Notable examples include that warriors are compared to mothers several times in the *Iliad*, and Odysseus is compared to a lamenting woman in the *Odyssey*.
16. Note that competitions for a bride feature in a variety of Greek myths, perhaps most notably in the Helen and Atalanta myths.
17. Note that in addition to first, second and third person, ancient Greek has an additional one called the dual to specifically reference two people.
18. See Olga Levaniouk's 'Penelope and the Pandareids' for a discussion of the myth variant employed in Penelope's prayer and its significance within the oral traditional system.
19. See 'Tracking the *Odyssey*'s Plot Through Dawn's Epithets'.

Afterword

1. See his '"Reading" Homer Through Oral Tradition'.
2. A few notable examples: at Troy, the Achaean camp suffers grievously because Agamemnon does to Achilles what Paris did to Menelaos: he unlawfully appropriates Briseis from Achilles. Achaean Diomedes and

Trojan ally Glaucus have a sacred family connection that precludes them from fighting each other. Until Hector kills Patroclus, Achilles has no personal grievance against the Trojans and declares this openly. Though he supports the Achaeans, Poseidon intervenes to prevent Aeneas from being killed because it is not his fate to die at Troy, and Poseidon understands that Fate must be respected, regardless of his personal preferences.

Appendix 1

1. This is the first phrase Zeus utters in the *Odyssey* as he recalls the destruction of Aegisthus.
2. For example, the reference to the Aesopic race between the turtle and the hare implied in Demodocus' song about Hephaestus catching Ares and Aphrodite.
3. For example, after Penelope asks where Odysseus is from, she adds, 'But now, tell me your race, from what place you are / for you do not come from a tree, neither from a rock, as was spoken long ago' (book nineteen, lines 162–164).
4. A favourite expression of my grandmother's comes to mind: 'With Athena and your own hands move', which captures the confluence of human will and divine favour that immortalises heroes in Homer.
5. A notable example from the *Iliad*: when the Trojan women pray to Athena, she lifts her head in denial, the opposite of what may be expected by modern readers, for whom nodding up and down is a gesture of agreement and shaking one's head side to side indicates disagreement.
6. The women heroes in the *Iliad* do not die, thus it is always 'he' and 'his'.
7. The issue of what colours people saw in the ancient world is a fascinating field of study all its own, and studies have suggested that cultures evolve toward greater specificity with regard to naming colours. While this is important and revelatory research, my biggest influence translating Homer's 'colours' was noticing that each 'colour' word had a physical presence in the observed world, and this is what I wanted to draw attention to.
8. See *In and Out of Mind: Greek Images of the Tragic Self*.

BIBLIOGRAPHY

Aeschylus, *Prometheus Bound and Other Plays*, translated with an introduction by Philip Vellacott, Penguin Classics, 1961.

Aeschylus, Sophocles, and Euripides, *The Greek Plays: Sixteen Plays by Aeschylus, Sophocles, and Euripides*, new translations edited by Mary Lefkowitz and James Romm, Penguin Random House, 2016.

Aesop's Fables, translated by V. S. Vernon Jones, Word Cloud Classics, 2013.

Alexiou, Margaret, *The Ritual Lament in Greek Tradition*, Rowman & Littlefield, 1974.

Alexopoulou, Marigo, *The Theme of Returning Homer in Ancient Greek Literature: The Nostos of the Epic Heroes*, Edwin Mellen Press, 2009.

Ali, Seemee, 'Seeing Hera in the *Iliad*', *CHS Research Bulletin* 3, no. 2 (2015).

Anhalt, Emily Katz, *Enraged: Why Violent Times Need Ancient Greek Myth*, Yale University Press, 2014.

Apollodorus, *Library of Greek Mythology*, translated with an introduction and notes by Robin Hard, Oxford World's Classics, 1997.

Apollonius of Rhodes, *Voyage of the Argo*, translated with an introduction by E. V. Rieu, Penguin Classics, 1971.

Apollonius of Rhodes, *Jason and the Golden Fleece*, translated with an introduction and notes by Richard Hunter, 1993.

Apollonius of Rhodes, *Jason and the Argonauts*, translated by Aaron Poochigian with an introduction and notes by Benjamin Acosta-Hughes, Oxford World's Classics, 2014.

Apuleius, *The Golden Ass or Metamorphoses*, translated with introduction and notes by E. J. Kenney, Penguin Classics, 1998.

Aristophanes, *The Birds and Other Plays*, translated with an introduction by David Barrett and Alan H. Sommerstein, Penguin Classics, 1978.

Aristophanes, *Clouds, Women at the Thesmophoria, Frogs*, translated with an introduction and notes by Stephen Halliwell, Oxford University Press, 2015.

Aristophanes, *Frogs and Other Plays*, translated with an introduction and notes by Stephen Halliwell, Oxford World's Classics, 2015.

Aristophanes, *Lysistrata and Other Plays*, translated with introduction and notes by Alan H. Sommerstein, Penguin Classics, 2003.

Aristotle, *Poetics*, translated with an introduction and notes by Malcolm Heath, Penguin Classics, 1996.

Arnold, Matthew, *On Translating Homer*, Barnes & Noble, 1861.

Babrius and Phaedrus, *Fables*, Loeb Classical Library edition translated by Ben Edwin Perry, Harvard University Press, 1965.

Bakker, Egbert, 'Homeric Discourse and Enjambment: A Cognitive Approach', *Transactions of the American Philological Association*, 1990.

Barber, Elizabeth Wayland, *Women's Work: The First 20,000 Years, Women, Cloth, and Society in Early Times*, W. W. Norton & Company, 1994.

Barker, Elton and Joel Christensen, *Homer* (Beginner's Guides series), Riverwalk Books, 2013.

Bergren, Ann, *Weaving Truth: Essays on Language and the Female in Greek Thought*, Center for Hellenic Studies, 2008.

Bertolin, Reyes, 'The Mast and the Loom: Signifiers of Separation and Authority', *Phoenix*, Spring/Summer 2008.

Blondell, Ruby, *Helen of Troy: Beauty, Myth, Devastation*, Oxford University Press, 2013.

Bottino, Aldo Paolo, 'The *Pharos* of Laertes: Weaving the Fabric of Epic', Center for Hellenic Studies, n.d.

Brann, Eva, *Homeric Moments: Clues to Delight in Reading the Odyssey and the Iliad*, Paul Dry Books, 2002.

Brown, A. S., 'Aphrodite and the Pandora Complex', *The Classical Quarterly*, 1997.

Burgess, Jonathan S., *Homer* (Understanding Classics series), Bloomsbury, 2015.

Burkert, Walter, *Greek Religion*, Wiley-Blackwell, 1991.

Calder, L., *Helen: The Evolution from Divine to Heroic in Greek Epic Traditions*, Brill Academic Publishers, 1976.

Carson, Anne, *Eros, The Bittersweet*, Princeton University Press, 1986.

Classical Literary Criticism, translated by Penelope Murray and T. S. Dorsch with an introduction and notes by Penelope Murray, Penguin Classics, 1965, 2000, 2004.

Classical Women Poets, translated with an introduction by Josephine Balmer, Bloodaxe Books, 1996.

Clayton, Barbara, *A Penelope Poetics: Reweaving the Feminine in Homer's Odyssey*, Lexington Books, 2004.

Cohen, Beth (ed.), *The Distaff Side: Representing the Female in Homer's Odyssey*, Oxford University Press, 1995.

Combellack, Frederick, 'Two Blameless Homeric Characters', *The American Journal of Philology*, Winter 1982.

Considine, P., 'Some Homeric Terms for Anger', *Acta Classica*, 1966.

D'Angelo, Frank J. 'The Rhetoric of Ekphrasis', *JAC*, 1998.

Dillon, Matthew, *Women and Girls in Classical Greek Religion*, Routledge, 2002.

Diodorus Siculus, *Library of History, Volume II, Books 2.35–4.58*. Loeb Classical Library edition, translated by C. H. Oldfather, Harvard University Press, 1935.

Due, Casey, *Variations on a Lament by Briseis*, Rowman & Littlefield, 2002.

Edmonds, Susan, *Homeric Nepios*, Center for Hellenic Studies, 2013.

Edmunds, Lowell (ed.), *Approaches to Greek Myth*, John Hopkins University Press, 2014.

Epictetus, *Encheiridion: The Manual for Living*, translated by George Long with an introduction by Odysseus Makridis, Barnes & Noble, 2005.

Epictetus, *Of Human Freedom*, translated by Robert Dobbin, Penguin, 2008, 2010.

Euripides, *Orestes and Other Plays*, translated with an introduction by Philip Vellacott, Penguin Classics, 1972.

Euripides, *Electra and Other Plays*, translated by John Davie with an introduction and notes by Richard Rutherford, Penguin Classics, 1998, 2004.

Euripides, *Trojan Women, Iphigenia Among the Taurians, Ion*, Loeb Classical Library edition translated by David Kovacs, Harvard University Press, 1999.

Euripides, *Heracles and Other Plays*, translated by John Davie with an introduction and notes by Richard Rutherford, Penguin Classics, 2002.

Euripides, *Heracles and Other Plays*, translated by Robin Waterfield, introduction by Edith Hall, notes by James Morwood, Oxford World's Classics, 2003.

Euripides, *Bacchae and Other Plays*, translated by John Davie with an introduction and notes by Richard Rutherford, Penguin Classics, 2005.

Euripides, *The Iphigenia Plays*, translated with an introduction by Rachel Hadas, Northwestern University Press, 2018.

Felson, Nancy, *Regarding Penelope: From Character to Poetics*, University of Oklahoma Press, 1994.

Finley, M. I., *The World of Odysseus*, introduction by Bernard Knox, NYRB Classics, 1982, 2002.

Foley, John Miles, '"Reading" Homer through Oral Tradition', *College Literature*, Spring 2007.

Foley, John Miles (ed.), *A Companion to Ancient Epic*, Wiley-Blackwell, 2009.

Fowler, Robert (ed.), *The Cambridge Companion to Homer*, Cambridge University Press, 2014.

Gaspa, Salvatore, Cecile Michel, and Marie-Louise Nosch (eds), *Textile Terminologies from the Orient to the Mediterranean and Europe, 1000 BC–1000 AD*, Zea Books, 2017.

Gilgamesh, translated with an introduction and notes by Stephen Mitchell, Washington Square Press, 2004.

Gilgamesh: A New Translation, translated by Gerald J. Davis, Insignia Publishing, 2014.

Gilgamesh: A New Translation of the Ancient Epic, translated with introduction and essays on the poem, its past, and its passion by Sophus Helle, Yale University Press, 2021.

Graziosi, Barbara, *Inventing Homer: The Early Reception of Epic*, Cambridge University Press, 2002.

Graziosi, Barbara, *Homer*, Oxford University Press, 2016.

Graziosi, Barbara, *Homer: Iliad Book VI*, Cambridge Greek and Latin Classics, 2010.

Graziosi, Barbara, *The Gods of Olympus: A History*, Metropolitan Books, 2014.

Graziosi, Barbara and Emily Greenwood, *Homer in the Twentieth Century: Between World Literature and the Western Canon*, Oxford University Press, 2007.

Graziosi, Barbara and Johannes Haubold, *The Resonance of Epic*, Bloomsbury, 2008.

Greene, Ellen, *Women Poets in Ancient Greece and Rome*, University of Oklahoma, 2005.

Greek Epic Fragments, Loeb Classical Library edition translated by Martin L. West, Harvard University Press, 2003.

Greek Poems to the Gods: Hymns from Homer to Proclus, translated with an introduction and notes by Barry B. Powell, University of California Press, 2021.

Haland, Evy Johanne, 'Athena's Peplos: Weaving as a Core Female Activity in Ancient and Modern Greece', *Cosmos*, 2006.

Hall, Edith, *The Return of Ulysses: A Cultural History of Homer's Odyssey*, Johns Hopkins University Press, 2008.

Harich-Schwarzbauer, Henriette (ed.), *Texts and Textiles in the Ancient World*, Oxbow Books, 2016.

Harris, William V., *Restraining Rage: The Ideology of Anger Control in Classical Antiquity*, Harvard University Press, 2001.

Hartwick, Kerry, 'Tracking the *Odyssey*'s Plot Through Dawn's Epithets', *Studies in Mediterranean Antiquity and Classics*, 2013.

Herodotus, *The Histories*, translated by Robin Waterfield with an introduction and notes by Carolyn Dewald, Oxford World's Classics, 1998.

Herodotus, *The Histories*, translated by Tom Holland with an introduction and notes by Paul Cartledge, Penguin Classics, 2013.

Hesiod, *Theogony and Words and Days, Theognis, Elegies*, translated with an introduction by Dorothea Wender, Penguin Classics, 1973.

Hesiod, *The Poems of Hesiod: Theogony, Works and Days, and the Shield of Herakles*, translated with an introduction and notes by Barry B. Powell, University of California Press, 2017.

Hesiod, *Works and Days*, translated with an introduction and notes by A. E. Stallings, Penguin Classics, 2018.

Homer, *Iliad*, translated with an introduction by Alexander Pope, Heritage Press, 1715–1720, 1943.

Homer, *Iliad* Books 1–12, Oxford Classical Texts edition, prepared by T. W. Allen and D. B. Monroe, Oxford University Press, 1920 (3rd edition).

Homer, *Iliad* Books 13–24, Oxford Classical Texts edition, prepared by T. W. Allen and D. B. Monroe, Oxford University Press, 1920 (3rd edition).

Homer, *Iliad*, translated by W. H. D. Rouse with an introduction by Seth L. Schein and an afterword by Adam Nicolson, Turtleback Books, 1938, 2007, 2014.

Homer, *Iliad*, translated by E. V. Rieu, revised and updated by Peter Jones with D. C. H. Rice, edited with introduction and notes by Peter Jones, Penguin Classics, 1950, 2003.

Homer, *Iliad*, translated by Richmond Lattimore with an introduction and notes by Richard P. Martin, University of Chicago Press, 1951, 2011.

Homer, *Iliad*, translated with an introduction by Robert Graves, Penguin Classics, 1959.

Homer, *Iliad*, translated by Robert Fagles, introduction and notes by Bernard Knox, Penguin Classics, 1990.

Homer, *Iliad*, translated by Stanley Lombardo with an introduction by Sheila Murnaghan, Hackett Publishing, 1997.

Homer, *Iliad*, Books 1–12, Loeb Classical Library edition, translated by A. T. Murray, revised by William F. Wyatt, Harvard University Press, 1999.

Homer, *Iliad*, Books 13–24, Loeb Classical Library edition, translated by A. T. Murray, revised by William F. Wyatt, Harvard University Press, 1999.

Homer, *Iliad*, translated with an introduction and notes by Stephen Mitchell, Atria Books, 2011.

Homer, *Iliad*, translated by Anthony Verity with an introduction and notes by Barbara Graziosi, Oxford World's Classics, 2011.

Homer, *Iliad*, translated with an introduction and notes by Erwin Cook, John Hopkins University Press, 2012.

Homer, *Iliad*, translated with introduction and notes by Peter Green, University of California Press, 2015.

Homer, *Iliad*, translated with introduction and notes by Caroline Alexander, HarperCollins, 2016.

Homer, *Iliad*, translated with an introduction and notes by Joe Sachs, Paul Dry Books, 2018.

Homer, *Odyssey*, Books 1–12, Oxford Classical Texts edition, prepared by Thomas W. Allen, Oxford University Press, 1917.

Homer, *Odyssey*, Books 12–24, Oxford Classical Texts edition, prepared by Thomas W. Allen, Oxford University Press, 1917.

Homer, *Odyssey*, translated by W. H. D. Rouse with an introduction by Deborah Steiner and an afterword by Adam Nicolson, Penguin Random House, 1937, 2007, 2014.

Homer, *Odyssey*, translated by E. V. Rieu, revised by D. C. H. Rieu, introduction by Peter Jones, Penguin Classics, 1946, 1991, 2003.

Homer, *Odyssey*, translated by Robert Fitzgerald with an introduction and notes by D. S. Carne-Ross, Farrar, Strauss and Giroux, 1961, 1998.

Homer, *Odyssey*, translated with an introduction by Richmond Lattimore, Harper, 1977.

Homer, *Odyssey*, translated by Robert Fagles with introduction and notes by Bernard Knox, Penguin Classics, 1996.

Homer, *Odyssey*, Books 1–12, Loeb Classical Library edition, translated by A. T. Murray, revised by George E. Dimock, Harvard University Press, 1998.

Homer, *Odyssey*, Books 13–24, Loeb Classical Library edition, translated by A. T. Murray, revised by George E. Dimock, Harvard University Press, 1998.

Homer, *Odyssey*, translated by Martin Hammond with an introduction by Jasper Griffin, Bloomsbury, 2000.

Homer, *Odyssey*, translated with introduction and notes by Stephen Mitchell, Atria Books, 2013.

Homer, *Odyssey*, translated with introduction and notes by Barry B. Powell, Oxford University Press, 2015.

Homer, *Odyssey*, translated by Anthony Verity with an introduction and notes by William Allan, Oxford World's Classics, 2016.

Homer, *Odyssey*, translated with introduction and notes by Peter Green, University of California Press, 2018.

Homer, *Odyssey*, translated with introduction and notes by Emily Wilson (paperback edition), W. W. Norton & Company, 2018.

Homeric Hymns, translated with an introduction and notes by Michael Crudden, Oxford World's Classics, 2001.

Homeric Hymns, Homeric Apocrypha, Lives of Homer, Loeb Classical Library edition translated by Martin L. West, Harvard University Press, 2003.

Homeric Hymns, translated by Jules Cashford with an introduction and notes by Nicholas Richardson, Penguin Classics, 2003.

Hyland, Drew A., 'Why Plato Wrote Dialogues', *Philosophy & Rhetoric*, Jan. 1968.

Jenkyns, Richard, *Classical Literature: An Epic Journey from Homer to Vergil and Beyond*, Basic Books, 2017.

Levaniouk, Olga, 'Penelope and the Pandareids', *Phoenix*, Spring-Summer, 2008.

Lightfoot, Jessica, *Wonder and the Marvellous from Homer to the Hellenistic World*, Cambridge University Press, 2021.

Lord, Albert, *The Singer of Tales*, Harvard University Press, 1960.

Lyons, Deborah, *Gender and Immortality: Heroines in Ancient Greek Myth and Cult*, Princeton University Press, 1997.

Marcolongo, Andrea, *The Ingenious Language: Nine Epic Reasons to Love Greek*, Europa Compass, 2019.

Marcus Aurelius, *Meditations*, translated with notes by Martin Hammond, introduction by Diskin Clay, Penguin Classics, 2006.

Marcus Aurelius, *Meditations with selected correspondence*, translated by Robin Hard with an introduction and notes by Christopher Gill, Oxford University Press, 2011.

Montanari, Franco, Antonios Rengakos and Christos C. Tsagalis (eds), *Homeric Contexts: Neoanalysis and the Interpretation of Oral Poetry*, De Gruyter, 2012.

Mueller, Melissa, 'Helen's Hands: Weaving for *Kleos* in the *Odyssey*', *Helios*, Spring 2010.

Nagy, Gregory, *The Best of the Achaeans*, Johns Hopkins University Press, 1998.

Nagy, Gregory, *Homer's Text and Language*, University of Illinois Press, 2004.

Nagy, Gregory, *The Ancient Greek Hero in 24 Hours*, Harvard University Press, 2013.

Nicolson, Adam, *Why Homer Matters*, Picador, 2014.
Nosch, Marie-Louise, 'The Loom and the Ship in Ancient Greece. Shared knowledge, shared terminology, cross-crafts, or cognitive maritime-textile archaeology?' In *Texts and Textiles in the Ancient World*, edited by Henriette Harich-Schwarzbauer, Oxbow Books, 2016.
Notopoulos, James A., 'Parataxis in Homer: A New Approach to Homeric Literary Criticism', *Transactions and Proceedings of the American Philological Association*, 1949.
Ovid, *Heroides*, translated by A. S. Kline, Poetry in Translation, 2001.
Ovid, *Metamorphoses*, translated by Frank Justus Miller, edited with an introduction and notes by Robert Squillace, Barnes & Noble, 1916, 2005.
Ovid, *Metamorphoses*, translated by Rolfe Humphries, annotated by Joseph D. Reed, Indiana University Press, 1983, 2018.
Ovid, *Metamorphoses: A New Verse Translations*, translated by David Raeburn with an introduction by Denis Feeney, Penguin Classics, 2004.
Pache, Corinne Ondine (ed.), *The Cambridge Guide to Homer*, Cambridge University Press, 2020.
Pantelia, Maria C., 'Helen and the Last Song for Hector', *Transactions of the American Philological Association*, Autumn 2002.
Pausanias, *Guide to Greece 1: Central Greece*, translated with an introduction by Peter Levi, Penguin Classics, 1979.
Pausanias, *Guide to Greece 2: Southern Greece*, translated with an introduction by Peter Levi, Penguin Classics, 1979.
Pindar, *Odes*, translated with an introduction by C. M. Bowra, Penguin Classics, 1969.
Pindar, *Nemean Odes, Isthmian Odes, Fragments*, Loeb Classical Library edition translated by William H. Race, Harvard University Press, 1997, 2012.
Pindar, *The Complete Odes*, translated by Anthony Verity with an introduction and notes by Stephen Instone, Oxford World's Classics, 2007.
Plant, I. M. (ed.), *Women Writers of Ancient Greece and Rome: An Anthology*, University of Oklahoma Press, 2004.
Plato, *Ion*, translated by Andrew J. Mihailoff, Kindle Library, 2013.
Plato, *Phaedrus*, translated with an introduction and notes by Christopher Rowe, Penguin Classics, 2005.
Plato, *Republic*, translated with an introduction and notes by Robin Waterfield, Oxford World's Classics, 1994.
Plato, *Symposium*, translated with an introduction and notes by Robin Waterfield, Oxford World's Classics, 2009.

Plato, *The Last Days of Socrates: Euthyphro, Apology, Crito, Phaedo*, translated with introduction and notes by Christopher Rowe, Penguin Classics, 2010.

Pomeroy, Sarah B., *Goddesses, Whores, Wives, and Slaves: Women in Classical Antiquity*, Schocken Books, 1995.

Porter, Andrew, 'Human fault and "[Harmful] Delusion" in Homer', *Phoenix*, Spring/Summer 2017.

Powell, Barry B., *Homer*, Wiley-Blackwell, 2009.

Reynolds, L. D. and N. G. Wilson, *Scribes and Scholars: A Guide to the Transmission of Greek and Latin Literature*, Oxford University Press, 2013.

Rynearson, Nicholas C., 'Helen, Achilles and the Psyche: Superlative Beauty and Value in the *Iliad*', *Intertexts*, Spring/Fall 2013.

Sappho, *If Not, Winter: Fragments of Sappho*, translated with an introduction by Anne Carson, Vintage, 2002.

Sappho's Lyre: Archaic Lyric and Women Poets of Ancient Greece, translations with introduction and notes by Diane J. Mayor, University of California Press, 1991.

Schulte, Rainer and John Biguenet (eds), *Theories of Translation: An Anthology of Essays from Dryden to Derrida*, University of Chicago Press, 1992.

Slatkin, Nancy, *The Power of Thetis and Selected Essays*, Harvard University Press, 2011.

Sophocles, *Three Theban Plays*, translated by Robert Fagles, Penguin Classics, 1984.

Sophocles, *Four Tragedies: Ajax, Women of Trachis, Electra, Philoctetes*, translated with introduction and notes by Peter Meineck and Paul Woodruff, Hackett, 2017.

Sophocles and Aeschylus, *All That You've Seen Here Is God: New Versions of Four Greek Tragedies, Sophocles' Ajax, Philoctetes, Women of Trachis, Prometheus Bound*, translated by Bryan Doerries, Vintage, 2015.

The Greek Histories: Essential Selections from Herodotus, Thucydides, Xenophon, and Plutarch, edited and annotated by Mary Lefkowitz and James Romm, translated by Carleton Brownson, Richard Crawley, Mary Lefkowitz, Pamela Mensch, Bernadette Perrin, James Romm, and Samuel Shirley, Modern Library, 2022.

The Epic Cycle, translated by Gregory Nagy, The Center for Hellenic Studies, n.d.

The Epic of Gilgamesh, translated with introduction by N. K. Sanders, Penguin Classics, 1972.

Theocritus, *Idylls*, translated by Anthony Verity with an introduction and notes by Richard Hunter, Oxford World's Classics, 2002.

Thucydides, *History of the Peloponnesian War*, translated by Rex Warner with an introduction and notes by M. I. Finley, Penguin Classics, 1954, 1972.

Thucydides, *The Landmark Thucydides: A Comprehensive Guide to the Peloponnesian War*, a newly revised edition of the Richard Crawley translation with maps, annotations, appendices, and encyclopaedic index edited by Robert B. Strassler with an introduction by Victor Davis Hanson, Simon & Schuster, 2008.

Tsagalis, Christos (ed.), *Theban Resonances in Homeric Epic*, De Gruyter, 2014.

Vergil, *Aeneid*, translated by Allan Mandelbaum, Bantam, 1970.

Vergil, *Aeneid Book VI*, translated by Seamus Heaney, Farrar, Straus and Giroux, 2016.

Vergil, *The Aeneid*, translated with an introduction and notes by Shadi Bartsch, Modern Library, 2021.

Vergil, *The Aeneid*, translated by Sarah Ruden with an introduction by Susanna Braund and notes and glossary by Susanna Braund and Emma Hilliard, Yale University Press, 2021.

Usher, M. D., *Homeric Stitchings: The Homeric Centos of the Empress Eudocia*, Rowman & Littlefield, 1998.

Warwick, Celsiana, 'The Maternal Warrior', *American Journal of Philology*, Spring 2019.

Wilford, F. A., 'DAIMON in Homer', *Numen*, September 1965.

INDEX

achaea, achaeans, 4–9, 11, 16–17, 37–40, 43–45, 47, 50, 55, 57–60, 62, 64, 68, 70, 72, 77–78, 90, 100, 102, 107–108, 111–113, 117–119, 124, 132, 139, 151, 154, 167–168, 170–182
Achilles, 4, 6–7, 9–11, 13–17, 34–45, 47, 53–55, 57–60, 62, 70, 76–78, 80, 90, 97, 100–102, 104–106, 111, 117–118, 134–135, 139–140, 147, 162, 167–168, 170–180, 183–185, 187
Actaeon, 61
Adrasti, 50
Aeacus, 77
Aeaea, 83, 169, 184–185
Aegean, 160
aegis, 9, 30, 56, 75, 77–79, 81, 100, 180
aegisbearer, 79
Aegisthus, 70–71, 180–181
Aeneas, 53, 63–64, 66, 74–75, 154, 168, 174, 176
Aeneid, 147, 154–155
Aeolus, 22, 83, 87, 184
Aeschylus, 69, 155–156
aetiology, 24, 159
Agamemnon, 4, 6, 34, 36–38, 40, 57–60, 70, 80, 117, 126, 168, 170–171, 175–181, 184, 187

Agave, 61
aitia, 115, 159
Ajax, 172, 177, 180, 185
Ajaxes, 100
Alcandre, 50
Alcinous, 20–21, 76, 91–92, 94, 96–98, 181–184
Alcippe, 50
Alcmene, 117
Alexandria, 154
Ali, Seemee, 11
allotted, 70, 104, 163–164
allusions, 89
Ambidexter, 2, 24
ambrosia, 10, 41, 65, 72, 111, 119, 121, 179
Anchises, 63, 68, 168, 174
andra, 91
Andromache, 3, 13–14, 17–18, 28, 35, 38, 48–49, 76, 90, 96, 99–101, 103–107, 109–112, 115–116, 135, 137, 160, 162, 173, 177, 180
Andromache, 101, 173
antagonist, 4, 60, 66, 93, 117–118
anthologies, 44, 142, 155
anthropos, anthropoi, 91
Anticleia, 12, 18–19, 171
Antinous, 116–118, 121, 125, 131, 181, 185–187
antiphonal, 60, 111

antiquity, 157, 162
Antony, 154
aoido, 56
Aphrodite, 5–6, 8, 23–24, 34,
    45–47, 53–54, 63–64, 66–68,
    70, 74–76, 84, 107, 119, 127,
    139, 145, 168, 170, 172, 174,
    176, 179, 183
Apollo, 4, 6, 11, 15, 21, 41, 54,
    57–59, 65–66, 73–74, 94, 128,
    130–131, 150, 168, 170–171,
    174–177, 179–180, 186
Apollo, 131, 173
Apollonius, 156
apportion, 114–115, 163
archaic, 1, 38, 44, 53, 56, 97,
    149–151, 153, 155
Arete, 19–22, 91, 96–98, 160,
    183–184
Argives, 14, 17, 60, 71, 111, 123,
    154, 175
Argos, 8, 102, 113, 139, 172
Argus, 25, 72, 85
Ariadne, 150
Artemis, 49, 63, 94, 98, 100,
    126–128, 130, 168, 183
assembly, 3–4, 11, 31, 40–41, 53–54,
    69–70, 72, 92–93, 115, 117, 121,
    168, 175–176, 179–182
Astyanax, 99, 101, 103–104,
    108–109, 116, 173
Atalanta, 150
Athena, 1–3, 5, 7–10, 12–13,
    19–22, 24–25, 27, 30, 36, 42–43,
    49, 52–57, 62–64, 66, 68–79,
    81–82, 84, 92–97, 99, 103, 105,
    113–115, 117–119, 121–122,
    125–128, 130, 132, 134–136,
    139, 146, 164, 166–167,
    172–174, 176–183, 185–187

Athena, 78, 172
Athenian, 155
Atlas, 71, 169
Atreus, 51, 58–59, 73, 100,
    170–171
audience, 87, 149, 165
Augustus, 154
authoritative, 92, 165
authoritative story, 165
Autonoe, 61

Babylonian, 145, 152
bacchae, 61
bard, 26, 45, 54–59, 62, 79–80,
    87–88, 97, 99, 101, 106, 110,
    112–115, 121, 123, 130, 136,
    144, 149–150, 175–181,
    183–184, 187
Bellerophon, 174
Bertolin, Reyes, 114
blameless, 39, 122
blessing, 95, 109
boundless, 48–49, 72, 112,
    118, 122
breath, 15, 40, 55–56, 58, 72, 91,
    108, 115, 158
Briareus, 4
Briseis, 4, 6, 23, 33–36, 59,
    170, 175

Cadmus, 60–61, 169
Caesar, 147, 154
Calypso, 54, 70, 79–82, 84–85, 97,
    122, 169, 181–183
captive, 13, 23–27, 29, 31, 33, 35,
    37, 39, 41, 43, 45, 47, 49, 51,
    70–71, 80–82, 91–92, 143, 169,
    181, 183
causality, 7, 28, 35, 37, 43, 45–46,
    48–49, 57, 66–67, 69–71, 81,

103, 106, 112, 114–116, 118, 126–127, 159, 170–171, 175, 179, 181
Charybdis, 185
Chronos, 150
Chryseis, 4, 6, 23, 170, 175
Chryses, 4, 59, 170, 175
Cicones, 83, 183
Cilicia, 99
Cilicians, 100
Circe, 22, 83–88, 121, 150, 169, 184–185
Cleopatra, 154
Clytemnestra, 70, 126, 150, 170, 181
coherence, 58, 147–148, 166
cohesion, 60
communal, 106, 150–151
companion, 15, 17, 22, 32, 39, 58–59, 78, 80–81, 83–86, 94, 110, 118, 121, 140, 145, 158, 162, 171, 180
compensation, 15, 19, 40, 48, 100, 112, 136, 175
complementarity, 2–3, 19, 36–37, 54, 58, 68, 74, 138, 155, 167
consciousness, 9, 14–15, 17–18, 20–21, 24, 31, 34, 39, 42, 45–51, 59, 63–65, 67, 70, 72–73, 77, 80, 85, 94, 96, 100, 102, 104, 108, 114, 117, 119–121, 123, 125, 127, 131–132, 134–135, 137–139, 144, 147, 158, 160–161
Considine, P., 5
contest, 44, 57, 72, 126, 128, 130–131, 133, 176, 186
cosmic, 1, 3, 5–6, 8, 10–11, 25–26, 35, 37–38, 41, 43, 54–55, 57, 60, 62, 69, 96–97, 105–106, 117–119, 128, 143, 146–147, 154, 162, 169
counterpart, 4, 21, 31, 44, 92, 102, 130
crafts, 2, 24, 92, 167
Crete, 87, 185–186
Cronus, 1, 7–8, 17, 20, 24, 36, 38, 42, 71–72, 167–168
cult, 48–49, 54, 60, 62, 89–91, 98–99, 110
culture, 1, 23, 48, 52, 56, 89, 143, 147, 149, 153, 157–158
cyclicality, 7, 23, 35, 107
Cyclops, 72, 83, 184
Cypria, 38, 41, 44
Cyprus, 64
Cytherea, 119

dactylic hexameter, 148
daimon, 5, 8, 11, 46–47, 67–68, 90, 99, 104, 120, 123, 127–128, 137, 140, 146, 161, 163
Danaan, 17, 47, 56, 58, 64–65, 67, 114, 154, 175
Dawn, 63, 127–128, 160, 179–180
deathless, 2, 24, 42, 45, 54, 75, 78, 81, 92, 120, 123, 164
Delos, 94–95
Delusion, 139, 179
Demeter, 53–54
demigod, 54, 68, 145–146
Demodocus, 56–57, 113, 144, 149, 183
destiny, 11, 18, 61, 64, 74, 100, 107
Dia, 145, 164, 168
Diomedes, 53, 64–66, 74–75, 84, 172, 174, 176–178
Dione, 54, 145, 168
Dionysus, 61–62

disconnected, 11, 32, 41, 59, 76, 80, 96, 105–107, 118, 126, 161–162
distaff, 49–50, 96, 104–105, 114–116, 118, 132, 177, 181, 186
divine, 52, 58, 97, 127, 153, 162–163
dmoee, 28, 107, 165
Dolios, 31
dualities, 23, 63, 89, 158
Dulichium, 123

Eetion, 99–101, 107
Egypt, 49–50, 52, 181
Elektra, 150
Elysium, 109
enchanted, 84, 87, 121, 184
enelusion, 109
Enkidu, 145
ennepo, 56
enslaved, 4, 13, 23–24, 28, 31–34, 96, 106–107, 116, 124–125, 142, 165, 170, 181, 184–186
enslavement, 13, 19, 23, 28, 96, 102, 105, 130, 165
enya, 64, 66
ephemeral, 144
epic, 1–10, 12, 14, 16, 18–20, 22–28, 30–32, 34, 36, 38, 40–46, 48–50, 52–60, 62, 64, 66, 68, 70, 72–74, 76, 78–80, 82, 84, 86, 88–90, 92, 94, 96, 98, 100, 102, 104, 106–108, 110–112, 114, 116, 118, 120, 122, 124, 126, 128, 130, 132, 134, 136, 138, 140, 142–158, 160, 162–166, 168, 170, 172–174, 176, 178, 180, 182, 184, 186

epigraph, 165
epiphany, 97
epithet, 28, 57, 121, 128, 159, 161, 163–164
eternal, 15, 19, 23, 35–36, 41–43, 54–57, 69, 78, 82, 89–91, 98, 102, 105–106, 110, 112, 144, 152, 162
ether, 77
Ethiopians, 37
Eumaeus, 23, 31, 130–131, 135, 185, 187
Eumenides, 69
Euripides, 50, 61, 155–156
Eurycleia, 23, 26–33, 125–126, 130–131, 133, 135–137, 159, 170, 181–182, 186–187
Eurylochus, 83–84
Eurymachus, 31, 120, 131–132
Eurymedon, 20
Eurynome, 119–120, 122, 125
Eurystheus, 69

faithful, 9, 114
fame, 8, 19, 23, 25–26, 37, 48, 50, 55, 57–58, 74, 89, 91, 98, 102–103, 109–110, 113, 117, 120, 122–124, 140–141, 162, 168, 171, 173, 181
fame in song, 37, 102, 117, 120, 122–123, 162, 181
fate, 13, 16, 24–25, 35, 41, 104, 107, 109, 114–116, 120, 124, 127, 159, 163–165, 174, 177–178
fated, 16, 36–37, 63, 71, 96, 105, 108, 110, 127, 174, 176, 182
Fates, 3, 45, 70, 87, 98, 112, 163
feminine authority, 1, 3, 99, 114–116, 118, 123

festival, 12, 23, 58, 60, 143, 147, 149, 154–155, 165
foresight, 83, 159
forever, 38, 40, 72, 82, 113
formula, 7, 21, 27, 35, 55, 139, 148
funeral, 14, 16, 49, 60, 73, 106, 110–111, 172, 179–181, 185, 187
funeral song, 60, 110–111
Furies, 127

Ganymede, 63, 68
genealogy, 8, 20, 26–27, 44, 61, 69, 100, 146, 178
generations, 3, 17, 47, 52, 63, 172, 187
Gilgamesh, 145–146, 152
girdled, 16, 103
glaucos, 164, 172, 174, 177–178
glaukopis, 164
glaux, 164
glory, 15, 42, 70, 124, 162
goddess, 1, 3, 5, 10–12, 23–24, 30, 34–36, 38, 40–47, 53, 55–59, 61–67, 71–72, 76–78, 80, 82, 84, 86, 93–94, 98, 119, 122, 126–128, 134, 160, 167–169, 173, 175, 182–183, 187
goddesses, 3, 10, 12, 24–25, 36, 42–43, 53–55, 57, 59–61, 63, 65–69, 71, 73, 75, 77, 79, 81, 83–85, 87, 152, 167, 182
godinspired, 57, 113
godlike, 34, 40, 45, 48, 51, 67, 70–71, 77–78, 113, 117, 121, 124, 126–129, 136, 164, 171
goos, 60, 110
Gorgon, 79
Graziosi, Barbara, 143–144, 146–147, 149

Greece, 34, 90, 110, 149–150, 157, 160
grief, 4, 10, 15, 19, 23–25, 31, 35–37, 39–43, 48–49, 53, 60, 63, 68, 85, 97, 100, 102, 105–108, 110–113, 118, 122–124, 128, 135, 139, 141–142, 171, 180–181, 186
guest, 21–22, 28, 56–57, 73, 97, 123, 131–132, 148, 174, 177, 181, 184

Hades, 16, 54, 58, 60, 89, 100, 104, 108, 169, 184–185
harmony, 3, 9, 17, 21, 28, 31, 91, 99, 130
hearers, 22, 62, 121, 149
hearth, 96, 134, 187
Hector, 12–17, 23, 34, 40–44, 47–49, 54–55, 62, 76, 90, 96–97, 99–112, 115, 117, 130, 133–135, 137, 139
Hecuba, 3, 12–18, 21, 23, 28, 38, 48–49, 99, 102, 105, 112, 163, 173, 177, 179–180
Helen, 3–6, 8, 23, 26, 34, 43–52, 57, 59, 63, 66–67, 76, 79, 95–96, 99, 106, 112, 133, 139, 147, 154, 160, 168–169, 171, 173, 176–177, 180, 182, 185
Helenus, 12–13, 99, 177
Helios, 78, 86, 162, 169, 185
Hellas, 113
Hellenistic, 153, 155
Hephaestus, 1–3, 6, 9, 24, 36, 40–41, 47, 51–52, 148, 167–168, 170, 175, 177, 179, 183
Hera, 2–12, 35–36, 41–42, 51, 53–54, 62–63, 69–70, 78,

93, 98, 118–119, 127, 162, 167–169, 174–179
Heracles, 109–110, 160, 172, 179
Hermes, 24, 72, 81–82, 84, 87, 92, 169, 180, 182, 184, 187
Hermione, 169
hero, 6–7, 9–10, 14–15, 17, 19–21, 23, 26–28, 36, 38–41, 44, 48–49, 51–52, 54–59, 62, 64, 66, 68, 70, 73–76, 78–80, 89–101, 103, 105–107, 109–111, 113, 115, 117–119, 121, 123–127, 129, 131, 133, 135, 137–143, 146–148, 150–155, 158, 161, 164–165, 167–173
Herodotus, 50
heroism, 174
heros, 89–91, 165
Hesiod, 1–4, 20, 24–25, 44, 54–55, 68–69, 89–91, 96, 106, 144, 146–147, 152–153, 155, 166
Hestia, 63, 134
histemi, 94, 97, 101, 114
histion, 92
histos, 92, 114
homecoming, 12, 59, 72, 113, 133, 151, 167, 180–181
Homer, 1, 3–4, 12, 19, 23–26, 28, 33, 51–56, 58, 60, 63, 66, 74, 80, 89–91, 96, 98, 111, 121, 128, 141–160, 162, 164–166, 168
homeric, 43, 53, 58, 63, 68–69, 88, 142, 144–151, 153, 161
Homeric Hymn to Demeter, 53
Homeros, 143
Homers, 153
hora, 7
hospitality, 22, 31–32, 51, 95, 120, 131, 154, 158, 173, 184–185

humanity, 112, 121
humans, 26, 91, 142
hymn, 53, 63, 68–69

Icarius, 113
ichor, 65
identity, 15, 23, 31, 35, 59, 63, 79–82, 87, 97–98, 113, 135, 138, 144–145, 158–159, 172, 183
Idomeneus, 100
Iliad, 3–6, 9–13, 15–17, 23, 26–27, 34–36, 41, 43–45, 47–50, 52–55, 57–59, 62–64, 66, 68–69, 73, 75–76, 78–79, 82, 92–94, 96–97, 99, 101, 109, 115, 117, 119, 123–124, 130, 133–134, 138–139, 142–143, 145–146, 148–150, 152, 157–158, 162, 164, 167–171, 173–175, 177, 179–181, 183, 185, 187
Iliads, 149
Ilium, 39, 56, 99, 102, 104, 120, 123, 151
Imbros, 15, 41
immortal memory, 55
immortalisation, 109–110
immortalised, 25, 62, 89, 160
immortalises, 15
immortalising, 10–11, 121, 160
immortality, 10, 38, 63, 145, 171, 182
imperishable, 37, 42
initiation, 49, 91
Ino, 60, 62, 82, 86, 92, 160, 169, 182
inspiration, 115, 157–158
intention, 5, 7, 9, 11, 25, 28–29, 36, 38, 43, 54, 62, 76, 81–82, 86, 90, 97, 103, 116, 119–122,

125–126, 130, 150, 154,
157–158, 162, 165–167, 178,
181–182, 185–186
interconnection, 24, 91
interdependent, 3, 74
invocation, 35, 55–57, 70, 175
Ion, 165
Iris, 41–44, 65, 168, 176–177,
179–180
Irus, 32
Ishtar, 145
Isthmian, 36–38
Ithaca, 18–19, 22, 49, 51, 54, 56,
58, 71–73, 81–83, 87, 97–98,
113, 115, 118–119, 122–123,
130, 132, 136–137, 144, 149,
163, 170–171, 181–182,
184–187
Ithacan, 83, 98, 172

judgement, 83, 159, 161

kelainefis, 160
kleos, 15–16, 19, 22, 38, 48–49,
102–103, 106, 110–111,
117–118, 122–124, 135,
138–139, 141, 162–163, 165
kudos, 15, 162–163, 165
kyaneos, 160

Lacedaemon, 46, 67
Laertes, 3, 18, 27, 30, 49, 53, 82,
86, 116, 124, 170–171, 181, 187
Laestrygonian, 83, 184
lament, 14–16, 28, 34–35, 37,
48–49, 60, 102–103, 105,
108–112, 116, 122–124, 128,
139, 148, 163, 173, 179–180
lamentation, 15, 49, 86, 102,
104–105, 111–112

lamented, 104–105, 126
lamenting, 39, 43, 71, 82, 108, 111
lanthano, 5
Latinised, 143, 175
leader of men, 34, 58, 173
leader of women, 23, 173
leaders, 1, 3, 6, 45, 55–56, 91,
93, 110, 118, 136, 143, 172,
174–176, 178
leadership, 21, 92–93, 118,
145, 171
Leda, 44, 168
legend, 17, 151
legends, 145, 147, 151
Lemnos, 15
leto, 59
leuko, 160
leukothea, 160
lifetime, 158
lightfoot, 97
lion, 61, 83, 93–94, 123
listeners, 55, 142, 148
literacy, 56, 143, 146–148, 153
literate, 57–58, 147, 150, 152–153
literature, 143, 145–150
loom, 19, 44, 84, 102, 104–105,
114–116, 118, 124, 132, 177,
181, 186
Lycaon, 73–74
Lycia, 73, 174, 179
lyre, 56, 136, 149–150
lyric, 148

macro, 69, 146
madness, 61–62
maenad, 107
Maeonia, 46, 67
maidens, 33, 105, 127
makaron nesoisie, 147
manifest, 90–91, 115, 118

marriage, 35–36, 52, 93, 101, 124, 126–127, 130, 138, 167, 185
martial, 76, 171, 187
masculine authority, 1, 3, 30, 114–115, 118, 133
mast, 92, 114–115, 182, 185
Mediterranean, 152, 154
Medon, 182, 187
Megapenthes, 51–52
megas, 161
melanthius, 31
melantho, 23, 26, 31–32, 186
meleager, 177
memory, 19, 27, 34–35, 52, 55–56, 58, 60, 63, 90, 98, 106, 110, 112, 135, 150, 165, 170
Menelaos, 6–7, 44–47, 49–52, 59, 67, 69, 73, 75, 96, 168–171, 176–177, 181–182, 185
menis, 45, 162
menos, 115
mentality, 93, 96
Mentes, 73, 115, 181
messenger, 17, 24–25, 46, 72, 105, 123, 168
metaphorically, 116
Metis/metis, 2, 68–69, 78, 167
metonym, 91, 123, 130
metre, 128, 146
mne, 115
Mnemosyne, 55, 150
Moira, 163–164
Moirai, 163
mortality, 23–24, 145, 158, 162
multiform, 145, 149
Muse, 55–60, 70, 80, 111, 180
Muses, 55–60, 111–112, 150, 176
mutable, 3, 33, 35
mutatas, 155
Mycenae, 8, 117, 170–171, 187

Myntos, 34
Myrmidons, 35, 180
myth, 23, 34, 45, 49, 54–55, 58, 60, 62, 69, 89–91, 109, 128, 135, 144–147, 150–156, 160, 165, 177
mythology, 150, 152–155
mythos, 165

Nagy, Gregory, 47, 80, 89, 98, 109, 115, 147–149, 153, 158, 160–161, 163–165
narrative, 1, 3, 6, 22–23, 25, 34, 36–37, 39, 44, 50, 53–54, 59–60, 62–63, 69–70, 81, 87–88, 91–92, 98–99, 105, 107, 109, 113, 121, 125, 146, 148, 158, 168, 171–172, 180
narratives, 23, 38–39, 50, 53, 55, 59, 88–91, 109, 135, 142–147, 151, 155, 167, 175, 177, 179, 181, 183, 185, 187
Nausicaa, 22, 68, 76, 90–99, 101, 109, 114, 167, 182–183
Nausithous, 20
necessity, 102, 157
Nemesis, 44, 169
nepios, 106, 161–162
Nereus, 35, 39, 170
Nestor, 172, 176, 178, 181
noos, 165–166
nostos, 81, 91, 98, 111, 139, 158–159
Notopoulos, John, 148
nymph, 4, 35–37, 72, 80, 100–101, 169, 171, 182

oath, 8–9, 29–30, 47, 82, 84–85, 182, 187
ochtheo, 5

Octavian, 154
ode, 36, 147
Odysseus, 3, 12, 18–22, 25–26, 28–33, 43, 49–50, 53–62, 68, 70–73, 75–76, 78, 80–88, 90, 92–99, 101, 109, 111, 113–116, 118–141, 144–147, 149, 158–159, 162–163, 167–172, 176, 178, 180–187
odyssey, 3, 5, 10, 12, 19, 22–23, 25, 28, 43, 49, 51, 53–60, 63, 68, 70, 73, 75–76, 78–80, 83, 87–88, 91, 99, 111–112, 123–124, 140, 142–146, 149–150, 152, 157–159, 164–165, 167–173, 175, 177, 179–181, 183–185, 187
Ogygia, 72, 92, 169, 182, 185
Oikoumene, 150
olbioi, 147
Olympian, 36, 53, 56, 68, 71, 167, 175
Olympians, 4, 6–7, 12, 146, 164
olympus, 3, 9, 11, 25–26, 35–38, 42–43, 46, 53–55, 65, 67, 69–70, 73, 93, 117, 127, 137, 164, 167–169, 175, 178–180
omen, 17, 26, 75, 99, 126, 173, 176–178, 180
oracle, 58
oral, oral tradition, 39, 43, 69, 143, 145, 147–150, 153
orality, 153
orally, 143–144, 147–149
Orestes, 70, 170, 180
oversaw, 101
Ovid, 44, 154–156
owl, 1–2, 24, 68–72, 74, 76–77, 105, 114, 119, 132, 164

Pallas, 1, 25, 74–75, 77, 113
Panathenaea, 143
Pandareus, 127–128
Pandarus, 64
Pandora, 24–25, 90–91, 96, 119, 146–147
Pantelia, Maria C., 49
paradox, 1, 43, 47, 103, 142
Paris, 3–6, 44–47, 53, 66, 69, 73, 75, 96, 154, 168, 170, 173, 176–177
Patroclus, 10, 13, 15–16, 34–35, 39–41, 76–78, 118, 134, 167–168, 171, 174, 178–180
patron, 68, 93
patronage, 53, 64, 68, 73–74, 76–78, 172, 176
pattern and variation, 28
Peleus, 36, 39, 57–58, 77, 170–171
Penelope, 3, 5, 10–11, 18, 25, 28, 30–32, 49, 52–53, 57, 68, 76, 79–82, 87–88, 90, 97–98, 111–126, 128–141, 146, 149, 159–160, 162, 165, 167, 171–172, 181–182, 184–187
Pentheus, 61
pepnoumai, 115
perception, 9, 11, 16, 18–19, 21–23, 27, 29–32, 36, 39–40, 42–43, 69, 90, 94–95, 102–103, 108, 116–120, 125–128, 137, 143, 161, 164
performance, 145, 149–150, 153, 155
performances, 145, 148–149, 153–154
Periboea, 20
periphron, 28, 121, 159
permeable, 23, 151
Persephone, 53
personified, 150, 163

perspectives, 150, 156, 159
Phaeacian, 19, 56, 76, 91, 144, 167, 182
Phaeacians, 18–22, 56–57, 61, 83–84, 86–87, 92–93, 95–98, 121, 141, 145, 163, 169, 183, 185
Phaedimus, 51
Phemius, 56–57, 113, 132, 144, 149, 181, 187
Phoenix, 177
Phorcys, 72
phren, 161, 164
Phrygia, 46, 67
Phyllo, 50
Pindar, 36–38, 155
Pisenor, 27
Pisistratus, 181
pity, 13, 16, 61–62, 86, 99–100, 104, 108, 169
Placus, 99–100, 108
plague, 6, 11, 59, 70, 168, 170, 175
pledge, 143, 150
poem, 56, 143–144, 146, 148, 151, 154–155
poet, 36, 44, 144, 154–156
poetry, 97, 142, 145, 153–155, 168
poikilon, 79
Polybius, 50, 52
Polydamas, 101, 178
Polyphemus, 72, 83, 168, 184
polytropos, 163
portent, 13, 79, 106
portion, 14–15, 37, 42, 47, 57, 61, 82, 104, 108, 163–164, 186
Poseidon, 9, 11–12, 20–21, 36, 54, 57, 61, 70–72, 83, 92, 140, 168–169, 174, 177–178, 180–185
potions, 121, 169

prayer, 12–15, 26, 40, 55, 74–75, 96, 98–99, 103–105, 108–110, 128, 130–131, 177
Priam, 3, 7–8, 12–14, 16–17, 28, 43, 45, 49, 97, 102, 105–106, 108, 110, 139–140, 163, 173, 176, 179–180
prize, 4, 6, 13–15, 19, 34, 38, 129, 165, 170, 175, 177, 180
Prometheus, 1, 3, 24, 54, 147
prominent, 93, 131
prompt, 34, 49, 68, 75, 131, 135, 170, 175, 177
prophet, prophets, prophecy, 37, 68, 134, 140–141, 144, 168, 171, 177, 184–185
psyche, 80, 158
Ptolemaic, 154
public speech, 3, 114, 132–133, 165, 181
Pylos, 29, 57, 72, 172, 181
pyre, 49, 73, 110
Pythia, 35, 171
Python, 58

Quintilian, 143

reader, 14–15, 22, 54, 56, 63, 83, 87–88, 121, 142–143, 147–148, 150–151, 158, 161–162
receiver, 7, 12, 88, 128, 149, 156
reception, 143, 153–155, 157
recipient, 76, 90, 99
recitations, 58, 143
reciting, 142, 149
reconcile, 145, 158
reconciliation, 28, 55, 173
reintegration, 118, 139
repetition, 7, 9, 95, 107, 132–133, 137, 139, 147, 150

Index

resonance, 70, 146–147
resonances, 7, 50, 152, 158
responsibilities, 15, 52, 93, 122
restoration, 11, 98, 130
restrain, 12, 14, 133, 159, 162, 187
retelling, 1, 43–44, 55, 69, 155, 177
retribution, 15–16, 136
reunion, 3, 18, 31, 58, 125, 134–135, 140–142, 172, 185
reunite, 6, 53, 128, 138, 187
reverence, 13, 16, 50, 94–95, 97, 101, 106
rhapsode, 59, 149
rhapsodes, 56, 58
Rhexenor, 20
Rhodes, 156, 172
rites, 14, 16, 49, 110, 179–180
ritual, 48–49, 51, 54–55, 89–91, 120, 125–126, 143, 145, 147, 150–151, 153, 173
Rome, 154

sacred, 1, 12, 14, 22–23, 32, 48, 54–60, 71, 73, 80, 86, 95, 102, 112, 120, 131, 134, 143, 145, 151, 154–155, 158, 162–163, 173, 185
sacrificial, 150, 163
Salamis, 172
Samos, 15, 41, 123
Sappho, 156
Sarpedon, 172, 174, 178–179
Scamander, 99, 179
Scamandros, 168
sceptre, 47, 150, 176
scribal, 145
scripts, 145, 149
scripture, 153
Scylla, 185
seasonality, 7, 23, 167

seasonally, 89, 147, 150
seer, 12, 91, 144, 185
sema, 101
Semele, 61
Shakespeare, 147, 149
shield, 45, 74, 179
shimmering, 113, 129
shroud, 106, 116, 124, 172, 181
Sidon, 52
Sidonians, 51
simile, 66, 75, 93–94, 122–123, 128, 138, 140
singer, 149
Sirens, 185
slaves captured in war, 165
Sophocles, 155
sorrow, 18, 24, 36–37, 59, 80, 82, 108, 158
Sparta, 4, 6, 8, 29, 46, 49, 51–52, 72, 154, 169–171, 173, 181–182, 185
Spartan, 44, 49, 169, 171
spear, 45, 64–65, 69–70, 72–73, 78–79, 102
speech, 3–5, 7, 13–14, 16, 18–19, 22, 24, 27–28, 35, 37, 60, 81–83, 88, 92–93, 95, 98, 101, 103, 111, 114–115, 117–118, 121–122, 124–125, 130, 132–133, 135–139, 159, 165, 181
stability, 4–6, 11, 35, 37, 41, 66, 152
steadfast, 124, 138
storytelling, 50, 88, 147–148, 150, 155
strife, 2, 4, 6, 44, 58, 65, 71, 75, 79, 112–113, 117–118, 152, 175–176
Styx, 82

subdues, 72, 79
subvert, 12, 81, 114, 185
suitor, 116, 138, 181
suitors, 10, 26, 29, 31–33, 55–57, 70, 72, 78, 113–126, 128–131, 133–136, 162, 169, 172, 181–182, 185–187
superhuman, 5, 15, 45, 78, 90, 146, 161, 163
supplicating, 145, 183
supplication, 38, 94, 139
survivors, 91, 183
swineherd, 31, 142, 185
swooping, 9, 73
symbol, 34, 138
symmetry, 3, 19

tale, 87, 90, 163
tapestry, 79
Taphians, 73
technology, 1, 144
Telamon, 172
Telemachus, 18, 26–33, 49–53, 57, 68, 73, 91–93, 95, 114–118, 120, 122, 126, 131–137, 139, 146, 165, 167, 170–172, 181–182, 185–187
temporal, 112
tension, 31, 130, 134
textual, 143, 153
thauma, 97, 115
Theano, 13, 99
Theban, 54
Thebes, 20, 50, 61, 99–100, 108, 147
thematic, 39, 53, 60, 146
theme, 25, 36, 38–39, 79–80, 145, 147, 155
Themis, 11, 36, 169
Theogony, 1, 3, 24–25, 54, 68, 146

Theogony, 146
theory, 133, 144, 149
theos, 15, 164
Thetis, 4–6, 9–10, 23, 34–44, 53–54, 60, 62, 69–70, 74, 111, 117, 167–168, 170–171, 175, 178–180
thnetois, 91
Thoosa, 72
threneo, threnodies, 60, 110
throne, 128, 160
thumos, 160–161, 164
thunderbolt, 26, 37, 81, 109, 160
timber, 48, 138
timeless, 56
Tiresias, 86, 140, 184–185
Titan, 169
Tithonus, 63, 68
Tlepolemus, 172
totality, 39, 57–59, 91, 154
tradition, 1, 39, 43, 69, 143, 147–148, 150, 155
tragedians, 155
tragedy, 69, 101
tragic, 107
transcripts, 145, 149
transform, 44, 60, 84, 155, 160, 164, 169, 184
transitional, 55–56, 92, 98, 154
translation, 80, 115, 142, 157–159, 161–164, 175
translators, 148, 161
transliteration, 89, 154
transmission, 56
transparency, 43, 157
Trojan, 4, 6–9, 11–14, 16–17, 23, 28, 34–35, 38–39, 41, 44–47, 50, 52, 54–55, 57–59, 63–64, 66–70, 73–79, 96, 101–103, 106–109, 112, 118, 131, 135, 139–140,

143, 146–147, 149, 152, 154–155, 163, 165, 167–168, 170–179, 182–183, 186
Troy, 4, 6–8, 11–13, 16–17, 19–20, 28, 36–42, 44–45, 48–52, 59, 62–63, 66, 70–71, 80, 83, 85, 87, 96, 99, 101–106, 108–110, 112–115, 118, 120, 123, 125, 131, 139, 147, 154, 167–168, 171, 173–174, 176–184
truth, 50, 57, 106, 151–152
Tydeus, 65, 74, 100, 172
Tyro, 117

Ulysses, 147
unblemished, 40–41
unburied, 40, 107
underworld, 80, 86, 184, 187
unity, 91, 95, 97, 111, 130, 140, 143, 147–148, 150
unravelling, 116, 181
upbringing, 32, 105
Uta-Napishti, 145
utterances, 2, 21

variation, 4, 10, 12, 28, 59, 79, 107, 133, 137, 150
variations, 60–61, 98, 149
vengeance, 112, 171
Vergil, 147, 154–156
victors, 118, 176
violence, 5–6, 11, 16, 27, 31, 44, 175, 186–187
virtue, 16, 114
vulnerability, 123, 154

wandering, 18, 61–62, 83, 98, 141, 154, 163, 169, 182
warfare, 12, 66, 167
warlike, 73

warrior, 4, 12, 27, 76, 78, 92, 94, 100–106, 123, 139, 142, 168, 171–172, 175–177
warriors, 3, 10, 12–13, 17, 51, 65–66, 78–79, 93, 101, 142, 177, 179
way of understanding, 21, 59, 71, 80, 85, 121, 165
weaver, 3, 47, 52
weaving, 30, 44–45, 49–50, 52, 76, 78–79, 105–106, 109–110, 116, 123–124, 169, 172, 176, 180–181
web, 25
wisdom, 9, 19, 21, 30, 69, 101, 133, 161, 172
Works and Days, 54, 90
worship, 15, 48–49, 55, 60, 62, 142, 145, 150–151, 165
Woven garment, 52, 185
woven garment, 51–52, 185
wrangle, 46, 175
writers, 148, 153

Xanthus, 168

yearn, 17, 113
yearning, 9, 117

Zakynthos, 123
Zeleia, 73
Zephyr, 20
Zeus, 1–12, 17, 20, 24–26, 29–30, 34, 36–45, 47, 50–51, 53–56, 58–59, 62–63, 65–71, 73–75, 77–82, 86, 90, 93–94, 98, 100–101, 103, 106, 109, 114–115, 118–119, 124, 127, 130, 139, 145–147, 150, 154, 159–160, 162, 164, 166–170, 172–185, 187